THE MONTAGNARDS OF SOUTH VIETNAM

A Study of Nine Tribes

THE MONTAGNARDS OF SOUTH VIETNAM

A Study of Nine Tribes

by Robert L. Mole

CHARLES E. TUTTLE COMPANY: PUBLISHERS
Rutland, Vermont & Tokyo, Japan

Representatives
Continental Europe: BOXERBOOKS, INC., *Zurich*
British Isles: PRENTICE-HALL INTERNATIONAL, INC., *London*
Australasia: PAUL FLESCH & CO., PTY. LTD., *Melbourne*
Canada: M. G. HURTIG LTD., *Edmonton*

Published by the Charles E. Tuttle Company, Inc.
of Rutland, Vermont & Tokyo, Japan
with editorial offices at
Suido 1-chome, 2-6, Bunkyo-ku, Tokyo, Japan

Copyright in Japan, 1970 by Charles E. Tuttle Co., Inc.

Library of Congress Catalog Card No. 70-104198

International Standard Book No. 0-8048-0724-8

First edition, 1970
Second printing, 1970

PRINTED IN JAPAN

TABLE OF CONTENTS

ILLUSTRATIONS

THE TRIBES OF I CORPS

FOREWORD

Rudyard Kipling's 1889 "Ballad of East and West" declared, "Oh, East is East and West is West, And never the twain shall meet, Till Earth and Sky stand presently at God"s great Judgment Seat. "

If Kipling meant that the East and West have different patterns of thought, value-behavior and religions, he was correct. If he was inferring the existence of an unbridgeable chasm between the minds and hearts of the East and West, he was wrong. There are the same qualities of humaneness in both worlds in spite of differing patterns of logic and culture. Kipling concluded his ballad by noting, "But there is neither East nor West, Border, nor Breed, nor Birth, When two strong men stand face to face, Tho' they come from the ends of earth"

Now citizens of the East and West are joined together in a mutual struggle for survival. The citizens of the two cultures, with those of the numerous subcultures, are involved in a process that is revolutionizing the world of yesterday. Titanic forces are creating far-reaching changes in most of the world's communities. These massive forces include such concepts as: modern medicine with its germ theory of diseases; educational concepts and goals predicated on rational scientific attitudes; mass communication methods and means combined with a world trade that encourages the flow of both ideas and material objects; modern technology that promotes the rapid production of goods for a money market which in turn encourages the reorganization of life about factory production and industrial centres rather than agriculture; powerful ideologies which create new allegiances and political power blocks as part of their goals, aspirations and hopes as well as the wars which are essential to either achieve these goals or to thwart them; governmental programmes and policies which often accelerate and direct social changes; and, the resulting examination of tradiional value systems and religious viewpoints which may be either reinforced or changed as men strive for a new or deeper understanding of themselves with a changing concept of their place in the universe.

These changes, which often shake the foundations of society, create imperative demands that there be an ongoing examination of new perspectives which were once beyond traditional horizons. These tend to create disruptions within communal solidarity. The traditional role of the community elders may be undermined with some individuals gaining sufficient independence of the community so that they are able to innovate changes or become free of former group ties. Increased knowledge may also create radical changes in value systems, social status, standards of living and roles of work along with patterns of dress. The acquirement of scientific knowledge and attitudes may challenge beliefs in magic and in other unseen supernatural powers so that fear, anxiety, dread or superstition toward the unknown and the unexplainable are sharply reduced.

Depending on content, application and the particular community, change may be either constructive or destructive. Nevertheless, change seems to be inevitable for most communities of the world. However, the uncritical acceptance or adopting and adapting of material objects, values and behavior can cause such a blurring and loss of identity and distinctiveness unless adequate substitutionary roles are formed. Certainly this is true for many of the cultural minority groups caught up into the twentieth century without advance preparation through no fault of their own.

THE MONTAGNARD TRIBES OF SOUTH VIETNAM uses the term "cultural minorities" to distinguish the thirty-three tribal groups which dwell primarily in the mountains and highlands of South Vietnam. These ethnic groups constitute fairly homogenous units, or tribes, with each one having its own common language, ancestry, area of habitation, social structures primarily based on kinship and the lack of scientific knowledge and modern technology.

Many minority peoples develop a sense of inferiority when in contact with more developed and sophisticated cultures. This inferiority complex can develop toward either of two extremes. First, it may create such an excessive pride in the traditional ways of life that even the slightest proposed changes are opposed with deeply ingrained resistance no matter how good or valid. The opposite extreme is to accept values, behavior patterns and devices uncritically in an almost purely imitative manner. Then there may be confusion, conflict of community or personal values and loss of goals.

The traditional aspects of community life such as self-reliance, group-solidarity, resourcefulness, etc., ought to be promoted when attempting to create or promote changes in a society. They may also be a valid basis for group development. Economic, social, cultural and religious aspects of ethnic community life form a unity. Therefore programs of development and change must integrate all phases of life inasmuch as these will be affected for better or worse. In this respect, the community must be allowed to develop in harmony with its own genius. Consideration must be given felt needs, in lieu of a program imposed from outside of the community. More important than good intentions and unlimited funds in the requirement of trained personnel, who possess an understanding of the people with sensitivity to the community's traditional ways and thought patterns.

Success in Vietnam requires that personnel know and understand the people among whom they serve. Effective aid, for the tribesman beyond the sounds of battle, requires that we know his innermost desires. We must know how his culture and religion satisfy these before we can establish points of contact in terms he can understand and accept. In this way, bridges can be established over which new ideas may be effectively conveyed to him. Unless his innermost desires, his familiar symbols and word meanings are known, the danger of misunderstanding is great while the opportunity for penetrating his understanding is small.

Generally, it is safe to assume that preliterate peoples can be appealed too on the visual and emotional levels most effectively. Effective communication must be in words and symbols they understand, and which convey the desired meaning. Only by the thorough understanding of the cultural terrain and its subtle cues can Americans hope to establish sufficient empathy to bridge the differences of thought and action between themselves and those of other cultures.

The booby trap, designed to blend into its environment or to appear harmless, is a major danger in guerrilla warfare and counter-insurgency. These explosive devices, which inflict grave wounds and death, are of concern to all those who confront them. Likewise, potential booby traps are created by the intermingling of different cultures when citizens of two or more societies are yoked in partnership. Impr sions of familiarity in a different culture can permit or cause the unwa to have such a sense of security that disaster may occur without consci warnings. Likewise, "strange" behavior may seem so illogical as to defy ready attempts to understand and relate meaningfully to others.

Religion is at the very center of the life of the tribal people. It is, therefore, the most difficult of all phases of their life to effectively change. No part of the tribesman's life remains untouched by religious beliefs and rituals. Religion therefore, finds its concrete expressions in everything which occurs during the year so that as their religion changes, the total way of life is affected.

The tribesman, like all men, have been incurably religious sinc the dawn of history. In a real sense the drama of man and the story of religion have been inextricably intertwined. In fact, one of the basic functions of religion is to act as a cultural gyroscope by providing a stable set of definitions of the world in relation to the individual self. These, in turn, permit the individual or society to meet the transience and crises of life with some equanimity. Thus, religion, whatever its form, constitutes one of the strongest cultural determinants. It is essential, therefore, that Americans have an awareness of the dynamic forces deeply imbedded in the cultures of Vietnam.

To provide assistance in developing a knowledge of indigenous religions, customs, traditions, and people, the United States Navy and Marine Corps have instituted a transcultural endeavor known as Person Response. Personal Response is a systematic effort in intercultural attitude changes predicated upon awareness, understanding and appre-ciation of cultural-belief-value systems which determine behavior patte This cross-cultural endeavor is currently supported by the United State Marines, the Chief of Chaplains, United States Navy and by the Com-mander Service Force, United States Pacific Fleet. This new dimensie of the Navy/Marine Team in Southeast Asia seems to remedy the deficiencies of transcultural understanding between Americans and thei allies. Awareness, appreciation and consideration of value-belief-behavioral patterns can be of significant value in the achievement of objectives assigned to Navy/Marine personnel.

This volume is an experimental edition of NINE MONTAGNARD TRIBES OF THE REPUBLIC OF VIETNAM. Produced under combat conditions, it is less than perfect. Nevertheless, it is a beginning. The suggestions of its readers and those who serve among the peoples of this volume can aid to improve subsequent editions. The author assumes responsibility of all flaws in this edition. He believes it is better to begin the transcultural journey one step at a time rather than bemoan the difficulties that lie ahead.

ROBERT L. MOLE

ACKNOWLEDGEMENT

It is appropriate to acknowledge those who have contributed their support, encouragement and active participation in this volume. However, it would be impossible to include the complete number. That list would include many whose names are unknown, or even when known almost unpronounceable, but who served as escorts, guides and bodyguards in the rugged enemy infested mountains of I Corps, South Vietnam. Nevertheless, there are some beyond the authorities listed in the footnotes of this volume who ought to be mentioned. Without their support, encouragement and sponsorship, this and similar volumes would not be possible.

Lieutenant General Victor C. KRULAK, USMC, (Retired) was the first American Flag officer to accept the responsibility of translating Personal Response concepts of cross-cultural understanding for military personnel into reality. He was joined in the sponsorship of Navy/Marine Personal Response by Rear Admiral James W. KELLY, ChC, USN, Chief of Chaplains, United States Navy. Chaplain KELLY, in response to General KRULAK's request, assigned this writer as the first U.S. Marine Personal Response Officer for Southeast Asia from June 1965 to August 1966. Then at the request of Rear Admiral Edwin B. HOOPER, USN, Commander Service Force, U.S. Pacific Fleet, this officer was again extended the privilege of pioneering Personal Response for the United States Navy in Southeast Asia from September 1967 to September 1968. Navy sponsorship has continued through the deep interest and complete support of Rear Admiral Walter COMBS, Jr., USN who is the current Commander Service Force, U.S. Pacific Fleet.

The two Commanding Officers of Naval Support Activity, Saigon, during this second tour of duty, Captain B. W. SPORE, USN and Captain Max C. DUNCAN, USN have provided the fullest command support in logistics and in guidance for the implementation of Navy Personal Response.

Captain John CRAVEN, ChC, USN formerly Force Chaplain, Fleet Marine Force, Pacific and Captain Joseph J. TUBBS, ChC, USN, Pacific Fleet Chaplain provided supervision, technical assistance and guidance besides moral support and encouragement when the assignment appeared to be impossible. Their abilities to see rays of light and workable methods when all seemed hopeless, combined with their unfailing patience, have laid a firm foundation for cross-cultural understanding in the military environment. Numerous other line officers and chaplains have been involved in Personal Response, and indirectly in this volume.

Perhaps the more significant of these were Lieutenant General Lewis WALT, USMC, former Commanding General III MAF, who consistently demonstrated a keen interest in Personal Response concepts; Captain Francis GARRETT, CHC, USN, former III MAF Staff Chaplain who actively took part in Personal Response and strongly encouraged all Navy chaplains attached to Marine units in Vietnam to become participants; Captain Michael MACINNES, CHC, USN, Director of the Chaplain Corps Planning Group, who served as my supervisor during the year between the two Southeast Asian tours of duty, and whose Christian example had a deep influence on me; Captain Edward HEMPHILL, CHC, USN, with a unique personality that combines a keen ever-questioning mind and seemingly unlimited emergy; Commander Otto SCHNEIDER, CHC, USN and Lieutenant Commander Richard McGONIGAL, CHC, USN, inasmuch as both later followed my tour and served as Marine Personal Response Officers in Vietnam and made significant contributions to cross-cultural understanding. Commander Robert A. CANFIELD, CHC, USN was a source of Christian strength during the trying months of hostilities of the second tour. His buoyant spirit united with courage, a balanced sense of humor and a deep spiritual concern, served as a catalyst for maintaining the proper prospective for this task. Without such close association, this assignment would have been even more difficult. Moreover when workloads were too much for the small Navy Personal Response staff, he permitted EM3 John W. BERRY and YN3 John C. ADAMS to assist me.

This volume and the related activities of Navy Personal Response could not have been accomplished without the diligent efforts of a limited office staff who translated relevant materials, typed countless papers, and hand collated more than one half million pages of manuscript under combat conditions. So a word of appreciation to YN3 E.M. MORRIS, Mr Triệu Khả Kiên, and Miss Trần Thị Dậu. Then lastly, a public word of appreciation to my wife, Jeannette, who faced and mastered so many of life's problems while her sailor husband has been in foreign lands.

ROBERT L. MOLE

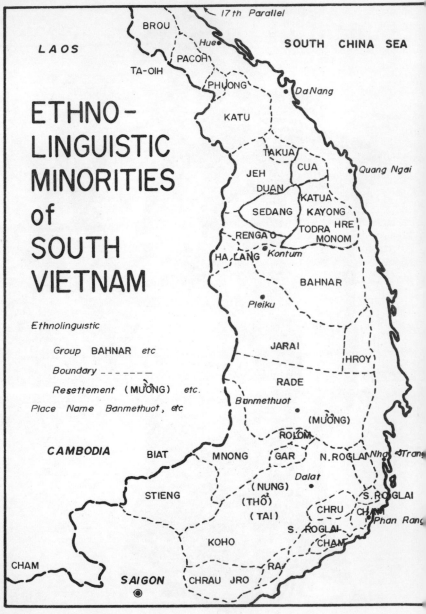

ETHNO-
LINGUISTIC
MINORITIES
of
SOUTH
VIETNAM

Ethnolinguistic

   Group BAHNAR etc

   Boundary _ _ _ _ _ _

   Resettement (MUONG) etc.

Place Name Banmethuot, etc

LAOS

BROU
PACOH
TA-OIH
PHUONG
KATU
TAKUA
JEH
DUAN
CUA
SEDANG
KATUA
KAYONG
RENGAO
TODRA
HRE
MONOM
HA LANG
BAHNAR
JARAI
HROY
RADE
(MUONG)
ROLOM
CAMBODIA
BIAT
MNONG
GAR
N. ROGLAI
STIENG
(NUNG)
(THO)
(TAI)
CHRU
CHAM
S. ROGLAI
KOHO
S. ROGLAI
CHAM
CHAM
RA
CHRAU
JRO

17th Parallel
Hue
SOUTH CHINA SEA
Da Nang
Quang Ngai
Kontum
Pleiku
Banmethuot
Dalat
Nha Trang
Phan Rang
SAIGON

2

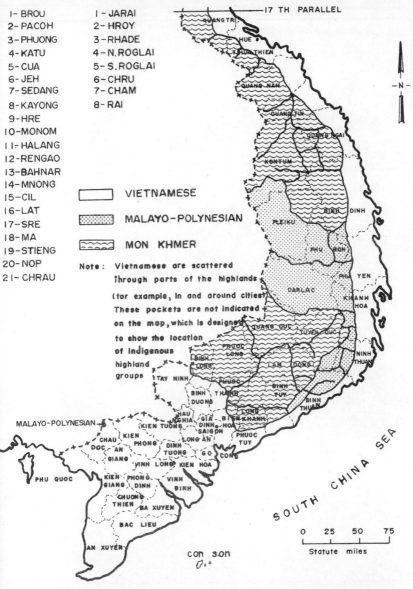

1- BROU	1 - JARAI
2- PACOH	2- HROY
3- PHUONG	3- RHADE
4- KATU	4- N.ROGLAI
5- CUA	5- S.ROGLAI
6- JEH	6- CHRU
7- SEDANG	7- CHAM
8- KAYONG	8- RAI
9- HRE	
10-MONOM	
11-HALANG	
12-RENGAO	
13-BAHNAR	
14-MNONG	
15-CIL	
16-LAT	
17-SRE	
18-MA	
19-STIENG	
20-NOP	
21-CHRAU	

☐ VIETNAMESE

▒ MALAYO-POLYNESIAN

〰 MON KHMER

Note: Vietnamese are scattered
through parts of the highlands
(for example, in and around cities)
These pockets are not indicated
on the map, which is designed
to show the location
of indigenous
highland
groups

17 TH PARALLEL

SOUTH CHINA SEA

0 25 50 75
Statute miles

ETHNO-LINGUISTIC GROUPS OF SOUTH VIETNAM

3

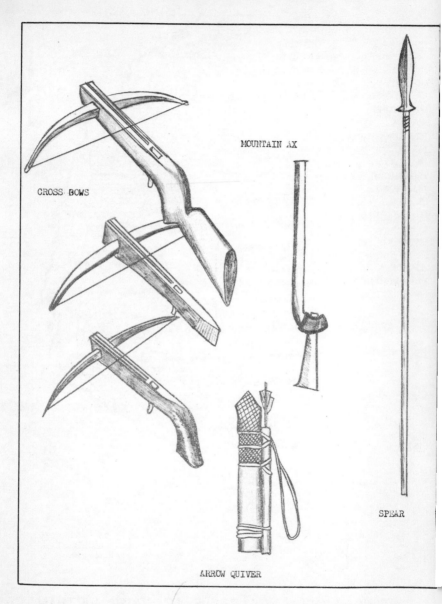

CROSS BOWS

MOUNTAIN AX

ARROW QUIVER

SPEAR

4

CHAPTER I

AN OVERVIEW OF THE

PEOPLES OF THE TRIBES OF SOUTH VIETNAM

The purpose of this study of the tribespeople of South Vietnam is to provide information which will help promote understanding, appreciation and constructive interaction between Americans and the minority ethnic groups of South Vietnam. Awareness and appreciation of the human dynamics operative in the lives of the ethnic Vietnamese and of the highland minority groups can help provide bridges across the chasms of cultural and ethnic differences. These chasms must be spanned if present nation building efforts are to be permanently effective.

An effort will be made herein to describe the various peoples who compose the thirty-three ethnic groups commonly known as Montagnards by most Americans. The belief-value-behavior patterns of the Montagnards will be analyzed so that American military personnel serving in a particular tribal area might be aware of, and grow to appreciate, the commonalities and differences in the lives of the tribespeople as compared with those of Americans, other tribal groups, and the ethnic Vietnamese.

The highly segmented culture of the Montagnards is extremely complex. Due to the subsistence economy and to the preliterate or semi-literate state of most Montagnards, their lives are highly conditioned by their immediate environment. Most of them are village oriented and have little idea of any higher levels of social or political loyalty. Therefore generalizations about the Montagnards are difficult and apt to be misleading to those who have a more complex vertical system of socio-political loyalties.

The assumption underlying this extended study of the Montagnards is that all human beings possess common basic physiological and psychological needs, but that these needs are met in a wide variety of ways by different societies in conformity with the requirements imposed by geographic location, economic conditions and cultural expectations. To a very large degree, the culture of a people is determined by geography, economics and religion. Religion, as herein defined, includes man's world-view and the individual's place therein, combined with efforts to achieve a harmonious relationship between himself and his supernaturally controlled environment.

It is hoped that this overview, and the subsequent chapters of this study will provide a frame of reference within which the American military observer can better bring to focus his own experiences and observations.

INTRODUCTION

South Vietnam like the rest of the Indo-China Peninsula, forms one of the most ethno-linguistically and ethno-culturally complex areas of the world. Generally, however, the societies of the whole area can be divided into two major segments, each of which has many subdivisions. The first of these two basic groups is composed of the people dwelling on the plains in the broader valleys, and on the deltas. The cultures of these peoples have been, and are, deeply permeated and strongly influenced by either the Chinese or Indian civilizations, or both. The major ethnic groups of mainland Southeast Asia in this category include the Vietnamese, the Thai, the Khmer, the Burmese, the Malay and the Lao. [1]

The second major segment of mainland Southeast Asian population is composed of the inhabitants of the highlands and mountains. These peoples, who differ both linguistically and culturally from the lowlanders, have remained comparatively aloof from other civilizations so that many elements of their cultures and histories are unknown. When contacts have taken place between them and the peoples who dwell on the lowlands, the experiences have generally tended to be unpleasant. Consequently, the highland dwelling ethnic groups of mainland Southeast Asia have not been too greatly affected by the "Great Traditions" (the highly formalized classical religious and cultural teachings) of the Indian, Chinese, Arabic or Judeo-Christian civilizations. Contrastingly, the Great Traditions of the foregoing civilizations have been determinative to varying degrees in the lowland belief-value behavior systems.

(6)

Name: The Vietnamese name for Vietnam's highland ethnic
minorities is "người thượng" (phonetically "newy tung") "highland
citizen", or người Việt-Nam Mới, "New Vietnamese citizen". The
French term for these tribes people who dwell in the mountainous
area of Vietnam is "Montagnards", "mountaineers", although some
French anthropologists refer to them as "Proto-Indochinois"
(Protoindochinese) meaning the first inhabitants in their particular
part of the Indo-China Peninsula. Any of these terms is preferable
to "mọi" (savage) which is considered a derogatory epithet, the use
of which often creates resentment and hostility.

Most of the peoples of the tribes, hereafter referred to by either
the generic term "Montagnard" or by the particular tribal name, tend
to identify themselves by the name of their village or geographic
location rather than as members of a particular tribe. This custom
is common among preliterate peoples whose thought patterns and
world concepts differ radically from those whose background is in
a Western scientific and technological society.[2] Nevertheless, when
a critical issue is involved, many Montagnards recognize ties based
upon language, blood lines, and common cultural factors which include
economic and religious elements. Therefore, the casual identification
with a self-sustaining local village is quite logical to the tribespeople,
who, having no formalized central tribal organization, are village-
oriented. The recognition that tribal names are imposed upon the
tribes externally can help Americans in the tribal areas to understand
this rather widespread practice.

Number: The number of Montagnards within South Vietnam is
estimated to be somewhere between 800,000 and 1,000,000. They
are divided into thirty-three different and distinct tribes distinguished
by linguistic factors.[3] Each of these tribes has customs, mores, and
religious beliefs which make it different from its neighbors.

Geographic Area: The Montagnards, while composing a small
percentage of Vietnam's total population, are of strategic significance
inasmuch as they are the primary inhabitants of about 50% of Vietnam's
land area. Similar to other tribal peoples of Southeast Asia, the
Montagnards live in the more remote highlands and mountainous areas
with rain forests and dense jungles dominating their environment.
The Montagnard tribal area is that of the Annamite Mountain Range
from the 17th Parallel to just north of Bien Hoa or about fifty miles

north of Saigon. On the east, the tribal area comes down to the plains of the narrow coast along the China Sea while it extends westward across the Cambodian and Laotian borders. While some of the tribespeople do cross the ill-defined international boundaries at will, and intermingle with other tribes to some extent, it is still possible to pinpoint rather definite areas for each tribal group.

Language: The Montagnards of South Vietnam are divided into several linguistic family groups. The two major linguistic groups are the Mon-Khmer and the Malayo-Polynesian, each with a number of tribal languages built on their linguistic base in much the same manner as Spanish, French, etc. are built on Latin. Mon-Khmer seems to be the larger language group of the whole former Indo-China area, and it is quite closely related linguistically to the current language of the Cambodians. The Malayo-Polynesian is related to the language spoken in parts of Indonesia and numerous islands of the Pacific.[4] Interestingly the Malayo-Polynesian groups are so located that they form a wedge which largely divides the Mon-Khmer speaking groups into north, central and south groups. This geographic factor appears to confirm the theory that the Malayo-Polynesian speaking peoples must have arrived in South Vietnam after the Mon-Khmer groups did.[5]

The Southern Mon-Khmer linguistic group is composed of the Chrau, Koho, Mnong, Stieng and some small-tribes; the central group is represented by the Bahnar, Halang, Monan, Sedang, Todra, Rengao, Bonom (Monom), Hre, Jeh, Cua and Kayong; and the Northern group has the Brou, Katu, Takua, Pacoh (Pakoh), Phuong and Tau-oi. The major tribes of the Malayo-Polynesian linguistic base include the Cham, Chru, Hroy, Jarai, Rade, Rai (Seyu), Northern Roglai, Southern Roglai and the Cac Gia Roglai.

In addition to the Mon-Khmer and the Malayo-Polynesian tribes, there are other ethnic groups such as the Man and the Meo of the Miao-Yao language family; the Muong, which closely resembles the Vietnamese language; the Nung (Nong), Nhang and the Tai of the Tai language family; and the Nung, which is basically a Chinese dialect.[6]

Despite such linguistic differences, intertribal communication

can be maintained. Many basic words resemble one another sufficiently
to remain mutually intelligible; a system of conventional signs has
also been developed to facilitate understanding. Moreover, in many
instances, intermingling occurs between contiguous tribes. This
proximity permits interchange of ideas, allows intermarriage, and
other types of transcultural influence. The result has often been the
appearance of small tribes which incorporate cultural elements
patterns of living, speech, customs, taboos, etc., from the surrounding tribes. These tribes then serve as a channel of communication
between the larger tribes. Thus ethnic groups in contiguous areas
are normally sufficiently familiar with the other's language for some
of the peoples to communicate without too much difficulty.

Some of the tribal groups with constant exposure to nontribal
influences, such as the French, Vietnamese or American, have
demonstrated an adeptness in learning languages other than their own.
Some tribesmen can fluently speak several tribal languages along
with French, Vietnamese and some English, but the great majority
of the Montagnards have not yet been exposed to opportunities to
learn any speech other than their own.

Characteristics: While the ethnic Vietnamese have borrowed,
adapted and absorbed many foreign cultural elements, the Montagnards
have not. Through sustained exposure to other civilizations, Indian,
Chinese, Arabic, European - the Vietnamese lowlanders have adopted
many foreign concepts or ideas that definitely affect their daily
behavior. The Montagnards, by remaining aloof, have generally
retained their traditional concepts and behavior patterns.

Moreover, geographic location and linguistic differences,
combined with mutual fears and distrust, have permitted the Montagnards to borrow very little from ethnic Vietnamese mannerisms,
languages or crafts. In fact, these conditions have been rather
effective barriers to communication among tribes so that each tribe
has tended to maintain its own particular sub-cultural characteristics.

It is not difficult to distinguish the ethnic Vietnamese and the
Montagnard in physical appearance. Not only is their wearing apparel
different under normal conditions, but so are their skin coloring and
facial features. The Montagnards generally resemble the Indonesians

(9)

and the Filipinos much more than they do the ethnic Vietnamese.
The Montagnard logic, unaffected by foreign influences, differs
radically from that of most ethnic Vietnamese. Thus, the possible
acculturation or assimilation of the Montagnards into Vietnamese
culture will require much effort, an extended time span and
exceeding patience by all concerned.

Similar to other Southeast Asian peoples, the Montagnards
believe in charismatic (divine or supernaturally inspired power)
qualities. This quality is known in Vietnam as ae which means
mana or soul force' which, while possessed by all males to some
degree, can be definitely enhanced by the favor of the spirits.
The Montagnard lives in an environment which he believes to be
almost entirely spirit controlled. The physical qualities which
mark the presence of ae may be unusual virility, a heavy beard,
or great strength in comparison to other Montagnard men. These
physical qualities give credence to qualities of prestige, leadership and wisdom. The amount of ae can be increased or reduced,
so that the individual possessing this quality can lose positions of
leadership if troubles afflict his people, or if his judgment seems
to be poor in the minds of his villagers.

THE VILLAGE

The village is the most important economic and political unit
in the usual experience of the Montagnards. The inhabitants of a
given village normally produce what they need, and whatever is
produced is consumed with very little remaining for trade. Politically the village is the highest level and most cohesive Montagnard
unit inasmuch as the Montagnards do not generally have formal
tribal-wide organizations. While there have been, and are,
instances of larger than village hegemony under a ruling group
of families, these are exceptions to the rule. Among some tribes,
such as the Bahnar, there are well-defined territories called toring
collectively claimed by the village within the boundaries of the area.
Generally, these are associations to safeguard village farming,
fishing and hunting rights rather than political units. [8]

Tribal villages vary from the very small, consisting of a dozen or so people, to the very large which may have a population of several thousand. Some Montagnards, such as the Tring, who are a small tribe, fear to live in villages and are scattered in isolated houses among the mountains of their area. Their fear is based upon their belief in evil spirits. They are convinced, for example, that if two families were to use the same water source, the spirits of the two families would fight. [9]

Typical Montagnard houses are made of natural jungle products. Bamboo is the most popular building material, and is split for studs and rafters, or plaited for walls and roofs. Where bamboo is unavailble or impractical, thatch or other available varieties of wood may be utilized. Houses are generally built on stilts with the floor of the house several feet above the ground. Entrance to most homes is gained by means of a ladder or a notched log. Raising the house on stilts not only provides protection from wild animals and the moist ground during rainy season, but also creates a space below the house which may be used for storage, animal pens, children's play, or as a shady escape from the hot sun. When the cooking fire is in the house, it is often contained in a dirt or mud-filled box supported by its own heavy pillar, and may be either at floor level or higher.

Some of the Montagnards utilize "longhouses" which may be more than a hundred yards in length. These tribal "apartment houses" provide living quarters for a number of families so that more than a hundred people may live in a single longhouse. Normally the inhabitants of the individual longhouse are related by blood or marriage and are thereby members of the extended patrilineal or matrilineal family. Some tribes have nuclear houses which means that these are single family houses of the man, the wife or wives and children. The extended family homes may be either patrilocal or matrilocal, i.e., the newly married couple live with the family of the groom or of the bride.

Most Montagnard houses are erected in harmony with local beliefs about evil spirits. Just as many of the Montagnard villages erect protective devices against malevolent spirits, so does the individual family. Since evil spirits are thought to be able to approach the village only in one set direction, the houses may be built with all doors and windows on the opposite side of the house so that the spirits will not be able to enter and cause harm and havoc. In addition to this style of house construction, many of the tribal houses have other items which are utilized either to ward off the evil spirit or to appease it in case it has not been sufficiently frightened. Almost all Animistic tribesmen have one special pole, usually a basic supporting one, known as the spirit pole. This has an awesome sacredness for the tribesman and must not be defiled in any manner.

Many of the Motagnard villages have a communal house. Usually it is the most elaborate and ornate structure in the village. Normally taboo to women, the communal house serves as the ritual center of its village and as the residence of the village spirit. Quite often the skulls of sacrificed buffalo are attached to its walls. It is believed that the skulls are still the residence of the buffalo's spirit and that the buffalo's strength is retained in the village. The communal house, normally centrally located, is the place where the unmarried men sleep, and it serves as the indoctrination center for tribal lore and traditions.

A third structure typical of many animistic Montagnard villages is that of the spirit house or houses. The village spirit house may be dedicated to the spirit of the village, i. e., the spirit of the particular location, or there may be numerous spirit houses erected by individual households of the village. The latter are usually quite small - from just a few inches to perhaps four feet in length and width. Regardless of size, these houses have great significance to the Montagnard. Because he exists in an environment dominated by supernatural spirits, it is considered imperative that precautions be taken against giving offense to the various spirits and that sacrifical appeasement be made from time to time.

Another ritualistic feature of some Montagnard villages is the Sacrifice Pole. While individual sacrifices of chickens and pigs to the spirits require only small temporary sacrificial poles, water buffalo sacrifices require a larger pole or post. The heavy sacrificial post may be located in the center of the village, near the village burial grounds or in some other prominent place.

These posts are temporary in some tribal villages and are erected as the occasion demands; other villages have permanent posts. In either case, the sacrificial pole is the locus of major sacrifices as the community seeks to placate the spirits. These poles may be quite simple or very elaborately decorated or carved. In either case, the ritual significance attached to sacrifices to the spirits make these posts taboo or the objects of mystical awe.

SOCIAL STRUCTURES

Because of the religious influence of the sorcerers, they also exercise both political and economic authority. Their position as religious leaders and communicators with the supernatural world makes them members of any elite group which may exist in the community. The sorcerer, magician, shaman, witch doctor or "spirit-lady" have an aura of influence and importance which exceeds that of most religious figures in Western civilization. Discretion dictates that foreigners treat them with courtesy and consideration.

Every village seems to have some social stratification. This stratification often includes four classes of people: free men, foreigners, debtors and slaves. Foreigners are all the non-local tribal people who have been "adopted" by the tribe and are living in the community. These may be other tribespeople, ethnic Vietnamese, Westerners or Viet-Cong. Debtors are those who have borrowed for living expenses or to engage in some venture which was not profitable. These debtors live on "borrowed time" inasmuch as they may become slaves if their debts are not paid off, or if they die in debt, their children may be seized as slaves for payment. Sometimes a Montagnard man may sell his wife into slavery in order to meet a financial obligation imposed by his in-laws by tribal custom. Slaves may be prisoners of war captured in tribal conflict, debtors who failed to meet their obligations or orphans who are not adopted by relatives. However, the subsistence level of tribal living allows but little distinction and privilege among the various classes.

The family: Family structure within the thirty-three tribes of South Vietnam varies greatly from tribe to tribe. In some tribes, parents choose marriage partners for their children based upon alliances or economic factors. Others allow the male to choose his own bride or brides with the encouragement and economic support of the clan. A few tribes are so structured that the girl or her mother makes the choice of a groom. Thus, only as a particular tribe is discussed can there be any specificity regarding the Montagnard family structure.

The newly married couple may reside with the parents of the groom (patrilocal) in an extended family longhouse or in a single unit house in the groom's family village (neolocal). They may live in the same family village as the bride's family in a single family house or with the bride's family extended longhouse (matrilocal). In rare cases the newly married couple establish their home in a new community or in one unrelated to the parents of either groom or bride.

Some tribes require dowries of the husband; others, dowries of the wife, while some have no required payments. Marriage arrangements usually require the services of an intermediary in order to save "face" and act as buffer when marriage price bargaining becomes serious. When the marriage ceremony occurs, it is surrounded with prescribed rituals that must be followed for the villagers to consider the marriage properly begun.

When children are born, their name will be determined by whether the family is patrilineal (after the groom's family) or matrilineal (after the mother's family). Customs pertaining to divorce are so varied that specific statements require reference to a particular tribe in order to have factual relevance. However, in spite of such societal differences, the family has a central role in all Montagnard tribal life.

Political Structures: The village political organization of the various Montagnard groups is quite similar. Political authority is in the hands of the males even when matrilineal systems such as the Rhade, Jarai, and Mnong are involved. In such matrilineal systems, the women own the houses, domestic animals, and farm products. They hold title to the land and possession of the gongs and wine jars which are items of prestige and value.[10]

In the Montagnard village-centered society, customs and moral

(14)

code are deeply internalized. Villages tend to have a strong collective spirit since all the inhabitants share the same common style of life and subscribe to the same basic set of values. Because society is comparatively closed, breaches of custom do not go unnoticed and the opprobrium of the total community is brought to bear on offenders. Guilt may require reparations to the injured party and or to the community as a whole. While offenders are normally treated as individuals, some offenses require that the offender's entire family be punished. This latter procedure is normal among the Stieng, but much more rare among the other ethnic groupings.

Upon occasion, "tribal justice" may seem quite harsh to American observers. Instead of the Anglo-Saxon concept of "innocent until proven guilty" the tribespeople sometimes utilize "trial by ordeal" methods to determine guilt or innocence. If accused of crime, or of being a troublesome witch, the individual may have to prove his innocence by great risk or actual loss of limb or life. For instance, among some tribes a person accused of witchcraft may have hot lead poured into the palm of the hand covered only by the thickness of seven green leaves. If the molten lead burns through the leaves and through the palm of the hand and drops to the ground, it is accepted as positive proof of guilt.

Upon occasion an accused may have to undergo trial by water to "win" his case. This trial involves submerging both the accuser and the accused in water. If the accused comes up for air before his accuser does, it is accepted as proof of guilt. If the accused stays under water until he drowns, it is accepted as a proof of guilt also. In some tribal groups, if a sick person dreams that a particular individual or family is causing his illness by "stealing away his spirit", the accused ones may be quietly killed and buried without formalities of any kind. These and similar methods of disposing of troublesome problems are above and beyond the letter of Vietnamese law.

Exception to general observations regarding discipline or justice must be made for the Rhade. Among this large group, the senior females who hold title to the clan land by right of inheritance, have a certain jural authority. These individuals are called po lan, "proprietors of the land." As guardians of the territories which may include several villages, they grant permission to farm within the area. They are also responsible for the performance of rites honoring the souls or spirits of clan ancestors who reside in the territory. In addition, the po lan are obligated to walk the boundaries of their territory at prescribed intervals. Should the territory be violated in any way, or polluted by the occurrence of incest, etc., within it, the po lan demand that the traditional penalties be invoked. Normally the more "wealthy" families form a socio-political elite. Among the Rhade, the Mnong and some other tribes, these families tend to intermarry, thereby perpetuating their privileged roles.[11]

Nearly all Montagnard villages have a governing council composed of the elder males who are usually selected from the household heads. The headman of the individual village is selected either by consensus of the adult villagers or by the council of which he is always a member. Traditionally, the headman, assisted by the village council, is responsible for the administration of the village, protection of its inhabitants, and the various village rituals. When the French established their administration in the tribal areas, the headman became the avenue of liaison between the district authorities and his village. While wartime conditions affect the Montagnards, the village council and its headman continue to function in the traditional manner with rare exception.

The headman and the village council administer justice within the community. When family problems cannot be solved by its head, the chief and perhaps the council become involved. When conflicts occur between families, or violations of the village customs or taboo come about, the chief and council handle justice according to tribal tradition and such Vietnamese law as may apply. In those areas not under the firm control of the Vietnamese government, problems between the villages or inhabitants of different villages fall within the jurisdiction of the headmen.

By tradition, the headman or chief is considered to be the wealthiest man in the village. Likewise he is generally believed to be the most intelligent man in the community.[12] He is the recognized administrator, the senior counselor, the leader in war (except where the Vietnamese army is involved) and the dispensator of justice. The decision of the chief is final insofar as his villagers are concerned. The only recourse to what an individual may consider a grossly unfavorable or unfair decision is to remove himself permanently from the village. To follow this course means being admitted to another village, or living to oneself, as well as depriving oneself of free social exchange with his former village associates and relatives.

When the French adminstration moved into the tribal areas, they established systems of district chiefs to whom the village headmen were responsible. The Vietnamese follow the same basic pattern. If the district chiefs interfere too much with traditional life, they are resented, and on occasion the tribesmen have revolted against what they believed to be injustices inflicted on them. Even the Viet Minh and the Viet Cong have felt the backlash of tribal resentment from time to time because of reaction to rules interfering with traditional tribal customs.

The current policy of the national Vietnamese government is to utilize Montagnard district chiefs in tribal areas whenever possible. This minimizes misunderstanding of tribal and government relationships and provides avenues for increasing awareness of a central government. In the judicial system those serious crimes and offenses which cannot be settled within the village court are tried in district or province tribal courts where Montagnards preside or assist in the administration of justice. [13]

ECONOMICS

The major means of supporting Montagnard life include farming, hunting, fishing, and gathering wild jungle products. Members of some tribes work for wages on the rubber, tea and coffee plantations that are scattered throughout the mountains. Others now work in various capacities for the American military.

Farming: Except for some limited wet-rice farming, the major means of farming among the tribespeople is the slash-burn method. This type of farming is called swidden or , in both French and Vietnamese, "ray". In this type of farming the fields shift continually.

All the bushes, vines and trees in a chosen area are cut down, allowed to dry and then burned. Then various food crops - mountain rice, millet, corn, pumpkin, squash, manioc, etc., are planted among the stumps and larger trees which were not removed. Manioc, or cassava, is a wild or cultivated tropical plant with edible starchy roots which may be used as bread or for the making of tapioca.

On the appropriate planting day, the men with dibble sticks (sharpened poles which may be held in either hand) punch holes into the ground randomly or in rows. The women usually follow, drop seeds into the holes, and then close them with their feet. The rains, which make the growing season possible, also spawn weeds which must be removed from time to time. Each field is chosen in harmony with tribal lore and animistic beliefs. After the fields have been used for one to three years they are abandoned and allowed to lie fallow fifteen to twenty years which permits the jungle to reclaim them.

The principle gardens of vegetables and leafy plants are grown near the home; fields may be any where from an hour to a day's walk from the village. The crops must be guarded against wild deer, wild pigs, doves and blackbirds. The presence of the deer and pigs also attracts wild tigers to the area. The fear of tigers is predominant among the Montagnards so precautions must be taken to prevent attack.

Domesticated animals are raised for sacrificial purposes and as food. These include chickens, pigs, dogs and the water buffalo. Few families possess animals in great number, and since most Montagnards eat slaughtered animals only after ritual sacrifices to the spirits, not many have more than a skimpy supply of such food. The meat supply becomes even more scarce in those tribes in which the meat of the sacrificial animal is taboo to the family required to offer it.

Hunting, Fishing and Gathering: The ever-present jungle is utilized to provide essential dietary supplement. Game is captured or killed through the use of traps, the bow and arrow, spears and guns. Mountain streams and rivers provide a source of fish which are caught with lines, traps, gigs, seines; or by the use of jungle-grown poisons which paralyze the fish in still pools or shallow streams but do not ruin them as food.

Women and children of the village are the main food gatherers. The jungle and forest provide a wealth of wild foodstuffs and fuel for cooking. Common edibles include mint, saffron, roots, wild fruits, and berries, bamboo shoots, leaves and other wild plants which the Montagnards have learned to utilize in many ways.

Crafts and Trade: Inasmuch as the Montagnards are largely self-sufficient except in their need for salt and iron, trade or commerce is not a major industry. There is some barter and sales between the tribes and between the lowland Vietnamese, Chinese or Cambodians. Such items as salt, iron metal utensils, clothing materials, and wine jugs are obtained in exchange for jungle products like tea, cinnamon bark, bamboo, wild honey, and some lumber and money earned as laborers.

Because arts and skills mainly serve the practical needs of everyday life, most tribes have not developed residual aesthetic arts and crafts. However, this does not indicate a lack of capability. When given the opportunity, or when a need arises through interaction with foreigners, the tribes-people demonstrate exceptional skills. Some of the Montagnard tribespeople have high proficiency in making cloth, baskets, primitive jewelry and unusual weapons.

Labor: Typical of subsistence societies the world over, men, women and children all participate in earning a living. The male labors at clearing the fields, carpentry, metal work, hunting and fishing. Women plant, weed, gather food from the jungles, weave, cook, carry water, and care for the children. Harvesting is a joint male-female operation with children joining in as soon as they are old enough. Children are responsible for looking after cattle and buffalo, and caring for younger brothers and sisters. The tribespeople too feeble or old for heavy labor perform lighter tasks such as making bows and arrows or baskets. All the members of a family fill a useful role in the overall responsibilities confronting the community.

RELIGION

A basic ingredient in Montagnard life is the pervasive force of religion. Many definitions of religion are ethnocentric and consequently fail to appreciate the religious influences which affects Montagnard cultures. Religion, as used here, is a personal awareness, or conviction of, the existence of a supreme being, or of supernatural powers and influences, which control the destinies of man. [14] The awareness of the existence of such supernatural forces may be accompanied by emotions of reverence, humility, gratitude, desires to serve and obey, or it can lead to attempts to manipulate these forces in the creation of a meaningful identity consistent with one's personal world view. [15] Robert Redfield says "... religion and magic are ways men must have, being men, to make the world acceptable, manageable, and right. "[16]

Religion has a dominant role in the daily life of the Montagnards. While the 33 tribes differ in many of their cultural patterns, all have myths which relate the origin of their particular ethnic group or "race". These myths are ethnocentrically focused in that they relate the beginning of the teller's tribe as being the first "people" on earth. [17] Most Montagnards are animistic in belief. As adherents of animism they attribute conscious life and an indwelling spirit to every material form of reality including trees, plants, stones, rivers, mountains, particular bits of ground, and the sky. Such natural phenomena as thunderstorms, floods, fire are also thought to have spirits. Included in the Montagnard belief system is the concept of the continued existence of individual disembodied spirits of the deceased who are capable of exercising either benignant or malignant influences. [18]

These supernatural spirits constitute a large pantheon generally called "yang" by all the tribal groups in spite of their great variety of spoken languages. [19] Though some of the spirits are good, the greater emphasis is always on those spirits which may be malevolent toward the tribesman concerned. An awareness and understanding of this dominant phase of daily life is essential if Montagnard value systems, behavior, taboos and patterns of logic are to be appreciated.

Some animistic tribesmen believe that each individual has a

spirit, or spirits without which sickness and death would soon occur. Normally a sorcerer is required for the treatment of these spirits in times of illness since sickness is believed to be spirit-created. Because of the ability of the sorcerer or "witch doctor" or "spirit lady" to communicate with the "spirit world", the persons holding this office are held in awe and are prominent members of the village.

The continued existence and presence of spirits of the deceased make it necessary to deal with them. Spirits which are ignored, unappeased and unattended may become angry, bitter and revengeful. Such unhappy spirits may then create harm, havoc, sickness and death for the living. The normal propitiation of spirits is made through ritual offerings. These offerings may be of rice, wine, or "betel chews", or the sacrifice of a chicken, dog, pig, or buffalo. Among the Katu the practice of human sacrifice is still thought to exist in spite of non-tribal attempts to suppress it. [20]

Because the disembodied spirits are thought to be like humans in emotional qualities, the Montagnards think of them as greedy, deceptive, and unpredictable. But they can be neutralized through appropriate ceremonies, sacrifices and the observance of taboos. Good spirits are ignored in favor of placating the evil ones. Fear of the evil spirits, and the potential danger they pose, wins the attention of the tribesmen over any honor bestowed on good spirits, who are present also, but do not create anxieties.

The major deities of the animistic Montagnards have been classified as follows:

The "Nhang" or "Yang"

For the polytheistic Montagnards, the "Nhang" or "Yang" is a kind of supreme god, a type of all-powerful being who prevails in the life of each Montagnard. The cult devoted to Nhang has originated some particular traditions handed down from generation to generation.

a) Before undertaking an important transaction, it is fitting to make an offering to Nhang to solicit success;

b) Before the sowing, and after the harvest, ceremonies are held to ask favorable weather conditions for the crop or to show their gratitude to Nhang.

The Montagnards believe, in addition, that Nhang reigns permanently over the rice fields and cultivated lands. From this, stem several taboos that resist all attempts to reform the traditional methods of cultivation.

Divinities

For the Montagnards there exist divinities on a high plane, followed by divinities of a lower plane. The former, who created the universe and man whom they nurture, can be enumerated as follows:

1. Bok-Hoi-Doi (The Creator).

The Creator, whose habitat is beyond the clouds, in the heavens, is the absolute master of the universe. He governs all the divinities and all the genii, good or bad. He made the sun, the moon, and the stars. His embodiment is a patriarch with white hair.

2. La-Kon-keh (The Creator's wife).

The Creator, like all men, has a wife, La-Kon-Keh, who created the Earth and all the Creatures who people it. La-Kon-Keh appears in dreams in the form of an old woman dressed in rags, looking very dirty.

3. Bok-Claik (God of thunder and lightning).

The influence of the god of thunder and lightning is not as great as that of the Creator or his wife. Nevertheless, his name is often recited in the prayers. According to Montagnard mythology, the god of thunder and lightning lies in heavy sleep during the dry season and awakens only during the diluvian season of rains, when he noisily announces his presence.

4. La-Pom (The goddess).

This is the daughter of the Creator and the older sister of La-Bok, the ancestor of the human race. She has a reputation for being generous, and for this reason her name is regularly mentioned in the ritual ceremonies.

5. Yang-Sori (God of the rice field).

This divinity reigns in the rice fields, in the granaries, and sometimes in the kettles. The Montagnards praise her, hoping to be able to benefit from the favors which she distributes to them. This is understandable, since her favors are synonymous with abundance and good crops.

6. <u>Yang-Dak</u> (Water god).

In the Montagnard regions, each stream and river has its god, designated as Yang-Dak; and as already known, there are as many Yang-Dak as there are streams. The Yang-Dak are subordinated to a super- god known as the Dragon. In dreams, the Dragon appears in the form of a hairy man, just as the Serpent and Mortar gods appear respectively as a young boy with long hair and an old man with large eyes.

7. <u>Yangkong</u> (God of the mountain).

The Montagnards practice as well the cult of mountains, which are each endowed with a god. There is, moreover, a god of stone. According to a legend which still remains engraved in their memory, within the hierarchy of divinities, there are two goddesses of the mountain who teach the Montagnards the craft of sorcery.

The divinities of the lower plane are of animal or vegetable origin; among these can be cited:

1. <u>Bok-Klia</u> (Lord Tiger).

From fear and from admiration, the farmers have given lord Tiger a pseudonym, Mister Thirtieth, Mr. Thirtieth is able to imitate both the cries of other animals of the jungle and the speech of man.

2. <u>Roix</u> (Lord Elephant).

Lord Elephant is a very combat-hardened fighter who often aids the Montagnard clans in combat by making use of his powerful defenses.

3. <u>Ket-Droik</u> (Lord Frog).

If there is any basis for which the Montagnards practice the cult of the frog, it would without doubt be because at harvest time this animal appears from all sides, in the rice fields as well as in the granary, in search of food. This appearance has led them to believe that the frog is the animal which protects the harvest and which announces the maturity of the crop.

4. <u>Yang-Xatok</u> (Lord of the Jar).

Xatok is the term for a type of baked- earth jar, brick red, which is frequently used in the ritual ceremonies and whose daily use is forbidden. When a boy, or a girl, or both make their appearance in a dream,

this signifies to the Montagnard that the divine will is
ordering him to go buy some jars of the Xatok variety.

    5. <u>Yang-Long</u> (Lord of the Tree).

Since there are several varieties of trees, there must
be several tree lords. The Montagnards love to relate
how sometimes when working in the fields, they heard
the cries and laughter of these lords.

These divinities enjoy a profound veneration by the
Montagnards, whether of the higher or lower plane
of the hierarchical classification. Nevertheless, the
cult of divinities on the higher plane is practiced in
the framework of periodical ritual ceremonies, and
is, thus permanent, while that of the lower plane is
celebrated but occasionally and according to the
directions of the sorcerers.[21]

Fear, anxiety and dread are dynamic forces in Montagnard
animistic concepts. Only by controlling and channeling these concerns
can the tribesmen find a meaningful existence. Fear is always
present in the heart of the tribespeople. It may be fear of the spirits
of the house, the rice fields, the water, the mountains or those of
the kra monkey, the barking deer, or the fearsome tiger. There
is also fear of the witch, the spirits of the deceased and of the
sorcerer, medicine man or "spirit-lady" who can communicate
with the spirits inhabiting the supernatural world.

Fear determines where, when and how the tribesman will
prepare and plant his rice fields. Fear enters into the choice of
marriage partners. Fear even determines where and how the
tribesman will be buried in death. As an example, fear may cause
the Brou tribesman to throw his dead infant violently into its grave
so that upright stakes in the bottom of the grave will pierce its
small body in order to prevent the baby's spirit from returning to
the village. Similar fears cause Tring Tribesmen to bury their
dead with exposed feet so that the spirit of the deceased will not
be angered by being imprisoned in the grave.

It is this same emotion that cause villagers to retreat into their
own homes and leave a bereaved family to bury its own dead if
death came through what the Montagnard consider to be unnatural.

Unnatural may mean murder, childbirth, suicide or by tigers. Moreover the bereaved family's hardship and grief are compounded by the fear-imposed requirements that such a victim must be buried in the jungle apart from other village graves, and the unfortunate family must abandon their home at once.

Fear can be powerful enough that the animistic tribesman will abandon a newly cleared field or even one in which badly-needed rice is ready for harvest. It often dictates the location, construction and utilization of a tribal house. In most houses there is either a spirit pole or a special section dedicated to some particular spirit of which the family is in awe. Fear is so present in daily life that it may cause a host to poison guests toward whom he has no malice or to poison the village water source and obliterate the community. This anxiety may cause a new mother to starve her baby or a son to kill his unsuspecting father. [22]

The Montagnards place great emphasis on omens which may come in dreams or in signs. It is believed that omens are sent by the spirits to warn of future good or evil. Should a tribesman on the way to his field notice a perched bird, he will watch carefully to ascertain which way it flies. If it flies to the tribesman's left, the spirits are warning him of impending danger, and he feels compelled to return home immediately. If the track of a certain animal is seen on the trail or path, it is a sign that should the traveler continue his journey, he will surely meet the "devil" himself. To free himself, the traveler must consult the sorcerer to determine when it will be safe for him to continue. Any violation of such travel taboos will most likely result in a tiger eating the offender. Incidentally, it is fear that causes tribesmen to refer to the tiger as "Mr. Tiger" if the name must be used at all. Moreover, it seems generally accepted that some people have the ability to become tigers upon occasion, even as some tigers may revert to being men.

To the animistic Montagnard, all existence is one and the same thing so that there are no permanent divisions or distinctions of animate and inanimate, or human and non-human. Past and present are contemporary, i.e., only that of the past which is still present has value, while the future is unknown and unpredictable. The future can only be realized and appreciated as it becomes the present. This concept of being can best be characterized by the assertion that animism does not have the linear concept of time which is basic to civilizations influenced by Judeo-Christian thought.

Animism is basically non-ethical and non-moral, i.e., it does not attempt to change the ethics and character of its adherents. Rather, it results in attempts to create the proper atmosphere in which the spirits will comply with the will of the animists. Because of such concepts, animistic rites become methods which utilize fetishes, blood sacrifices, symbolic designs, magic works, taboos, etc. as techniques which cause the spirits to do the will of the worshipper. In this respect, the animistic adherent does not view himself as an entirely helpless or passive victim of the invisible world; rather, he perceives himself as one capable of using the right means or the correct religio-magic formula to achieve his own goals. In this procedure all rituals must follow the prescribed standard pattern in order to avoid causing discomfort to the spirits. Nevertheless, the animist expends much of his thought, effort, energy and resources in religious observances designed to channel the supernatural forces for his benefit. He is, therefore, constantly on the lookout for members of the spirit pantheon who may fit into the situation of the moment.

Many of the tribespeople give so much of their property, livestock and energy to sacrificial offerings and taboo requirements that poverty is common. Some tribespeople, when ordered to make a buffalo sacrifice to the troublesome spirits, make marks on their brass arm rings as "promissory notes" to the spirits that they will sacrifice a buffalo as soon as they can acquire one. The buffalo sacrificial requirements impose upon the Montagnards an economic drain quite similar to that which would be imposed on the average American by the destruction of his high-priced, but uninsured, automobile. Nevertheless these rites seem necessary to the animistic Montagnard and provide order and meaning for his life. Blood sacrifices are essential offerings to the proper spirits for such things as protection, health, prosperity, and events related to birth, marriage death, drought, warfare, etc. Each sacrifice has its own special and prescribed ritual which must be followed if desired results are to be achieved. Nearly all sacrificial rites to the spirits include the drinking of a special rice wine. In fact, some Montagnard tribes feel that the spirits would be unhappy if the rites were celebrated with the drinking of wine purchased from non-tribal sources. The Montagnard wine is normally consumed through long hollow reeds or bamboo tubes inserted in the top of the wine jugs Water is often added to the wine as drinking continues so that the jug stays full, but the alcoholic content is reduced.

Normally during the religious ceremonies, or on other special occasions, the Montagnard village is taboo to all non-villagers. On such occasions taboo signs will be prominently placed outside the village. These may be sticks lying across the main path or sticking on a bush or pole near the path, or anything which seems out of place in the area. Sometimes the village word for "forbidden" will be prominently displayed, and these taboo signs mean just that. [23]

Barriers are also often placed across pathways leading into the village in order to keep evil spirits from entering. It is important to keep them out for they will probably bring sickness, death, harm, danger or hunger to the community. Sometimes the barricade may be just a plank lying across the path in a place chosen by the sorcerer. At other times, it may consist of a maze along part of the path so that several turns must be accomplished in entering the village. Humans can figure out the mazes, but it is believed that the evil spirits cannot. On other occasions the path will feature elaborate temptations to lure the evil spirit aside. These may include a table and chairs for resting, attractive displays of foods believed tempting to the spirits, small jars of rice wine with hollow drinking tubes already inserted, or perhaps a floral display. Sometimes even steps are built from the path to these displays in order to make the spirit's climb easier.

In other cases- when attraction is thought to fail - attempts to frighten spirits are made. While one means may be a mirror which will frighten the spirit when he sees himself, another is the construction of a man's figure with a cooked bow and arrow pointed at the path. Sometimes these figures may have a sword or knife hanging from the loin cloth as an added threat. The Jarai place great faith in such grotesque figures. [24]

Each tribe seems to have its own taboo sign for the spirits or for unwelcome men. The Katu use a tree planted in the path, the Raday hang a monkey skin over the pathway, the Sedang have a maze of fetishes that block the village entrance, while other tribes have their own specialty. Whether a single sign or several, they all mean "KEEP OUT".

The chief declares a curse on anyone who leaves the village. The evil spirits will bring disaster on those who venture out - even to their rice fields. The chief warns that their own knives will slash them; bamboo will pierce their bodies; a snake or tiger will kill them. So the superstitious tribesmen stay home. If a tribal stranger ignores the warning and enters the village, he is taken captive and bound until the curse is lifted. By doing this, the evil spirits of the stranger's village are thus powerless to wage war on the spirits of the home village. Warfare between opposing spirits would bring horrible catastrophy upon the village. [25]

Similar devices are used in the home when a new baby arrives. During the first week of a baby's life the whole family may be isolated from the community by the use of a taboo sign of tree branches blocking the doorway. This is done to prevent the devil or evil spirits from slipping into the house to steal the spirit of the baby. Because the Montagnards fear the evil spirits, they give their babies such names as "pig", "dog", "naughty", "poor" and names of the sex organs. They think that evil spirits will not be interested in such badly-named children. Because male babies are more highly prized, yet have a higher death rate, they are often given girls' names and dressed in girls' clothing in order to fool the spirits. If a child is given a name, and many are not even named until the first and most dangerous year has passed, it may be kept secret and not used until the infant is much older. Protective sacrifices are offered for babies and additional devices such as charms or strings are tied about the baby's neck, arms, and ankles to keep evil spirits away. [26]

SOCIAL CUSTOMS AND BEHAVIOR PATTERNS

Fear is continually present in the daily life of most Montagnards.

Their religion is primarily an attempt to overcome it so that existence might have meaning and purpose. Even those tribesmen who become Roman Catholics or Protestants continue to cling to many conscious and subconscious animistic concepts and practices for a long time. But this is not too different from many western cultures where animistic notions are still in evidence. [27] However, as the tribesmen are exposed to other cultures where such ideas are not dominant, many of the characteristics of fearful behavior are often gradually overcome.

The Montagnards, like many other preliterate or semiliterate peoples, may conduct a feud for several generations - even long after the cause of the original fighting has been forgotten. Revenge will be carefully and patiently planned. When the moment is right the avenger will strike either openly or secretly as the occasion demands. Within the cultural heritage of the tribesman lurk the qualities that can make him either an unflinching friend or a deadly enemy.

Having an unfamiliar logical pattern, the Montagnard often reacts quite differently than a Westerner anticipates unless he has studied the behavioral patterns of these Vietnamese mountaineers. Consequently many foreign observers differ on the question of "truth" among the tribal peoples. Some declare that the Montagnards are as truthful as any other people on the face of the earth, and that any apparent failure to be truthful is based upon differences in logic rather than deliberate misrepresentation. Others insist that if the Montagnards do not "lie", they must have strange notions of what is fact and what is not. The differences in values, thought patterns and language probably explain most of the difficulties in this matter. Many American military privileged to serve with the Montagnards have the highest praise for their truthfulness, diligence and faithfulness under difficult circumstances. In this regard, it is of interest to observe that this is one of the major problems between the Montagnards and the ethnic Vietnamese. This attitude is largely based on tribal lore and unpleasant dealings with the Vietnamese tradesmen and military, rather than on massive interaction between the two cultures.

Montagnards are similarly concerned about the use and misuse of personal property. Living in a semi-closed community in which each individual has an integral role, tribesmen do not practice theft. While some foreigners have contrasting views pertaining to Montagnard exchanges of either wealth or property, primitive or semi-primitive people do not usually steal from their friends. Once again, an understanding of tribal logic and values explains the apparent discrepancies which trouble some foreigners. Sometimes the apparently gross differences in wealth between a tribesman and a foreigner may reduce the sense of urgency in the repayment of a loan, but this is not stealing!

Likewise, the borrowing of a water buffalo or tools may persist without any effort to return the loan. The tribal practice is to go and claim your loan when your need for it arises; in the meantime it is being looked after and serving a useful purpose. Upon one occasion the loan of a buffalo was lengthy enough for it to calve twice before its owner went and reclaimed his livestock, but there was no sense of injustice involved. But to take property without asking permission is a different matter. Moreover, the sharp dealings of the few merchants who abuse trading with the Montagnards tend to make them distrust all ethnic Vietnamese and brand them as thieves. The abuse which sometimes accompanies military activities in an area with a seeming disregard for the rights of others, and often the nonpayment for items consumed or wantonly destroyed, does much to build a wall of hostility between the Montagnards and the ethnic Vietnamese or other non-tribal peoples.

The average tribesman possesses but few personal items - crossbow, arrows, knife, wine jug, ax, loin cloth, etc. Due to tribal beliefs, these items are often disposed in or on the grave of the deceased. Even a cooking pot may be put at the grave of a woman. If not placed at the grave, those items considered personal are destroyed. The Montagnards claim that non-tribesmen in the area sometimes take these items which does much to perpetuate the distrust between the tribesmen and "foreigners" (all non-tribesmen). It is well to remember that the semi-isolated Montagnard has little actual contact with ethnic Vietnamese except for the tradesman and the soldier, so his ideas of the Vietnamese can be quite distorted.

GUIDELINES FOR UNDERSTANDING

While all cultures are unique, paradoxically all cultures have a basic sameness. Sharing a common framework predicated upon the humanness of man, cultures have vast differences of structure, and configuration. Kluckhohn, a noted anthropologist, believes that all cultures develop various solutions to questions posed by human nature in contrasting geographic, historical, economic situations. [28] Even though no single factor can be held responsible for the variability or uniformity of cultures, an understanding of the similarities and differences among them is essential to effective interaction.

Man s processes of logic are reflected in his value systems and behavior patterns. He acts and reacts toward the situations confronting him in a manner consistent with his most deeply ingrained concepts. Men usually respond to troublesome or threatening situations in one of four ways or in combinations or modifications of them. These four ways are to fight, flee, ignore or submit. In these responses the Montagnard is not much different from the American. Similarly, the biological needs -food, drink, rest, sex, etc. - do not differ from those of other people. He is subject to injury, disease, accident, death, anxiety, love, hate, fear, joy and sorrow just as are others. However, his unique culture determines how these needs and emotional requirements are to be met. The uniqueness of a particular culture is largely determined by geographical factors, economic realities and religious concepts.

Customs and beliefs peculiar to particular tribal or racial groups such as the Montagnards determine to a very large extent their viewpoints of life and behavior patterns. The relative isolation of the tribesman restricts his ability to understand readily or to appreciate concepts and objectives from outside his experienced realm of knowledge. Therefore, any attempts to alter Montagnard thought processes and living patterns radically must take cognizance of primitive living conditions and life patterns which have not previously required broader considerations. These circumstances are quite different than those known by most Americans. It becomes very important that the initial approaches to tribal peoples be carefully considered and correct procedures utilized. If Montagnard-American relations are to be effective, the approaches to the tribesman must be within the scope of his understanding. The recognition that he has previously experienced little need to adjust to anything larger than the immediate demands of his environment is no reflection upon his intelligence or abilities.

Normally the Montagnards are quick to grasp practical ideas and many demonstrate unusual abilities in languages, the arts, and mechanical skills. It must not be forgotten that his ingenuity has enabled him to exist in a hostile environment for many centuries.

The Montagnard is also a practical and rather successful psychologist within his own environment. It is imperative that those who would seek his cooperation be sincere. Insincerity or hypocrisy are quickly detected by the tribespeople. Outsiders who reveal any tendencies in this direction are rejected and despised. While the Montagnards are generally friendly, they will react with contempt and even hostility toward anyone with an ingratiating or obsequious manner. A good rule is to be yourself while maintaining a high degree of awareness regarding the customs and expectations of the tribesmen concerned. A sense of dignity must always be maintained in association with tribal peoples. To attempt to live and function at the lowest possible level "overdoes" the role of attempting to communicate. Moreover, it leaves nothing for the tribesman to "look up to", to admire, to desire to follow, or to perceive as an "authority figure". If the American is to be the "older brother" to the Montagnard, he must win their respect rather than their pity or scorn.

The fact that cultural customs contrast greatly does not mean that one custom is right and another opposite wrong. Neither does it render cooperation impossible. Rather, an understanding of the differences and their causes can help Americans to more fully appreciate the fundamental sameness of all peoples. The Montagnard requires time to think over ideas or to accept people. He wants the opportunity to explore his own mind and to consult with his fellow tribesman. "Ready-made solutions" are not generally acceptable to him but, given an opportunity to examine an idea, modify and execute it within the range of his own perception, the Montagnard will go to great lengths to make it successful. Under such circumstances, economic or physical hardship does not deter him from the determined course.

If programs of action can be understood by the tribesman -if the objectives have values and benefits which he can perceive,he will generally accept them. Because of the Montagnard concepts of time, he is not normally interested in some grandiose scheme that will benefit his people tomorrow. He lives in the "Now" and the goals of his efforts must be realistic enough to produce results within a relatively short period of time.

FOOTNOTES

1. Robbins Burling, Hill Farms and Padi Lands, Englewood Cliffs, N.J. Prentice-Hall, Inc., 1965. The whole book is concerned with the divisions of the Southeast Asian mainland population and why they exist. Other excellent basic sources on this subject are listed in the bibliography at the conclusion of this volume.

2. See Bronislaw Malinowski, Magic, Science and Religion, Garden City, New York, Doubleday Anchor Books, 1948.

3. This tribal number is that established by the Summer Institute of Linguistics, Saigon, Vietnam in their July 1966 listing of "Vietnam Minority Languages"; Frank M. Lebar, Gerald C. Hickey, John K. Musgrave, Ethnic Groups of Mainland Southeast Asia, New Haven, Human relations Area Files Press, 1964.

4. Confer Frank Lebar et al, Ethnic Groups of Mainland Southeast Asia.

5. Navy Personal Response Tape on Montagnards #30. This tape on the Primitive Tribes of South Vietnam is a part of the Navy Personal Response sponsored by the Chief of Chaplains, U.S. Navy, and includes the on-site research files of CDR. R.L. Mole, CHC, USN, 1965-66.

6. The tribal breakdown is based upon the Summer Institute of Linguistics, Saigon, "Vietnamese Minority Languages" List of July 1966; Lebar et al, Ethnic Groups of Mainland Southeast Asia; and Navy Personal Response Tape #30 "Primitive Tribes of South Vietnam".

7. Confer Bronislow Malinowski, Magic, Science and Religion, New York, Doubleday and Co., 1948 in discussion of mana; also.

Gerald C. Hickey, The Major Ethnic Groups of the South Vietnamese Highlands, Advanced Research Projects Agency Memorandum 4041 of April 1965.

8. P. Guilleminent, "La tribu bahnar du Kontum," Bulletin de l'Ecole Francaise d'Extreme Orient, Vol. 45, 1951-1952, pp. 393-561

9. Navy Personal Response Tape #30, "The Primitive Tribes of South Vietnam" by Les Smith. Also see Homer E. Dowdy, The Bamboo Cross, New York, Harper and Row, 1964; Laura Irene Smith, Victory In Vietnam, Grand Rapids, Michigan, Zondervan Publishing House, 1965.

10. L. Sabatier, Recuèil des coutumes Rhades du Darlac, Hanoi, Imprimerie d'Extreme Orient, 1940.

11. Personal Response Project Tape #36 by Ralph Haupers on the Stieng; also R. L. Mole, Fieldnotes 1965-66 on the Navy Personal Response; and T. Gerber, "Coutumier Stieng" Bulletin de L'Ecole Francaise d'Extreme Orient, Vol 45, 1951, pp. 228-269.

12. David A. Nuttle, The Montagnards of the High Plateau of South Vietnam, Saigon, USIA, 1962, p. 11.

13. Gerald C. Hickey, The Major Ethnic Groups of the South Vietnamese Highlands, Santa Monica, California, The Rand Corp., 1964, RM-4041-ARPA and R. L. Mole, Fieldnotes of Navy Personal Response 1965-66 (Unpublished).

14. Confer "Religion", Webster's Third International Dictionary Springfield, Mass., G&C Merriam Co., 1961, p. 1968.

15. Ibid

16. Robert Redfield in the Introduction to Bronislaw Malinowski's Magic, Science and Religion, p. 12.

17. Confer the various issues of Jungle Frontiers, News

magazine of the Vietnam Mission (Tribes Region) of the Christian and Missionary Alliance, 260 West 44th Street, New York; also Gerald C. Hickey, The Major Ethnic Groups of the South Vietnamese Highlands.

18.   See "Animism", Webster's Third International Dictionary, p. 86.

19.   R. L. Mole, Fieldnotes of Navy Personal Response for 1965-66 (Unpublished).

20.   Consult "Blood Hunt" in the chapter of this book titled "KATU" The practice is described in detail and gives references.

21.   Henri Maspero, Les Traits Characteristigues dans les Moeurs et Coutumes des Tribus Montagnards Au Sud du Vietnam, translated as The Montagnard Tribes of South Vietnam by the Joint Publications Research Service, Washington, D.C., 1962 pp. 80-85.

22.   Mole 1965-66 Fieldnotes, Navy Personal Response Tape #30 by Kenneth Smith, "The Primitive Tribes of South-Central Vietnam".

23.   R. L. Mole, 1965-66 Field-notes which include interviews with tribesmen, foreign students of tribal culture in Southeast Asia, and with Christian Missionary and Alliance missionaries in Vietnam.

24.   Evelyn Mangham, "Superstitions" Jungle Frontiers, Summer 1960, p. 10.

25.   Ibid

26.   R. L. Mole 1965-66 Field-notes; Navy Personal Response Tape #30, "The Primitive Tribes of South-Central Vietnam".

27.   Confer Eugene A. Nida, Customs and Cultures, New York, Harper and Row, 1954; also Eugene A. Nida and William A. Smalley, Introducing Animism, Friendship Press, 1959, for extensive elaboration of this factor in Western cultures. Also see the very fine discussion by Louis J. Luzbetak, The

Church and Cultures, Techny, Illinois, Divine Word
Publications, 1963, p. 214f "Secondary Aspects of Culture
Change".

28.   Confer Clyde Kluckhohn, "Universal Categories of Culture"
in A. L. Kroeber (Editor) Anthropology Today, Chicago,
University of Chicago Press, re-edited by Sol Tax, Phoenix
paperback edition, 1953, pp. 507-523 (p. 520).

IN VIETNAM'S HIGHLANDS

YOU WILL FIND THE MONTAGARDS
(ESPECIALLY THE BROÛ TRIBE)
ARE VERY FRIENDLY.

    —TAKE TIME TO SAY—
      "HELLO" : BAHN TAY !
   "THANK YOU" : SAH UNH
"I AM YOUR FRIEND" : KOOT LAH YOY AN
               YEE HAH

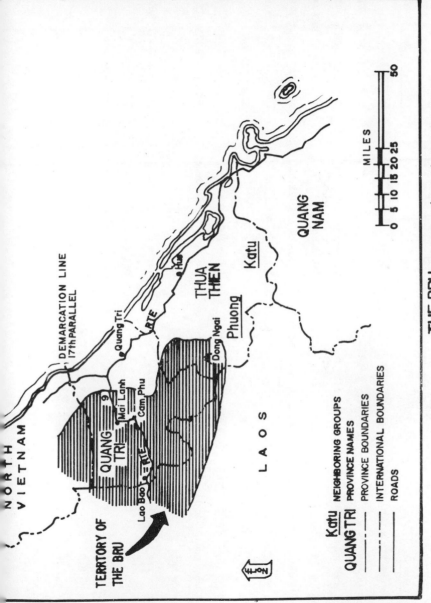

THE BRU MAP FROM/CRESS/CINFAC R-0426.

39

NAVY PERSONAL RESPONSE ELEMENTARY BRU PHRASE LIST

Vietnamese	English	Bru	(Phonetic Bru)
Chào ông (to a man)	Hello	Ban Te	BAHN TAY!
Tôi là bạn	I am your friend	Cuq la you anhia	KOOT LAH YOY AN YEEHAH
Tôi muốn gặp lãnh tu bạn	I would like to meet your chief	Cuq yoc ramoh arish	KOOK YAH RAHMUH ARYEE AYEEH
Các bạn là người lãnh.	You are good people.	Anhia coaî ᴏ.	AN YEEHAH KO EYE AH.
Người dân bạn tên là gì?	What's the name of your people?	Anhia la coai ntrdu.	AN YEEAH LAH KO E'E EN TROW.
Bạn cần đồ ăn không?	Do you need food?	Anhia yoc sana tau?	AN YEEAH YAHK SANAH DUH?
Đồ ăn này tốt đối với bạn	This food is good for you	Sana nai O.	SINAY NAY AH.
Bạn cần thầy thuốc không?	Do you need a doctor?	Anhia yoc bac-se	AN YEEAH YAHK BAHK-SHEE?
Tôi uống nước được không?	May I have water?	Cuq seiq nquaiq dauq?	KOOk SHAYT MEW OIT DUH?
Cảm ồn bạn	Thank you	Sa-aun	SAH UNH
Bạn có bán nỏ không?	Will you sell crossbows?	Anhia cheq tameang tau?	AN YEEAH CHAYT TOMEEYANG DUH?
Dạ có.	Yes	Op uuh.	OT OOH-UH
Dạ không.	No.	Tau boun.	DUH BUNH.
Bao nhiêu?	How much?	Maleq praq?	MALLET P-R-RAH?
Xin tha lỗi cho tôi.	Excuse me	Seiq Loih	SHAYT LOYICH.
Xin mời bạn đi ra.	Please come out.	Seiq looh	SHAYT LA-AH

CHAPTER II

THE BRU

The Bru have several names including Baroo, Brou, Van Kieu, Ca-Lo and Kalo. The latter two translate as "bosom-friend". The tribesman and the ethnic Vietnamese who know and accept each other may use these terms when speaking to one another. Although some authorities give additional names as Leu, Galler, Leung, Muong Leung, Muong Kong, Khua and Tri,[1] these appear to be similar peoples primarily located in Laos. The Bru use the term "Bru" when referring to groups like "Bru Radai, Bru Jarai, Bru Miq"(the American Indian), etc. Generally, individuals of the Bru ethnic group identify themselves as members of their particular village when questioned by outsiders. This is a common practice among the pre-literate peoples when villages are largely self-sufficient without higher centralized political structures. The village is the highest political organization except for the gradually imposed Vietnamese structures.

Language: The Bru are a full tribe even though their language is considered to be a subgrouping of the Katuic branch of the Mon-Khmer family of languages.[2] While being related to the speech of such Mon-Khmer tribes as the Bahnar, Sedang, Cua, Hre, Jeh, etc., it is more closely allied to that of the Katu. The Bru language, unlike that of the Vietnamese, is non-tonal.

The language of the Bru is currently being prepared as a written language for the first time. The task of preparing a phonetic alphabet for the Bru language is one of the roles of the Summer Institute of Linguistics in conjunction with Vietnamese National Department of Education. Moreover some Christian Vietnamese and foreign missionaries to the Bru are participating in the effort to establish means of written communication for this and other tribes in Vietnam.[3] In spite of being a preliterate people, some of the Bru near the Laotian border speak Laotian; others speak French and Vietnamese to a limited degree. A few of the Bru, who are associated with American military personnel, are beginning to use English also.

Population Estimates: There has never been an accurate census of the Bru. The estimates of foreign observers among the Bru range from forty to seventy thousand persons.[4]

Location: The Bru are located in the extreme Northwest corner of

South Vietnam and in the contiguous areas of Laos and North Vietnam. The tribal area of the Bru starts about fifteen miles inland from the China Sea due west of the city of Quang Tri. It extends westward across the Laotian border and North across the 17th Parallel. In Laos the Bru inhabit the Kha Leung plateau which is just west of the Laotian Annamite Mountains. In North Vietnam, they are just across the 17th Parallel in the rugged country almost identical to that of their kinsmen in South Vietnam.

The Bru tribal area extends southward almost to a line even with the ancient royal city of Hue so that National route 9 which crosses Vietnam is about the center of the tribal area. National Route 9 was, until the present conflict, the best land route from the coastal area of Annam with the cities of Danang, Hue and Quang Tri across the mountains to Vientiane, Laos. It can now be traveled only in heavily guarded military convoys with accompanying engineers to replace destroyed bridges and check for land mines. Most of the Bru travel routes are trails and paths that follow the rivers and the natural contour of the land. Especially is this so in the more difficult forest-covered steep mountains close to the Laotian border.

Within the region of the Bru, several high mountains dominate the skyline. North of National Route 9 are two major mountains: one of these is the 5,240 feet high Dong Sa Mui, while the other is the 5,820 feet high Dong Voi Mep which the French call Dent du Tigre. Towering over and dominating Route 9 in the southern tribal area is the 7,750 feet high Dong Quang Ngai.

The Bru region is affected by the May-October summer and the November-January winter monsoons. Rainfall in the higher elevations averages more than 150 inches while the lower levels receive more than 60 inches per year. This evenly distributed rainfall through most of the year promotes a rain forest in the higher regions. Here the trees are 75 to 90 feet high and form an almost continuous canopy. A second layer of smaller trees 45 to 60 feet tall form a second layer of foliage, while below this there is an abundance of saplings and seedlings. Because little sunlight penetrates to the ground level, not much ground cover exists to block the traveler's way in the dry seasons. However clinging to and suspended from the trees is an abundance of woody climbing plants known as lianas, with orchids, epiphytes and other herbaceous plants.

Where the foregoing primary rain forest has been cleared and then left uncultivated, the forest growth is smaller with an abundance of heavy ground growth of tall grass, lianas and other herbaceous climbers. The heavy dense grass may grow to a height of more than twenty feet so that penetration through such jungle is difficult and requires the almost constant use of a machete or bush-knife if one is not using the well-worn paths.

Three larger rivers are in the Bru area. The Song Bo Dien (Dỗq Crổng Ravúm in Bru) is the most northern and flows by Dong Ha to enter the China Sea. The Song Quang Tri (Dỗq Crổng Calang in Bru) transits the Ba Long valley and goes through the city of Quang Tri. The Song Pone (Dỗq Crổng Sapổl in Bru) flows westward into Laos toward the Mekong. In Bru, Doq Crổng means "big river" in contrast to a stream or brook which is called Doq Tum. Thus two smaller streams, Do'q Tum Labuoiq (Song Rao Quan in Vietnamese) and the Dỗq Tũm Calang in the higher Bru area form the headwaters of the Song Quang Tri. All the rivers furnish waterways for tribal travel while in the lower foothills and plains, they are used for both transportation and irrigation. In addition to these larger streams, there are others which serve the various villages as water sources, but none have been effectively harnessed for man's use.

Neighbors: The Bru neighbors to the East are ethnic Vietnamese, while the Cado and the Tau-oi (Taoih) are the tribal neighbors to the south. The Tau-oi are situated along the border of Laos immediately south of the Bru. The Pacoh are to the southeast of the Bru and due east of the Tau-oi so that the Pacoh area extends almost to Hue. The Bru and Pacoh share only a narrow common border area with mutual interchange of trade, language and numerous similar patterns of culture. West of the Bru are the Mang Cong, who are often thought to be Bru, except the Bru consider them not to be Bru even if closely related, and the CRAI who are Laotian in language and customs.

The estimated twenty-five to forty thousand Bru in South Vietnam are divided into several larger settlement areas of Quang Tri Province. For instance, it is estimated that about 10,000 live in the general area of Cam Phu, [5] some in the vicinity of Lao Bao (near Khe Sanh) on the

Laotian border, [6] with another 10,000 existing in the Huong Hoa District, [7] and others in the Cam-Lo District of Quang Tri Province. [8] Some of the Bru, not wishing to live in resettlement village area, apparently still live in scattered remote villages in terrain too rugged for ready access by non-Bru and too isolated for frequent contacts with anyone outside of their own village. The village of Khe Sanh is actually the Vietnamese government center in the area and is located on National route 9 about six miles from Laos and only a little greater distance to North Vietnam. In Khe Sanh the Bru and the Vietnamese intermingle in the affairs of daily life in the same area.

INDIVIDUAL CHARACTERISTICS OF THE BRU

The Bru men, whose height varies from about five feet two inches to five feet four inches, are generally stocky and powerfully built with an average weight of 115 to 120 pounds. Their size is roughly similar to that of the Vietnamese except the Bru tend to be more muscular. The women are just a bit shorter than the men. Most of the Bru have high cheekbones, black hair, dark brown eyes, wider noses than do the Vietnamese, and have light brown skin. [9] In fact, their skin coloring is quite similar to that of the Filipinos, the Indonesians or some of the American Indians.

Many of the Bru men and women have tatooed faces, and a number of them have their front upper teeth filed, or broken down to the gums. This may be due to their traditions pertaining to the spirits, or as "beauty treatments". Since long teeth are throught to make a person resemble an animal, the remedy is to cut off these teeth. This puberty rite makes it easier for the Bru male to acquire a suitable mate. This custom seems to be dying out as many Bru now retain their front teeth. The men do not normally wear ornaments, but may have pierced ears. Some of the pierced ear lobes of the women are stretched to permit inserts of wood, pewter or other ornaments with the latter sometimes including clumps of cotton. [10] The women may wear a silver ring about their necks or necklaces made of old French coins.

Normally, the Bru men and women pull their long black hair into a chignon, (a coil of hair made into a pad on the back or side of the head.) At times the women may wear their chignon in a tight spiral on one side of the head rolled in a colored cloth turban with at least one lock of hair allowed to hang free in back of the head.[11]

The normal apparel for the Bru men is a loin cloth. But as westernized civilization is exposed to them, a number now wear trousers over their loin cloths. Most of the men now wear shirts when they go to market or voluntarily deal with foreigners. The women wear skirts made of a piece of cloth which is wrapped around and tied into a knot at the waist. In warm weather, if a blouse is worn by the women, it is often left unbuttoned. Generally the jackets and blouses of the Bru women have sleeves. Certainly this is true of their "dress-up" blouse that often contains rows of coin sewed into place. In cold weather the Bru man may wear more clothing as protection against the cold, even using a blanket about his shoulders, but it is rare for a woman to do so.

Children up to the age of puberty wear very little clothing. After puberty young girls must wear blouses until they are married and have their first baby. After that, blouses are worn only as protection against the cold or for the benefit of "strangers" in town.[12]

Long-time foreign observers of the Bru consider them to be friendly, hospitable and cheerful.[13] The Bru people are a gentle non-warlike tribe with this characteristic trait shown in their sacrifices to the spirits. It is one of the very few Vietnamese tribal peoples who do not torture their sacrificial animals as they normally kill the animals quickly and mercifully.

Americans serving among the Bru consider them to be a hardworking intelligent people. However, their concept of labor is not governed by the clock, but rather the agricultural and jungle life of their environment. From earliest childhood the Bru are reared in the tradition of specific rules for all phases of behavior with the belief that the spirits will surely punish any violations of customary rules. Being psychologically enmeshed in these traditions, the Bru are ever alert to omens from the spirits.

Patterns of Bru thought include the family and clan, and then the individual. He seems to consider the effects of an action on his family and clan before he thinks of its effect on himself. Therefore, typical

of some other Montagnard tribes, decisions or acts are often post-
poned until consultations can be held with family and clan or village
leaders. Once these conferences are held and decisions are reached,
the Bru will hold to the agreed course of action regardless of the cost
to himself. 14

THE VILLAGE AND ITS BUILDINGS

The Bru people are village-oriented as there is no centralized
tribal organization. The Bru, being non-nomadic, generally prefer to keep their villages in one location. However, governmental
security plans have caused many Bru to be resettled in fortified
strategic villages. Even in these more compact settlements, the
Bru characteristic patterns of life continue. While the villages
are normally walled with bamboo fences, (stakes, punji sticks and
or barbed wire), the village area has many fruit trees - bananas,
coconuts, oranges, papayas, mangos. Coffee trees add both color
and shade.[15] The protective devices of the tribesmen predate the
presence of communism as ancient history of the area refer to
these defensive methods.

Bamboo is the primary building material for Bru houses, and
is used in many ways. It is woven or plaited for walls; split for
floors; used whole for rafters or wall studding; sliced and softened
for use in tying the various parts of the house together. Larger
pieces of bamboo may be used for joists and supports. In some
instances it may be split for shingles as the roofs may be of either
shingle or thatch.

Most Bru houses - even in fortified resettlement villages -
are built on strong posts with the floor being five or more feet off
the ground. Access to Bru houses is a ladder which may be removed if the occupants desire. Normally each Bru house has a
large uncovered porch which allows entrance to either of the two
rooms of most houses as the larger room is for the men and the
smaller one for the women. The large porch serves to keep the
inside of the house clean as mud and dirt are removed from the
feet before entering the house, and for drying such items as rice
grain, tobacco, coffee, etc. Unlike some tribes, the Bru have no

46

taboos that prevent either sex from entering the room of the other.

Each room may have a floor-level earthen fire box supported from below by a post. Fires in these open boxes may be used for cooking, for heating, for drying either food or clothing. Some houses have partial ceilings used for storage, while others have a small room or two that can be reached by the porch that are used for storage. Few of the houses have doors since the doorway is a primary source of natural lighting. When window spaces are added, these may have crude thatched or skillfully plaited shutters which may be closed when necessary. Many of the houses have a doorway with a small platform in addition to the large porch. This small platform was formerly a place which permited the mounting of elephants as a number of these were found in the Bru tribal areas as domesticated animals. Currently, conditions and changing times have altered this practice even though a few domesticated elephants still exist. Dimensions of the dwellings vary as does the number of persons living in each house. Ideally the house will have but one family. Now some may house several nuclear, but related, families.[16]

The major political unit in Bru social structure is the village with the central figure of the village being its chief. Each village is an autonomous governing unit as the tribes have never been united under a central chief or king.[17] While cooperation between villages may occur from time to time, this is only on special occasions. While the village chief is responsible to the District chief, and is therefore a government representative within the village, to the Bru, their chief is much more than this.

Often the chieftainship is inherited. When no eligible direct descendant is available, the office may go to another member of the former chief's clan. The village chief must be consulted on all matters pertaining to village life, including moving a household, marriage, funerals, sacrifices, location of fields, cutting down large trees, etc. He act as judge in those disputes between families and often as arbitrator within family disagreements. He has the authority to require all villagers to work on any needed community job, and he is the final authority on village traditions. His authority and judgments are never questioned. Since he is the court of last resort on village matters, the only recourse open to anyone who disagrees with his decisions, judgments, or authority is to leave the village, and move to another one or start a new settlement.[18]

Bru society is patrilineal so that family authority rests with the eldest male of each family. When purely family matters are involved, he can make the decision. On matters which involve more than one family group, the heads of each clan may meet with the chief if he desires. The village chief makes decisions that concern war, village movement, punishment for serious violations of tribal traditions and customs, arrangements for village sacrifices to the spirits, etc. [19] Disputes between individuals within a clan will be settled in the clan. Disputes between individuals of different clans will be settled by the village chief if they cannot be settled between the involved parties to the satisfaction of all. While the chief may consult with clan heads before rendering a decision, the final authority is his. He has an integral part in every marriage or funeral celebration for a member of his village. He is consulted when large sacrifices are to be made; when fields are to be moved, when large trees are to be cut down, etc. He represents the central government to the villagers and the village to all other agencies of government.

SOCIAL STRUCTURE

The kinship system of the Bru is patrilineal. Males occupy the prominent places politically, socially and religiously. They are afforded many rights and privileges denied to females. Within the Bru tribe, the clan (sau) is the most prominent and influential social unit inasmuch as the clan is responsible for the welfare of all clan members.

All the members of the clan have a common spirit (Yiang) that watches over them and that must be placated at various times with sacrifices that may vary according to "felt" needs. In fact, the attitude toward this particular spirit seems to be the basic unifying factor for the clan. Within the clan, great care is exercised to avoid offense to this spirit because it, normally thought of as "he", has the power to bring disaster on the offending individual and the clan also.

Each of the clans has one individual who has the primary respon-sibility of keeping the clan spirit placated. In meeting this obligation, he is free to call upon any clan member to provide sacrificial animals when ever these are deemed necessary.

The clan fills an important role in the major events of the life of its members. Life, birth, marriage, illness, death, all involve the clan. For instance, when a clan member marries, the entire clan is consulted. If it is a male member, the entire clan is expected to help meet the bride-price that is required. Upon marriage, girls become members of their husband's clan after the appropriate rites that are utilized to introduce her to the clan spirit. All children become mem-bers of the father's clan. A widow can elect to remain with or leave the clan. If she chooses to remain, she can become the wife of another clan member or remain single if she desires. If the latter is chosen, the clan is responsible to provide for her. Should she marry outside of her late husband's clan, or if she chooses to return to the home and clan of her parents, she automatically loses her privileges in her husband's clan. Should she leave the clan of her husband, the other members of his family may demand all or portions of her bride-price be repaid. [20]

While the Bru individual's main concern is for his immediate family, it appears that the clan is more important when it comes to the matter of traditional behavior patterns. When an individual of one clan offends someone of another clan, the matter becomes a clan affair rather than just a disagreement of two people. Likewise, marriages, business agreements, etc, are nomally handled as clan matters rather than on a family or village level.

Living Patterns: The Bru are patrilocal. That is, when a young man marries, he brings the bride to his father's village. The mothers-in-law, if they are still living, look forward to having daugh-ters-in-law so that they may ease the strain of the household chores. As the mothers-in-law grow older and weaker, their role becomes one of staying home and looking after the grandchildren while the daughters-in-law help with the heavy work in the fields.

Each child has its special place in the home. The little girls begin to carry younger siblings (brothers or sisters) on their backs almost

49

as soon as they begin to walk themselves, and to look after the
house while the mothers are away in the fields. The children also
learn to bring in water and firewood while very small. When there
are no girls in the family, the little boys may have to do these
tasks. [21]

Because the Bru social structure is patriarchal and based upon
the family, little boys early learn to hunt and fish and work with
their fathers. In this manner, they are taught the names and uses
of plants, the sounds of the jungle-forests, the use of the crossbow
and other weapons, the traditions of the tribe, etc. Children seem
to be much loved by the Bru. Because of a death rate that permits
seven or more of ten children to die before adulthood, the Bru
seek to placate those spirits that might harm the children.

Normally Bru children bear neither the paternal or maternal
name. It would be more correct to say that the parents carry their
children's name, inasmuch as the Bru have no surnames, i.e.
family names. Thus the Bru individual's name changes several
times during his or her lifetime. When one or two months old
the child will be given a name. This is not done earlier because so
many babies die. The name is often appropriate to the circumstances of birth. Then when a man marries, he will take the name
of the village from which he got his wife with the prefix of Khau'i,
which means "a married man who does not have children yet.
After his first born child is named, he will be called Mpoaq_____,"
Father of_____". If this child dies, the man will take the name
of his second child prefixed by Mpoaq_____. When his first grandchild is born and named, the man will become Achuaih_____.
"Grandfather of_____". A similar change of names occurs
with his wife as events change their status.

Bru children seem to require little physical discipline as by
nature the Bru are a gentle people. Many of the Bru children
are not weaned until about four years old, [22] yet a few years later
at puberty the end of childhood is signified by the rite of having
the front upper teeth filed.

From this time, that is, the reaching of puberty, boys and girls
no longer sleep in their parent's home. Instead, they sleep with

friends of their own sex or in a house of an older couple in the village or with some childless couple. The boys sleep in one part of the house while the girls sleep elsewhere in the home. In this way of living, the Bru believe the boys and girls get to know each other for a period of two to three years before they are ready for marriage and, are better prepared for life. At the same time this custom allows tribal parents a greater privacy while allowing their children to have an informal but correct schooling in Bru tradition.

Marriage: Bru men may have as many wives as they can afford, but most have only one. Many of the Bru males marry at about fifteen or sixteen years of age. As a matter of fact the practice of having a common house in each village where young boys and girls sleep is a factor influencing their choice of mates and early marriage. In some of the larger villages there may be two or three houses where this is done, but every village has at least one house for this purpose. Incidently these common houses are open to the young people of other villages also. In this way, the young people of other villages are provided opportunities to find a mate beyond the confines of their own village.

In these houses, the girls will occupy one room and the boys with the person or persons who own the house will occupy another room. In these houses filled with young people, there is much talking, playing of musical instruments, etc. When a young man becomes interested in one of the girls, the Bru custom is to make initial contacts through a friend. Through talk within each group and informal contacts between the two groups, it becomes general knowledge which boy is interested in a particular girl and her reaction to this interest. The use of such communication allows the male to know if it would be worth-while to make a direct bid for one of the girls. If it seems that it is, he will ask one of his friends to inquire through one of the girl's friends about her interest.

When a mutal interest is confirmed, it is permissable for the pair to separate themselves from the group and seek out secluded areas in the rice fields or forest. The relationship can rapidly move to the state that if the male offers the girl a small sum of money (in 1968 about fifty piastres or forty-five cents American money) and she accepts it as a token of his good faith in wanting to marry her, sexual union is permissable. Under these conditions, sexual relations are not considered as promiscuity since it is assumed that the couple will shortly become officially engaged.

Having once committed herself to a young man in this manner, the girl is no longer free to accept the attention of another man unless it is clear that she and her original partner have definitely broken off their relations. The couple going "steady" are permitted to have sexual relations as often as they desire without stigma as long as the girl does not become pregnant and the boy gives the stipulated sum of money each time to the girl. Should the girl become pregnant, pressures upon the young man and his family become so great that the couple marry inevitably.

Should the couple break their engagement before marriage, or should the girl be "unfaithful", the young man can reclaim all the money he has given the girl. Should the engagement continue and negotiations between the families reach agreement, the agreed bride price will be paid to the family of the bride.

The bride-price depends on the ability of the families to pay, as bride prices can range all the way from a few "dollars" to the exchange of buffalos and elephants. Sometimes the agreed price may be paid in money, pigs or precious jars, so that when agreement of price has been reached, the wedding date is set. While Bru boys and girls may select their own mates freely, custom demands that these choices meet family approval.

Because the Bru consider the primary purpose of marriage to the continuation of social, cultural and economic customs of the tribe, some children are betrothed by families while they are still infants. [23] Thus there are very few old maids or bachelors among the Bru.

During the wedding ceremony, it is customary to sacrifice one or more buffalos and to drink rice wine. If the bride-price has been fully met by the wedding day, the newly married couple move into their own home. Otherwise, the couple may have to live with his parents and work off the bride price if his clan has not raised it. [24]

Divorce: Divorce may be allowed under certain circumstances, but is relatively rare. The village chief has the authority to grant divorces, and to establish settlements, etc. If the husband opposes the divorce or if she is at fault, the wife must repay all the bride-price. When a man wishes to divorce his wife and he is at fault, he is not obligated to pay anything to the wife. If adultery is the basis for divorce, though it seldom is, the guilty party and the involved mate are required to give the wronged mate a large alimony. [25] However infidelity and the breaking of tribal customs are not punished by death in the Bru tribe as other tribes so often inflict punishment. [26] In cases of divorce, children may choose to live with the father's family or with their mother. Naturally a nursing child generally stays with its mother. [27] When parents cannot agree about where any small children shall live, the Chief makes the binding decision.

Adultery does not seem to be a major problem among the Bru since this is one area in which they seem to be extremely careful. While a married man is free to have any number of affairs with unmarried girls, the married woman is not allowed to have any extramarital interests. Should she do so, divorce would be the result as soon as her activities were known.

Birth: Pregnant Bru women are forbidden to have their babies in any house except her own or that of a clan member in her own village. The reasons may include the belief that only so many babies are to be born in the village during the year and the village wants those for itself. It may also be the fear that the spirits who come to eat the placenta may steal the spirits of other new born babies in the process. Delivery may be achieved alone or with the aid of elder relatives. Successful birth is an important event so that family or clan celebrations are conducted and sacrifices are offered to the spirits for the baby's benefit when it is introduced to the spirits for the first time. Likewise, when delivery is difficult or delayed, sacrifices are offered to the spirits in hopes that their assistance may help. [28]

Death Patterns: Typical Bru culture is that of the "survival of the fittest" Generally the Bru fail to comprehend any correlation between dirt and bad health habits with disease and death. Not only is infant mortality exceedingly high, but any serious illness almost invariably results in death for they have so little in the way of modern medication. Personnel of the Summer Institute of Linguistics, missionaries and military personnel are acting to remedy this situation, but much greater efforts are required before the death patterns can be permanently changed. [29]

When the Bru die, the clan join the family in mourning. The deceased are wrapped in cloth and then tied into a mat. The wealthy and elders have coffins made from a tree section which is split and hollowed out for this purpose. After the body has been placed in the coffin, it is sealed with a gum of the forest until it becomes airtight. The body may be buried immediately or kept for several days while friends and relatives lament over the body with occasional funeral chants. During this time, there are a number of taboos for both family and village members, but not applied to strangers.

When the lamentations have ceased, the body in either coffin or mat is buried in a shallow grave of three or four feet with such personal articles as jewelry, pipes, clothing, etc. [30] Similar to people who practice ancestral veneration, the Bru believe that the spirits of the dead become potential enemies if these are not hereafter kept happy. They seek to placate the departed's spirit by holding a satisfactory period of mourning. This need is so strongly felt, that another member of the family may die rather than the family break the taboo of leaving the home during the period of mourning. [31]

When a number of children die during an epidemic, their bodies may be thrown into the grave with some violence. This "strange" act is predicated upon the belief that the spirit of the deceased would be angry because it had been in the body such a short time. If it were not frightened away, it would surely come back and do evil to the family. Sometimes a stake is placed in the bottom of the grave and the child's body thrown upon the stake so the body is pierced. This is to impale the spirit in the grave so that it cannot wander around and create trouble. [23]

Sometimes the Bru funeral ceremony is elaborate and sometimes very simple. They are also rather rare. The grave ceremony includes a traditional funeral chant and a prescribed dance around the grave. After the grave has been covered, a small shelter or house is erected over it, and this is considered to be taboo-ground thereafter. If at a future time, the sorcerer decides that a certain ancestor has caused or is trouble, sacrifices and offerings will be made to that spirit so that it, figuratively speaking, will be laid to rest. The Bru, unlike the Vietnamese or some tribes, do not exhume the body of the dead.[33]

In many cases, formal funeral ceremonies may not take place for months or even years. Only the fairly rich seem to have an immediate formal ceremony. For the poor, the clan will "collect" a number of small pieces of bamboo with each piece representing someone who has died since the last ceremony. When the clan head decides that the time has come for a ceremony, and the economic conditions have much to do with this decision, people will come from far and wide for this occasion. At this time, all those who have died since the last ceremony will be properly commemorated.

The normal adjustment following the death of a mother or a father is basically a shifting in the line of responsibility of each one in accord with patterns of seniority and physical capabilities.

BRU ECONOMICS

The economics of the Bru is that of subsistence with farming, hunting, fishing and gathering the wild products of the jungle as conditions permit. Some minor trading is accomplished along with some of the tribespeople working on the coffee plantations in their area.

Farming: The Bru farm by the slash/burn (swidden/ray) method primarily. Location of the fields, which are village-owned, is made by the village chief, and the field user after the appropriate sacrificial rites have been made to the spirits. These rites help to choose the exact location as well as the proper day to start clearing the area, the day to burn the slashed and dry growth, and the day to begin planting.

On the appointed day, the tribesmen, using sharp mountain axes, clear bushes, vines, grass and small trees. The larger trees are left standing. When the cuttings are dry, they are set on fire on a date chosen after rites to appease the spirits. The larger logs, which do not burn, are then either left in place or placed as barricades about the field. Both men and women go to the field with pointed sticks and their seed upon the appropriate planting day. Holes are punched in the soil in rows or at random, seed dropped in, and the holes closed by stamping with the foot. The rains create the growing season of plants and weeds so that the latter must be removed from time to time with the use of a sharpened stick or other primitive tools. Such fields, enriched by the ashes, normally last for three or four years of rice growing.

When rice harvest time comes, it is women that must do this work generally. Different than many other peoples, the Bru do not cut the rice paddy. Instead, the women use their bare hands to strip the rice heads from the stalks. During this operation in some areas there must be no talking for fear of offending the rice spirit while other Bru do not have this taboo. The grain must then be hauled on their backs in baskets to the sometimes distant village where it may be hulled by having the buffalo walk on it or by flail and wooden mortar, and then winnowed. This unpolished rice is quite nourishing, and when used with greens of the garden, products of the jungle or with available meats, it forms the major part of the Bru diet under normal conditions. [35]

The major crops of the Bru are mountain rice, pumpkin, gourd, beans, peas, potatoes and manioc. Manioc or cassava is a tropical plant which grows either wild or is cultivated, and which has edible starchy roots which may be used as bread or for the making of tapioca. While rice fields must be changed every three to four years, the other crops may be planted in the same field for year after year. [36]

Domesticated Animals: Some of the Bru have buffalo and elephants. These animals can be an economic drain rather than a help if sacrifices are not equated as being of value to the total community. This is true of the elephants which are not used for labor generally. Rather, the elephant is treated as a member of the family with some member of the family required to guard and care for them and to keep them out of mischief. Because of the attitude toward the elephant by some Bru, suggestions for disposal of an elephant could create hostility. [37]

The buffalos are used as meat, but not as draft animals by the Bru. However the only time a buffalo is killed is for a sacrifice for some consider the spirit of the buffalo to be representative of the spirit of man. When used for sacrifice, the buffalo represents the desires and grievances of a family, a household or a village. The consumption of the buffalo, which is divided among the spirits to which it is offered, and among the family and the village, symbolizes a type of communion which unites them all.

Other domesticated animals include pigs, chickens, dogs or an occasional goat. But meat from such sources is too scarce to provide sufficient protein for the tribes people. Other sources must be sought and utilized.

Jungle Products: The jungles provide an additional means of livelihood for the Bru. Growing wild is the betel palm with its nut which the Bru use and which they also use as an item of trade. The betel palm may be any one of a number of closely related tropical palms which have a smooth trunk, feathery crown of leaves, fragrant white flowers and orange-colored nutlike fruit. Such palms are normally called areca palm. The fruit of this palm mixed with a small amount of lime and the leaf of the betel-climber (normally a vine pepper plant) is widely chewed in Southeast Asia. One of its effects is to turn the user's teeth a shiny black. This plant provides a chew much like that of tobacco in the United States.

The jungle also provides cinnamon bark, wild bee honey, scented leaves and herbs for tribal use and for trade with the Vietnamese. Some lumbering is done for sale or trade, with the latter greatly restricted due to the conditions of war.

Fishing: The rivers and streams in the Bru area are sources of fish. To catch these, the Bru utilize traps, nets, spears, gigs, baskets, and sometimes use their bows and arrows for this purpose. The nets may be homemade, obtained by trade or through the United States Aid Program or from military personnel in the area. [38]

Hunting: Hunting of the various wild animals is accomplished by the use of spears and arrows (often poison tipped), by the use of traps and both nets and pits. The ingenious tribal traps are used to catch anything from elephants or tigers to mice in the houses and fields. The small game traps are made of bamboo with fine string-springs. There are other traps which are placed along the path or trail of animals with trip-strings so that when something hits the trip-line, a fixed crossbow may shoot an arrow or project a spear into the target. This device is often used to kill wild boar. Often the gigantic bamboo spear has a poisoned tip to ensure effectiveness. Their major method of capturing or killing tigers and wild elephants is to dig a deep pit and in the bottom plant bamboo spears, or if they merely wish to capture the animal alive the spears are omitted. Then a light natural cover is placed over the hole so that it looks natural. When the heavy animal tries to cross, its weight causes the cover to collapse, and it cannot escape. [39] Normally the village chief will be given a part of any large game which is killed, while other villagers may be given some of the game killed by the individual hunter. This practice is of his own choosing and is not an enforced requirement.

Employment: Some of the Bru become wage earners by working on coffee plantations as coffee grows well in the Bru tribal area. The average wage in 1965 averaged 30 to 50 Vietnamese piastres (with the official military rate being 118 piastres to the dollar). Some Bru earn money working for the American military forces in their area, and are generally considered to be good workers by the Americans.

Crafts: The Bru are makers of beautiful sturdy baskets which can be used in many different ways. Each basket weaver makes one kind of basket with this usually being of double layer strength so that it is quite substantial. Their art work is a bit primitive although some do carve designs in their crossbows or their baskets. This lack is not due to ability, but knowledge and opportunity. [40]

Some of the Bru weave cloth for use as loin cloths, skirts and blankets. These materials are dyed with natural dyes drawn from the jungle. Likewise the Bru make and use pipes for tobacco smoking, with some of the finely wrought silver pipes being rather highly prized. Some of the children seem to start smoking about the time they are weaned as tobacco is another product grown in the tribal region.

The Bru culture includes music, and the more popular musical instruments, locally made, include a four-string banjo, a mountain violin, a flute made of a single piece of straight bamboo, and a reed instrument made of bamboo or other woods and perhaps a little tin or silver. In the hands of the skilled Bru, these instruments can produce rather amazing musical sounds. [41] Gongs also provide musical sounds which the foreign hearer can never forget.

RELIGION

Religion is a dominant factor in the lives of the Bru. From birth to death Bru life is wrapped up in, and controlled by, spirit worship. In fact, the religious beliefs of the Bru are centralized around the concept of spirit appeasement. Spirits may be those of deceased persons as each human is thought to possess a non-dying spirit, or any of the other numerous spirits which create great concern among the Bru.

Although there has been no systematic study of these spirits, there seems to be an almost unlimited number of them. The road or path, the forest, the air, moon, sun and earth all have individual spirits even as do features of the terrain which includes prominent rocks, unusual trees, streams, rivers and mountains. Moreover, the Bru believe that spirits inhabit animals and household objects such as the family hearth, tools, the rice-mill and especially the rice wine jugs. However the spirits which necessitate the greatest attention of the Bru seem to be those of the sky, the rice paddy and the village.

Not too worried about the good spirits who are thought to need little attention, the Bru constantly seek to ascertain which spirits may be causing their current woes and troubles. For these, rites of appeasement are undertaken even as precautionary taboos are observed to prevent hostility by offending spirits, and to provide placation for those who may be resentful of infringement on their "rights". Because the Bru believe that the spirits like to eat, most of the tribesmen stay quite poor trying to satisfy the appetite of these supernatural powers.

The spirits are believed to be responsible for every major and minor catastrophy. The concept that the spirits will punish any and every violation of prescribed conduct provides sanction for the Bru code of behavior as the tribesmen live in continual fear of punishment imposed by the spirits. [42] Fear of the spirits is an ever-present terrifying factor even for the few Bru who have become Christians. Terror of offending spirits, symbolized by objects representing special spirits in their homes, prevent the Bru from discarding these symbols. Not only would their houses become homes no longer because of the absence of these, but their clans would disown them. They would be severely ostracized if their household "spirit representations" were relegated to obscurity. [43]

Many of the Bru believe that there is one spirit named "yiang sursei" who is superior to all the other spirits. He is the all-powerful and all-good spirit who created everything. His nature precludes the necessity to either worship or appease him. It is the lesser spirits who are evil and it is because of the harm which they may do that they must be placated. [44]

Interestingly, the Bru have a story of the "Creation and Flood" which is the following:

> In the beginning God (Yuang Sorsei or Yiang Sursei) created a man and a woman. The man and woman lived together very happily. Every day they hunted wild animals and looked for fruit. Only one thing troubled them - they had no children. One day as they wandered in the woods God met them and he promised them children.
>
> God's promise was fulfilled and the woman gave birth to eight sons at one time. Now they were more troubled than before, for as the children grew they ate more and more until the parents were unable to support them. In desperation they took them to a high mountain and abandoned them.
>
> In the course of time one of the young brothers acquired a precious and beautiful sword having remarkable powers. When the handle was grasped securely rain would fall, and when the blade was held the sun would shine.
>
> One day the young lad who owned the sword

became very hungry. He went about looking for food. On the bank of a river he saw a fig tree and a civet cat eating the figs. He went to the civet cat and asked for something to eat. But the civet cat said, "This is not your kind of food. If you want to eat these figs you will have to become a civet cat like me". He brought out a civet cat skin and the boy put it on. He became a civet cat, eating figs and sleeping in the shade of the tree.

The chief of all that area was called Anha. One day the youngest daughter of Anha was paddling a canoe along the river. She came to the place where the fig tree stood and saw the civet cat beneath it. She took the civet cat home with her as a pet, and the animal (or boy in disguise) was very happy to go.

God spoke to Anha, the chief, and told him that there was going to be a great flood. He commanded him to build a boat. Although the chief tried to hire workers to help him make the boat, no one was willing, not event to escape a flood. When the boat was finished. Anha took his family into it. With him were his wife, four daughters and two sons eight people in all, plus the civet cat that the youngest daughter took with her. God commanded the civet cat to grasp the precious sword by the handle several times. A violent rainstorm followed. It rained for eight days and eight nights. The water rose destroying everything on the earth. The water rose up to the heavens, and the fish nibbled at the stars.

The flood receded and the land dried off. The youngest daughter of Anha fell in love with the civet cat, realizing that he was actually a person. She asked her father for permission to marry him. At the wedding ceremony, while the buffalo was being barbecued, the civet cat removed his disguise. His bride threw the civet cat skin into the fire. He turned into a handsome young man who lived thereafter with his wife, the youngest daughter of Anha. [45]

The Bru have a number of medicine men, magicians or shamans. These may from time to time handle those rituals and supernatural matters too complex for the individuals tribesman. Nevertheless, these do not have such prominent roles among the Bru as are found among other tribal groups in South Vietnam, and insufficient study has been done to identify their roles with any degree of accuracy. [46] Moreover, such practitioners do not seem to be overly successful as disease and death are daily occurences even when war is not a factor.

Bru sacrifices seem to increase in proportion to their desperation. These sacrifices vary from such simple offerings of an egg to the slaying of a buffalo, along with rice, wine and other items which may involve a great deal of work. While most Bru sacrifices are associated with the agricultural cycle of clearing the forest and the planting and harvesting of rice, other sacrifices occur as the needs arise.

Although the individual family or the individual members of a family can conduct rites for the family or themselves, the village chief presides in those sacrifices which are for the community as a whole. The particular cause for a sacrifice may be to gain the favor of a particular spirit so that greater benefits may be derived, or to serve for the placation of certain spirits after some taboo has been broken so that epidemics, crop failure or other disasters may be avoided. Because such spirits are thought to control nature, both good and evil spirits can create misfortune in the form of accidents, illnesses and deaths when the spirits are offended. [47]

The sacrificial rites include invocational prayers addressed to the relevant spirits inviting them to attend and partake in the sacrifice. These prayers also state the reason and desires of those engaged in the sacrifice. Accompanying such invocations will be the ceremonial killing of the sacrificial animal be it a chicken, pig or buffalo.

A basic element of the sacrifice is the offering of the blood and flesh to the spirits by displaying them in pans and bowls accompanied by offerings of rice, wine, and other foods believed to be liked by the particular spirit. Also in instances of sickness, blood may be placed on the ill person. The display of the sacrificial elements is followed by the drinking of rice wine and the eating of the sacrifice inasmuch as the Bru believe the spirits draw their nourishment from the intangible elements of the offerings. Through the eating of the food, all Bru participate actively in the sacrifices thereby sharing the efficaciousness to be gained through such rituals.

> The clamour and noise which go along with some of the sacrifices for disease are enough to cut the balance and send the patient over the line into death. Also the social custom of the Bru is that when a close friend is seriously sick, it is the duty of the well friend to go and watch him. Thus when a patient should be left alone to rest his sick body, instead he will have friends crowded into the house all around him perpetually pestering him .... "Are you dead yet?" "Oh, he is dead; he is dead already! Thus if a patient does drop into a much needed sleep, he is not allowed to stay there. [48]

Since the animistic religion of the Bru is predicated on fear and the desire to manipulate the supernatural world, Bru life seems to be an almost continuous round of sacrifices. With a fear motivated base, Bru religion involves a larger share of wealth, time, importance and concern than most non-tribesmen believe possible. But to the isolated preliterate and semiliterate tribespeople, it provides the only means by which they can make sense of an otherwise senseless world.

In conformity with religious beliefs, Bru life is regulated by numerous customs and taboos. While most Bru cannot give detailed reasons for observing the taboos other than it is expected, the code of behavior has been transmitted from generation to generation until it has the force of tribal law. Since broken taboos require sacrifices in order to regain the good graces of offended spirits, existence for the Bru is complex and complicated in spite of what seems to most foreigners to be very primitive living conditions. For instance, all tribesmen present during an animal sacrifice must participate in the drinking of rice wine. Otherwise the sacrifice is thought to be ineffective as the spirits will be offended. [49]

One important taboo in some Bru areas is that no one may speak while engaged in the ricefield harvesting the grain from the stalk by using their bare hands to pull the grain loose as the rice-stalk must not be cut during the harvest. Talking during this operation would make the rice-spirit unhappy and calamity would surely result. [50] Moreover, to insure good crops and continuing fertility of the soil, taboos prohibit allowing paddy, i.e. unhusked rice, to fall into the fire or to be deliberately burned, as the rice spirit would be gravely offended. [51]

Some Bru believe that the spirits accept the buffalo to be representative of man. For this sacrifice, the animal's head is tied very securely to the sacrifice pole so that it cannot move its head. Then at the appropriate time, its throat will be slit so that it will quickly bleed to death. The eating of the flesh of a sacrificed buffalo (and this is the only time that the Bru kill buffaloes) is believed to be consumed by the spirits as well as by both the family who offer the buffalo and the village inhabitants, and serves to constitute a uniting communion for all those involved. The sacrificial animal represents the desires and grievances of those who offer it and those of the community also. It thus has many of the connotations found in the animal sacrifices of by-gone centuries in other lands.

The Bru believe that evil or offended spirits cause illness and therefore the most effective cure is to offer sacrifices to the offended spirits. Rather than blindly sacrificing to all spirits, the Bru sorcerers, who may be either a man or woman, determine by divination the responsible spirit and the required sacrifice through which a cure may be achieved.

To promote good relations with the spirits the Bru have taboos that include prohibitions against the use of certain subjects or words which they believe offensive to the spirits. Likewise they have prescribed methods for the utilization of certain objects which denote supernatural interests to them. Thus the Bru must never sleep with his feet pointed in the direction of the family altar or any "sacred" objects. [52] The Bru family altar is found on the wall of the house to the left of the entrance-way, and on it may be several small objects of woven bamboo or other artifact for religious purposes. All visitors are presumed to know of this strict taboo so that the breaking of this religious rule will certainly frighten and offend the host to the extent that the visitor may be compelled to leave the house either through a felt hostility or an expressed wish of the host so that the spirits will not harm him or his.

The Bru prefer to keep their villages in one location even though they may have to walk many miles to their fields. However if sufficient omens are given through dreams, the village will move in compliance to such supernatural warnings. Also due to causes believed to be supernatural, a village or a field may be taboo from time to time. The sign of such a taboo is a leafy tree branch suspended horizontally from a stake planted in the middle of the village path of entrance. In a similar manner, a house may show that it is taboo, i.e. entrance is forbidden, when a leafy branch is on the doorway or when the ladder to the porch has been withdrawn and is out of sight.

GUIDELINES FOR RAPPORT

The Bru have neither cultural nor ethnic ties with the Vietnamese, and little with those of their neighboring tribes. Some of the Bru feel that the Vietnamese with whom they have had unpleasant contacts were "too skillful at trading" and feel "cheated"; moreover some express the belief that the Vietnamese deal with them with a sense of Vietnamese superiority. This attitude creates hostility, resentment and contempt.

The Bru are not sympathetic toward the Viet Cong inasmuch as the Bru do not like the Viet Cong tactics of terror, intimidation, or rumored style of communal living. However, at present, the Bru think the South Vietnamese to be little better since both are Vietnamese. The Bru would prefer to just be left alone and unmolested by either side of the current conflict. But since this does not seem possible, most have chosen to be free of communist domination, and live in fortified villages in order to stay alive, while yearning to return to a way of life that existed prior to the coming of the Viet Minh.

Generally, foreigners have been well received by the Bru inasmuch as there is no sense of exploitation present at this time where foreigners are concerned.

Within the Bru culture, stealing and lying are considered to be bad and strongly disapproved inasmuch as the Bru are gentle people in relation to some of the tribes of Vietnam. The Bru have no dreams of being an independent governing people, but do appreciate fair and kind treatment.

It is imperative that promises never be made which cannot be fulfilled. Moreover once a promise has been made, it is essential that it be executed, otherwise the Bru lose faith, and this cannot be easily regained. This applies to little items as well as to major concerns.

The Bru must have time and opportunity to see, hear and consider the meaning of all attempts made in his behalf. He must be able to formulate his own opinions without undue haste or a sense of pressure imposed by the American desire to "get the job done". Haste is foreign to the Bru. Likewise, the excited, loud-speaking overbearing individual who attempts to "bulldoze" his way among the Bru is usually doomed to fail.

Initial visits to the Bru settlements ought to be formal. Through initial contact with the village elders, the chief and other village personalities will be included. Essential to any success is the willingness to realize that trust takes time to develop and requires patience, tact, understanding and personal integrity. Even when confronted by apparent apathy or resentment, the visitor must remain good-natured, have patience and proceed in a slow deliberate manner.

Projected projects should have sufficient short-range goals which can be achieved and thereby aid the Bru to comprehend the value of doing something differently than has been the custom. It is better to have several small projects which meet "felt" needs than large projects which offer no immediate returns for efforts expended. At all times, care must be taken to give credit to the village leaders, even as the foreigner must work with and through them to the fullest extent possible.

If the Bru offer hospitality drinks or food, this is a signal of honor and should be accepted. A sip of the drink - coffee, tea water, etc. - is not offered lightly by the Bru, so must not be slighted. The worse that one could receive is a bit of diarrhea, and this can be cured more quickly than rejection of Bru friendship, as demonstrated by the offer to share what little he has. Few foreigners will be so accepted that offers of food or drink will be made by the Bru, so make the most of it.

Never treat the Bru adult as one who does not deserve treatment as an adult. A superior and patronizing attitude will quickly be detected and while not giving a public indication of it, they will discuss this among themselves to the discredit of the foreigner.

Medical help is a dire necessity among the Bru. Likewise, the need of formalized schooling to replace the traditional tribal transmission of knowledge is essential as the twentieth century comes uninvited to the Bru. Vocational education, to help master the skills necessary to meet and answer the challenges and opportunities presented by the current war, would be a blessing to the Bru for generations to come. Some effort is now being directed toward this goal, but a much greater effort must be undertaken if much is to be achieved.

Foreigners ought to treat Bru property just as carefully as they desire their own to be handled by strangers. This applies to property, animals, women and children. Never enter a home unless invited and accompanied by an inhabitant of the home to avoid later difficulties. Great care ought be taken to avoid damage to Bru rice crops, fruit trees etc., as a few dollars paid as compensation does not erase the damage, and the normal time gap between damage and payment creates resentment. Be careful in regard to taboo and religious ceremonies. Stay away from these unless invited for otherwise you are not wanted. Warning signs for taboos are normally placed near or in the main entrances to a settlement. In a similar manner, when a house is taboo to non-inhabitants, the ladder is usually lifted up on the porch.

When entering or leaving a Bru home, be sure to always use the front entrance and not a backdoor. The Bru believe that the rear of a house is continually watched or guarded by a spirit. The use of a backdoor may allow harmful spirits to enter the home or offend friendly spirits. This belief about spirits is one of the reasons that most Bru homes are built so that their backs face the backs of other homes, although war conditions have created changes in some places.

The establishment of a trading center with posted fixed prices in English-Vietnamese and Bru agreed upon by the village chief and the appropriate military command can do much to reduce and avoid difficulties created by unregulated commercial transactions between the Bru and non-tribal peoples. Supervised centers would provide a market for the Bru items at a fair price established by village authorities and the military. It would make desirable souvenirs available to purchasers under conditions which they understand. This and similar working agreements could include any personal work done by the tribes people for those outside of their culture. This would do much to prevent unnecessary resentment and hostility to all parties. It would also promote those arts which could form light industries for the tribal peoples.

The Bru consider blue to be one of the most attractive colors. They often work it into the various clothing designs of their garments.[53] When making gifts of friendship that include clothing-materials include blue clothing or designs that contain this color. Such considerations, may often seem to be petty. Yet it is often the small things of life that determine so much of the inter-personal affairs of man rather than "headline events."

The Bru love life and are a friendly, gentle and coloful people. As a rule their food is more varied than other tribes; their clothing more decorated; their houses better built. In spite of every difficulty, foreigners have been received with greater hospitality by the Bru than in many of the other tribes.

Bru, being non-tonal, presents opportunity to learn at least a few phrases. This effort will more than repay for itself in the sense of acceptance and in better communication between you and the Bru.

The Bru are experts in many things which the American knows little about. They can therefore be of real assistance in ways of existing and living in an area that is alien to Americans. The Bru are easy to work with because they have much the same frame of reference and their sense of humor seems quite identical to that of Americans. The things that make them laugh are those that make Americans laugh. Moreover, they have a cooperative spirit and an open mind toward foreigners, and will generally accept the foreigner at face value until he proves himself unworthy of this trust. [54]

FOOT - NOTES

1. Frank M. Lebar, Gerald C. Hickey, John K. Musgrave, Ethnic Groups of Mainland Southeast Asia, New Haven, Human Relations Area Files Press, 1964, p. 128; CRESS, Minority Groups In the Republic of Vietnam: Ethnographic Study Series, Department of the Army Pamplet No 550-105, 1966, p. 55; Summer Institute of Linguistic's List of July 1966, p. 1, "Vietnam Minority Languages".

2. Ethnic Groups of Mainland Southeast Asia, p. 138; Navy Personal Response Tape by Miss Eugenia Johnson on The Bru as a member of the Summer Institute of Linguistics, Saigon, July 1966.

3. Rober L. Mole, On-site Field Notes of Navy Personal Response 1965-1966, and discussions with Summer Institute of Linguistics members, missionaries of the Christian Missionary Alliance, the Worldwide Evangelization Crusade, U. S. Army Special Forces at Khe Sanh and personal observations among the Bru.

4. Ibid

5. United States Information Service, Montagnards of the South Vietnamese Highlands, (Saigon, U. S. I. S. July 1962) P. 17

6. Exeley, "Returnee Response to Questionnaire on the Montagnard Tribal Study" Fort Bragg, North Carolina, U. S. Army Special Warfare School, January 1965.

7. Montagnards of the South Vietnamese Highlands, p. 17

8. Pastor Leroy Josephsen of the Christian Missionary Alliance Mission in Vietnam in his taped discussion of the Bru for the Navy Personal Response. This interview was recorded 31 March 1966.

9. Josephsen, Ibid; E. Johnson's Bru Tape for the Navy Personal Response; Mole, Unpublished Field-notes.

10. Ibid; Laura Irene Smith, Victory In Vietnam, Grand Rapids, Michigan, Zondervan Publishing House, 1965, p. 88.

11. Ibid, p. 88.

12. Josephsen, BRU, Tape for Navy Personal Response: E. Johnson, BRU Tape for Navy Personal Response. Mole, On-site Field-notes 1965-1966

13. Recorded Interview with John and Carolyn Miller, 27 Feb 1965.

14. E. Johnson, Bru Tape for Navy Personal Response.

15. Mole, Field-notes of 1965-66

16. Smith, op, cit. p. 140; J. Hoffet, "Les Mois de la Chaine Annamitique, Terre, Air, Mer; La Geographie, LIX (1933) pp. 27-8 Mole, Field-notes of 1965-6

17. E. Johnson's Bru Tape for PRP.

18. Ibid; John Miller Interview; Mole, Field-notes 1965-6.

19. Noel Bernard, "Les Khas, peuple inculte du Laos francais: Notes anthropometriquest et ethnographiques", Bulletin de Geographie Historique et Descriptive (1904) p. 370; Dam Bo (Jacques Dournes), "Les Populations montagnards du Sud-Indochinois" France-Asie (Special Number Spring 1950) pp. 1086-87; Mole, Field-notes of 1965-6 (The Montagnards palaver over matters for what seems to be an extended period of time to most Americans. To force a more speedy decision is often to lose the battle the foreigner seeks to win, so patience is essential.)

20. John Miller Interview previously noted; George M. Maspero, Montagnard Tribes of South Vietnam, Washington, D.C. Joint Publications Research Service (No 13443, 1962) pp. 4 and 7.

21. E. Johnson, Bru Tape for Navy Personal Response

22. Mole, On-site Field-notes 1965-66.

23. E. Johnson's Bru Tape for Navy Personal Response: Mole, Field-notes of 1965-6

24. John Miller Interview; Mole, Field-notes of 1965-6.

25. Noel Bernard, op, cit. pp 355-356; E. Johnson's Bru Tape.

26. E. Johnson's Bru Tape for Navy Personal Response

27. Noel Bernard, op. cit. pp 356-357.

28. Ibid, p. 358

29. Mole, Field-notes 1965-66

30. Mole, Field-notes of 1965-6.

31. E. Johnson's Bru Tape

32. E. Johnson's Bru Tape Mole, Field-notes 1965-6.

33. Ibid, Mole, Field-notes of 1965-6.

34. Ibid; Mole, Field-notes of 1965-66.

35. Josephsen, Bru Tape

36. Mole, Field-notes for 1965-66.

37. E. Johnson's Bru Tape

38. Mole, Field-notes 1965-6.

39. Josephsen's Tape on The Bru

40. Johnson, Ibid; Josephsen, Ibid; Mole, Field-notes of 1965-6.

41. Josephsen, Ibid; Mole, Field-notes

42. Special Operations Research Office, Ethnographic. Studies Series: Selected Groups In the Republic of Vietnam: The Bru (Washington, D. C. SORO, Feb. 1966) p. 7; also Mole, Unpublished Field notes of 1965-6 of the Navy Personal Response.

43. Johnson's Bru Tape for Robert Mole (1966) In the Navy Personal Response.

44. John Miller Interview; Josephsen, op. cit; Johnson, op. cit ; Mole, 1965-66 Field-notes.

45. Bui Tan Loc, "Creation and Flood in Bru Legend" Jungle Frontiers, News Magazine of the Vietnam Mission (Tribes Region) of the Christian and Missionary Alliance, Summer 1961, Number 13 p. 8 (Mr. Loc is a long time Vietnamese missionary to the Bru).

46. Mole, Field-notes of 1965-66; Johnson's Bru Tape of 1966.

47. George M. Maspero. Montagnard Tribes of South Vietnam (Washington, D. D. Joint Publications Research Service (No. 13443) 1962, pp. 6-7.

48. E. Johnson Bru Tape (1966) for Navy Personal Response

49. Mole, 1965-66 Field-notes

50. Josephsen, 1966 Bru Tape for the Navy Personal Response

51. Maspero, op. cit. pp. 8-9; Mole, 1965-6 Field-notes.

52. Maspero, op. cit. p. 9

53. Laura Irene Smith, Victory In Vietnam Grand Rapids, Michigan, Zondervan Publishing House, 1965, p. 88

54. E. Johnson's Bru Tape (1966) for Navy Personal Response also Mole, 1965-6 Field-notes.

BRU TRIBESMAN WITH CROSSBOW

BRU MOTHER AND CHILD

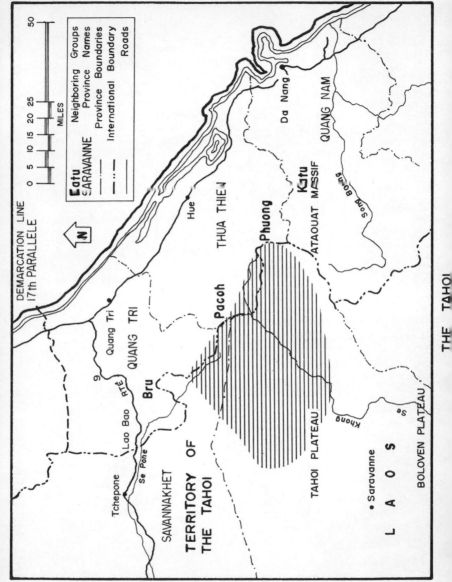

THE TAHOI

CHAPTER III

THE TAU-OI

The Tau-oi have several synonyms which include Ta Hoi, Tahoi, Ka-Ta-Oi, Ta-oih and Toi-Oi. [1] One French authority believes that the Tau-oi are descendants of an ethnic group known as Teu and are therefore related to the Van-Kieu who are the Pacoh of Quang Tri and Thua Thien provinces in south Vietnam. [2] There does exist an ability to understand each other's language as well as a greater mixing of tribal customs than found among many of the other ethnic groupings. [3]

Language: Linguistic authorities believe that the Tau-oi language is a Bruan sub-subgrouping of the Katuic subgroup from within the Mon-Khmer family of languages. This belief is generally adhered to in spite of the fact that it seems quite similar to that of the Souei who are a Laotian tribe located near Thateng in the Laotian province of Saravanne. [4] While a few of the Tau-oi understand Vietnamese, the Tau-oi language has not been reduced to writing yet. [5]

Population Estimates: The majority of the Tau-oi live in Savananakhet and Saravanne Provinces in Laos while an estimated six to ten thousand live in South Vietnam. Due to their geographic isolation, modes of tribal organization and factors of war, the estimates are guesses based upon limited census work. [6]

Location: The Tau-oi, while primarily in Laos, are found along the Laotian-Vietnamese international border in an area extending eastward in Vietnam some five to twenty miles in depth. The whole Tau-oi tribal area is in the form of a rough triangle with the northern apex fixed on the international border on the level of the city of Hue. The eastern side of the rough triangle extends southeastward to a line about even with Danang, some eighteen to twenty miles from the Laos border to the west and about five miles to the Laotian border in the south as the Tau-oi are found at the head of the A-Shau Valley. The southeastern point of the Tau-oi tribal area is that of the Ataouat Massif, and from this point the southern tribal line extends across the Tau-oi Plateau of Laos. From there it runs northward to the apex to form the whole tribal boundary. Thus the Tau-oi tribal area in South Vietnam is in the extreme southeast corner of Quang Tri Province and the strip along the western border of Thua Thien Province except for about five miles in the southwest of that province.

The Tau-oi tribal terrain is composed of contrasting alluvial plains, a high grassy plateau and steep rugged heavily forested mountains. While the Annamite Mountain Chain of the international border area drops off into "a collection of deeply eroded plateaus dominated by isolated peaks" in Laos, [7] in Vietnam it does not. While the western side of the Chain facing Laos has gentle slopes that vary from 2300 to 4500 feet, the Vietnamese side is much more rugged. For instance, in the southeast corner of the Tau-oi area is located the Ataouat Massif which is over 6,000 feet and composed of granite and gneiss. [8] Gneiss is "a laminated or foliated metamorphic rock corresponding in composition to granite or some other feldspathic plutonic rock and often named for a conspicuous mineral constituent". [9]

The Tau-oi area is drained on the western side of the Annamite Mountain Chain by two rivers, the Se Pone and the Se khong which flow into the Mekong. On the eastern side of the Chain, the numerous small streams become part of the Song Da Giang (River of Hue) and empty into the Pacific.

Seasonal mcnsoons dominate climatic conditions in the Tau-oi area so that streams and rivers form an essential element in the life of this isolated tribe. The summer monsoon from May to October brings wind and rain from the southwest while the winter monsoon (November through January) brings winds from the northeast. Although November through March is the "dry season", typhoons cause some rain fall, but much less than the rainy season which starts in April and reachs a peak of about 20 inches of precipitation in July and August before tapering off so that the annual rainfall for this area averages 60 to 80 inches.

The Tau-oi area in Quang Tri and Thua Thien Provinces in South Vietnam is largely covered with monsoon forests. Monsoon forests thrive in tropical areas where the precipitation averages 60 to 80 inches with a dry season of several months duration. In contrast to the rain forests covering much of the South Vietnamese mountains the monsoon forests have much more open growth, although there are often dense spiny thickets. The numerous tree seedlings, saplings, epiphytes and lianas (woody climbing plants) characteristic of rain-forests are usually rather scarce if not completely absent in monsoon forests also. Instead, ground cover in the Tau-oi area is largely composed of Tranh, a tall coarse tough grass (Imperata Cy lindrica) which can rather effectively bar the progress of anyone who seeks to walk through it. The indigenous tree which seems to predominate in the Tau-oi area belongs to the Dipterocarpaceae family and is called ca chac by the Vietnamese. Ca Chac, after losing their leaves from November to December, begin to blossom in February, and provide a change of color to the mountains and valley. Because the dry season allows numerous forest fires, only those trees that are most fire resistant seems to flourish, and it seems apparent that the ca chac has this quality. When the tribal cultivated fields are abandoned, wild herbs, bamboo, bananas and tranh rapidly take root so that the areas are quickly reclaimed by jungle growth. Within a short time the secondary forest growth begins to smother out even the persistent bamboo stalk that elsewhere might be called the "king of the jungle".[10] Other than minor paths made by wild animals and the tribesmen, few roads exist in the tribal area except those constructed as a result of the war effort. There is one minor trail along the Se Khong which connects Hue with Saravanne,[11] and another between Pakse and Paksong in Laos.[12]

Neighbors: Within South Vietnam the Tau-oi have the Bru as their neighbors in the north while the Pacoh and the Phuong are to the east between the Tau-oi tribal area and the Vietnamese who dwell on the coastal plains. The southern Tau-oi tribal border is contiguous with that of the Katu, a tribe feared by those who know of the Katu tribal character.

Tau-oi Tribal History: An early twentieth century Frenchman thought the Tau-oi to be of Malay descent,[13] but others believe them to be of the Northeast Mon-Khmer linguistic and ethnic family that includes such tribes as the Bahnar and Sedang tribes of II Corps in South Vietnam.[14] It is generally thought that the Lao peoples moved into Indo-China from the area of what is now South China during the 14th and 15th centuries. As they did, they gradually replaced the ancient Khmer domination of the area that is now Laos. As the Khmer power waned and the Lao increased, the tribespeople, such as the

77

Tau-oi were forced from the lowlands and took up the less desirable heights of the hinterlands. [15]

About the same time other peoples, from what is now South China, also migrated west of the Mekong to establish the Kingdom of Siam in what is now central Thailand. Thus in 1431 the Khmer capital was conquered by the Siamese and the presence of the Siamese forces caused the Khmer peoples to retreat into the more remote mountainous terrain. About the same time, the Cham peoples were being pushed into the Annamite mountains by the Vietnamese as their kingdom expanded southward along the east coast of the Indo-China Peninsula. By the 15th century the Lao began to penetrate the mountain areas also. Therefore, from time to time strife would occur between the "invaders" and the tribesmen, with Tau-oi raids on Laotian settlements being followed by reprisals in an almost unvarying pattern. [16]

Inasmuch as the advancing Vietnamese settled only on the coastal plains, they did not attempt to move into the higher mountains of the Annamite range where the Tau-oi lived. [17] In fact, the only Vietnamese penetration of the mountains near the Tau-oi seems to have been the pass of Ai Lao near Khe Sanh. This pass contains the route that starts at Quang Tri, north of Hue, and connects Quang Tri and the Vietnamese central coast with the Mekong and Vientienne, Laos. Even though the royal court at Hue used this route to send troops and other royal agents to the Mekong Valley, apparently the Tau-oi tribal area was largely by-passed.

In the chaotic conditions resulting from the Siamese (Thai) seizing land along the Se (River) Don in 1886, the more belligerent Tau-oi, Sedang and Jarai tribes, began to engage in slave trade. This activity was patterned after the examples of the Khmer, Siamese and Lao slave traders operating in tribal areas. While killing anyone who resisted, the Tau-oi kidnapped women and children of neighboring tribes and supplied Montagnard slaves for the markets at Bassac, Attopeu, Phnom Penh, Bangkok and other trade centers. Even the Vietnamese were not safe from raids by these tribes and are reputed to have paid for safe conduct through tribal areas. [18]

The Tau-oi helped the Siamese establish military outposts in some of the tribal areas until the French colonial forces in Vietnam arrested the Siamese advance. Finally, in 1890, the French captured Ai Lao pass and forced the Siamese to retreat westward. The resulting treaty in October 1893 made Laos a French Protectorate and defined the boundaries of the Annamese-French territory insofar as the Siamese were concerned.[19] Although completely independent until the French occupation, the Tau-oi accepted French sovereignty and domination with the first Tau-oi-French negotiations starting in 1897. Though ending the Tau-oi slave trade and the violence it caused, the French opened the Tau-oi area to both Annamese and Laotian trade convoys.[20] But in spite of this, and because of geographic, psychological and economic reasons, the Tau-oi have been left to themselves until the present time.

TAU-OI CHARACTERISTICS

Physical: The Tau-oi have the same basic color and build of most Montagnards; well built muscular bodies with well-developed muscles. However, due to poor diet and disease their endurance is much less than their physical appearance would indicate. Moreover, because of diet defficiencies and similar factors, the Tau-oi seem to have a rather low resistance to the diseases of the area.[21] Since malaria, typhus, cholera, typhoid, yaws, tuberculosis, dysentery and other parasitic infections are prevalent, the Tau-oi who reach adulthood have survived in spite of a very high infant mortality through repeated exposure to the numerous endemic diseases. Village sanitation is just as rudimentary as is the personal hygiene of the tribesman. Sexual mores permit venereal diseases to spread unchecked and untreated by any tribal or scientific methods that are effective.[22] Moreover the use of dishes, separate eating bowls or plates and the use of chopsticks were unknown among the Tau-oi until recently.[23]

Tau-oi Apparel: Tau-oi men generally wear a loin-cloth called "kho" while the women wear a skirt, "yeng" and a short blouse much like that worn by Laotian women.[24] Tau-oi clothing is handwoven, simple in style and dyed with indigo. The women's clothing is a skirt which covers the knees and loose-fitting short sleeveless blouse.

Both men and women normally wear their hair long and roll it into a chignon or "bun" in the same fashion as that of many Vietnamese. Sometimes variety is effected by forming eye-brow length bangs. Some of the Tau-oi have their front teeth filed to the gumline, and have pierced earlobes which are stretched to permit inserts of wood or tin earrings. A large tuft of cotton as ear decorations is thought to be the mark of highest elegance. The Tau-oi are fond of jewelry and wear large bracelets and collars of brass wire formed in spirals. The collars are so tight that they tend to confine and limit any movements of the head. [25]

THE VILLAGE AND ITS BUILDINGS

The Tau-oi customarily construct their villages in harmony with a circular basic design. The communal house, reserved for men only, is in the center with individual long-houses radiating like the spokes of a wheel about it. The rim of the wheel is composed of a protective perimeter fence that encircles the village. [26] The Tau-oi individual house, like that of most South Vietnamese tribal groups, is built on wooden piles so that the floor of the house is several feet above the ground. [27]

Normally, Tau-oi houses are built as longhouses with some of them being over 600 feet in length. These longhouses are usually subdivided by interior partitions so that each of its nuclear families (husband, wife and children) have their own room. [28] The size and need for space of the extended family determines the length of the longhouse provided the village has sufficient room. Since the lizard is the favorite motif of the Tau-oi, each house reflects this design in some way. Sometimes the lizard motif is intricately carved on the ends of the main roof beam as a work of art. [29] In this regard the Tau-oi seem to have a talent of woodworking and skillful carving that surpass that of most other tribes. They also demonstrate a well-developed talent to fit pieces of wood together so that the material's full strength may be realized which is a talent that seems uncommon among most Montagnards. [30]

Within the Tau-oi village, in addition to the longhouses and the communal house, is a small house dedicated to the "phi", village spirit. It is here that the village ritual for sacrifices takes place, as the buffalo to be slain is tied to one of the wooden columns that surround the "phi" house.

Mores combined with religious beliefs necessitate an additional structure for many Tau-oi communities which is not found in other ethnic groups. Among the Tau-oi, the adolescent unmarried girls are permitted to engage in sex relations with the young men of the village with this practice being known as "Di-sim" or "Tam-bon", which literally means "sleeping on the water".[31] However it is taboo for the unmarried to participate in sex within the village enclosure as this is believed to anger the phi, the village spirit. An angered phi may cause a severe punishment for the whole village. This behavior taboo therefore causes the Tau-oi in the larger communities to erect a hut just outside the entrance gate to serve as a place of rendezvous for unmarried sex participants.[32]

SOCIAL STRUCTURE

The Tau-oi are patrilineal with the various communities socially structured as patriarchies upon the extended family and clan rather than on the village or tribe. With no tribal structure evident, the village seems to be the highest effective social and political organization so that the extended patriarchal family is the most cohesive unit. Inasmuch as the male members inherit property, it seems natural that the oldest male rules the family[33] This form of social structure encourages a hereditary system of administration in which the roles of a father become the functions of his son. Thus when the Tu-Truong "Tribal Leader", is unable to function, his son serves in his place. The same procedure is followed when the Village Chief "Xuat Vin", may be ill. The hereditary tradition of these roles cause the Tau-oi to believe the men in these offices to be very important people.[34]

Under normal circumstances, administrative officials are treated with deference by the Tau-oi. When they visit a tribal community, the most copious dishes are prepared for them even as the most highly prized objects are placed at their disposal for the duration of the visit. Likewise, the visitors must accept all gifts which are offered so that offense to the giver may be avoided.[35]

The division of roles of Tau-oi men and women is quite distinct. The women have the duties of planting, harvesting, processing foods, preparing meals, gathering products of the jungle including firewood, and carrying water. She thus seems to be the most essential worker of the community. Even the birth of a child does not alter her work patterns for long.

The birth-practice of the Tau-oi helps to explain why only two or three out of ten newly born babies survive. The Tau-oi are among the Southeast Asian tribes who believe it imperative that each woman in labor must deliver her baby unattended. To do this, she normally chooses a secluded spot outside her village in the forests. There she is expected to bring forth her baby, to sever the unbilical cord and the placenta as well as give the first cares to the newly-born baby. She cannot be physically aided by a midwife or anyone else. However, when child labor is exceedingly long and difficult, her family may make an offering of eight piglets to the spirits for their help.

If the mother survives this ordeal, she is allowed to "rest" for several days before resuming her normally strenuous activities with the newly born baby wrapped in a blanket strapped to her back. Incidentally, during her period of known pregnancy, it is taboo for her to enter or move into any village except her own. Thus, it is little wonder that Tau-oi women twenty-five years old seem to be quite "faded". [36]

The Tau-oi men seem to work in a more leisurely manner. They fish, hunt and trap game, cooperate in the construction of longhouses when such occasions arise, clear jungle areas as fields, and wield male authority to settle either family or village problems. Only a careful analysis of the total Tau-oi life would reveal the actual status and effort of individual tasks. Some of the tasks so nonchalantly performed by Tau-oi men might require long training and persistent effort on the part of foreign participants.

Marriage: In spite of the custom of "Di-sim", "Tam bon", Tau-oi girls maintain a certain modesty and normally hide in their homes when strangers are in the village. When choosing a girl as a prospective wife, the man makes her acquaintance and at a propitious time offers her a gift. The acceptance of the gift, which may be either a particular item or a bit of money, is tacit consent of marriage by the girl. After this, the girl may be presented to the man's parents, and if they approve, the couple are engaged.

The actual betrothal must be sealed by a deposit that may eventually be the equivalent of over 300 dollars. After the first formal presentation, the family of the future bridegroom start the serious collection of the dowry so that the marriage can take place. The dowry may be made up of some cash, two or three buffalo, copper kettles, gongs and other utensils deemed useful or desirable. In the case of an extremely poor bridegroom's family, the dowry may be reduced by consent of the bride's family but it must always include at least one buffalo and some food. These are to be used in the presentation ceremony in which the newlyweds are formally presented to all members of the families and to the ancestors of the groom's family.

Should the bridal family be unable to agree among themselves as to how the dowry is to be shared, each member may come to the groom's family and seek to obtain their share directly. This may necessitate "a marriage on credit" which can put the new household in debt for several generations. The dowry is so important to the Tau-oi that incompatible couples are required to delegate maternal grandparents the right to marry off their nieces and receive the dowries for themselves.[37] Likewise, in marriages that produce only boys, parents must will the boy's maternal grandparents the right to marry off the boy's future daughters so that they might receive the dowry benefits.

The enormous expense of such marriages does much to encourage the Tau-oi tribal custom whereby the oldest brother wills his wife to a younger brother after his death, or for a father to will his concubine to either his son or to a male relative. If the widow refuses to comply with the terms of the will, she is required to repay the full dowry as well as the engagement price. This of course is impossible so that submission to the will is her only course of action in all except the most rare instances.

Polygamy is an accepted Tau-oi matrimonial pattern. Prosperous men may acquire a number of wives while many men are unable to contract a marriage and so remain bachelors all their lives. Sometimes the richer men, in order to insure their ability to marry as many wives as they desire, will buy nine and ten year old girls and make them their wives when the girls are older.[38]

The Tau-oi, unlike other ethnic groups, often marry girls of other tribes. The bridal price of a Tau-oi girl, depending upon her family status and her health may be as high as fifteen buffaloes, while that of neighboring tribes is more often two buffaloes. In a society in which plural marriages indicate wealth, creates prestige, and brings additional workers into the family, the Tau-oi tribesmen often consider marriage to young women of neighboring tribes to be a wise bargain.[39]

Intra-tribal marriage between two Tau-oi may impose additional requirements upon the tribespeople. For instance, every Tau-oi girl who marries a man from another village than her own is subject to a "breach of promise" custom. This custom requires her to name all her former "lovers" to the prospective groom before marriage. Should she fail to do this, or fail to name everyone, and the groom learns of this after the marriage has been consummated, he may lawfully demand two buffaloes from the bride's parents as payment for this fault.[40]

In spite of the custom of "Di-sim" or "Tam-bon", Tau-oi society disapproves of adultery and imposes fines upon the guilty when they are detected. However, there does exist some violations of tribal mores so that the use of traditional fines is recognized. If detected or if pregnancy occurs, the man - be he married or single - must sacrifice a buffalo to the village phi for his redemption. Until this offering has been made and consumed, the guilty man and woman are taboo to entering any village except their own. If this restriction should be violated, the offender must pay an additional fine of one pig. However, once the sacrificial buffalo has been eaten by the villagers, the man has fulfilled his tribal obligations to his society, to the woman, and to any possible children.[41]

<u>Death and Burial Patterns</u>: There is a difference between the Tau-oi and the Bru death and burial practices. [42] When a Tau-oi dies, the village is considered taboo, "Khalam", until the burial has taken place. After a natural death, the corpse must be left outside and underneath the house for the first night. Normally the villagers come in their finest dress for burials and contribute to the occasion by bringing alcohol, ordinary rice and a specially prepared gluey rice.

Because the village is taboo from the time of death until after the burial, an outsider entering the village must offer a buffalo as the appropriate sacrifice to the village phi. Likewise, the non-villager who encounters a funeral procession must join it, participate in the funeral and return with the cortege to the village, or be fined one buffalo by the family of the deceased. Should this fine be refused, it is necessary that the family must sacrifice one of its own buffaloes to appease the spirits.

When death occurs from accidents such as: being killed by a falling tree; wounds of a marauding tiger; murder; etc; which are thought to be supernaturally caused, the funeral party must stay in the jungle for three nights following the burial. After this, they may return to the village, sacrifice a buffalo, and the funeral cycle is complete. Should death occur during or from childbirth, the woman's body must be guarded for three days. During this period tambourines are shook and gongs are struck frequently about the body. This Tau-oi practice is believed to be efficatious in guarding other prospective mothers against the spirits that caused the childbirth death.

Tau-oi burial usually takes place in remote areas of the forest, in random, but, suitable places. Only those Tau-oi who live along the right bank of the Se Khong utilize predetermined funeral sites. Whenever burial takes place near streams or flowing water, the head of the deceased is placed in the direction of the current. [43] The coffins are only about half buried or covered up, and this condition continues for three years. [44] The predetermined funeral sites are normally marked by being surrounded by a number of tree trunks which have been carved into various silhouettes. [45]

As in most tribes, the burial of a Tau-oi village chief requires special effort and attention. A village chief's coffin is hewn from a tree section with sufficient room being chopped out for the body. The lid of the coffin is carved with various designs. Moreover, the personal possessions of the dignitary (clothing, weapons, pipes, jewelry) are placed in the coffin. [46] If not placed in the coffin due to lack of space, they are put in the grave with the coffin. Over the grave will be erected a bamboo roof several feet above the ground supported by decorated wooden statuettes with the Tau-oi lizard motif undoubtedly found as one of the carvings. Should anyone violate the grave, the necessary payment is one white and black buffalo, a bracelet, a chicken, a pig and an armload of red cloth.

Three years after the initial burial, the Tau-oi exhume the ramains from their shallow grave. These are then buried in a deep grave which is then filled and leveled. At this time the "true" funeral ceremony takes place with the sacrifice of fowls, pigs, buffaloes and rice wine. [47] After this ceremony the deceased is apparently forgotten and receives no additional attention. Incidently, the Tau-oi mourning period for a widow is twelve months and for a widower is two months. The period of mourning is computed from the day of the first funeral.

ECONOMIC

Similar to the other Montagnard peoples discussed in the Overview of Chapter One, the Tau-oi subsistence economy is based upon the cultivation of dry grown or upland rice. This is grown in fields cleared from the forest and jungle areas by the technique known as slash and burn. Among the Tau-oi the winter months are used to cut down all the growth and to allow it to dry and then be burned. The ashes resulting from the dry vegetation is the only fertilizer which the Tau-oi, use as they believe that the spirits of the rice and of the field would be unhappy if other forms of soil enrichment are used.

In spite of the potentials for simple dams and irrigation pos-sibilities residual in the Tau-oi tribal area, they depend solely on rainfall for their crops. Thus the steep hills combined with the simple farming methods and the lack of soil enrichment results in such damage to the fields, that they are abandoned within a few short years. Thus even as old fields are used, new ones must be prepared.

The forests are a source of scented leaves, edible roots and fruits. Streams and rivers provide ready sources of fish. These are caught by gig, hook, net baskets, etc. Nevertheless, the Tau-oi diet would be considered an insufficient diet by most "civilized people".

The Tau-oi practice the crafts of woodworking and carving, of basket weaving and making, and the weaving and dying of blue and red cloth for their various needs. In addition, a few of the Tau-oi work as laborers on non-tribal sponsored projects. [47]

RELIGION

The Tau-oi religious beliefs are animistic with the exception of the few who have become Christians. Their religious practice involves the relationship between themselves and the supernatural powers known as phi or genies. These all powerful spirits control all the forces of nature. The Tau-oi believe their strongest spirits to be the Spirit of the Sky and the Spirit of the Paddy. These two spirits are thought to control the destiny of the tribe. Because the Tau-oi are in perpetual poverty with food an ever-present need, the Spirit of the Paddy remains the most "venerated" of all the supernatural forces.

The Tau-oi believe that the spirits work through, and control, the various natural forces so that harm or prosperity may be given to an individual or the village as the spirits please. Therefore, the Tau-oi seek to gain the favor of the spirits; to placate them when this is needed; and to secure their cooperation when possible. These goals cause the Tau-oi to build a house for the phi that resides in their village; to observe very carefully all the taboos, and by continually offering appropriate sacrifices. [48]

Always fearful of the destructive powers of the spirits, the Tau-oi offer sacrifices to prevent accidents of all types; to obtain redemption due to violated taboos through placation of the spirits; and to enhance personal favor with the spirits by showing them respect. The Tau-oi see in almost every occasion a need for offerings; if the harvest is good; if it is bad; if sickness occurs; if omens are indicative of potential harm, and many other events of daily life.

An offering ceremony includes the making of appropriate sets of bamboo shelves upon which is placed the offerings and parts of the blood sacrifices. One of the more venerated Tau-oi village elders squats facing this small altar and begins to recite the appropriate prayers. This phase of the ceremony is terminated by earnestly entreating the spirits to make known their acceptance or rejection of the offerings. The knowledge of the spirits' reaction is obtained by throwing two coins into a dish. If the coins fall so that one shows "heads" while the other shows "tails", the offering is believed to be accepted. However, if the coins do not fall in these positions, another offering must be made. [49]

Small sacrifices may consist of offerings made of brass rings, alcohol, rice and or the ritual slaying of chickens and pigs, with the food items subsequently being consumed. Larger sacrifices require that a buffalo be sacrificed with appropriate ceremonies. For this ritual, the selected buffalo is firmly tied to one of the columns which surround the small village phi house. Then the young men of the village, with spears, swords and long tribal knives or axes, dance and sing about the buffalo. The rest of the village are also participants as they gather about to shake their tambourines, strike their symbols or beat upon their gongs with the base of their palms as essential elements of this rite. Suddenly, one of the young men in passing behind the buffalo's back legs will use one blow of his sharp weapon to sever the tendons. The buffalo, unable to stand on its hind legs, is now tortured as tribal spears are repeatedly thrust into its body. Accompanied by the various musical instruments, the shouts of the women and children and the songs of the men, the Tau-oi young men continue their dancing and stabbing of the buffalo until it is dead.

To the Tau-oi, each part of the ritual has its purpose and is done in conformity to that purpose. The beating of instruments and the shouting is to make sure that the spirits are aware that the sacrifice is being made for them; the dance and the song is to make the spirits understand that this is for their honor and benefit;

the torture of the buffalo is to make it cry out as it cannot bellow. This noise is thought to be most pleasing to the spirits as is the sight and odor of sacrificial blood is believed to delight the spirits. Entrance to Tau-oi villages is taboo during such ceremonies.

Under certain conditions, the Tau-oi village may feel itself unprotected and declare itself taboo to all non-villagers. The events that necessitate making the village khalam, "taboo", are activities or circumstances that interrupt the daily routine. These may include the preparation of a new trail in the nearby forests, the repairing of a long house, a fire that destroys part of the village, a trapped tiger, the absence of a village war party, etc.

Since a village is taboo during the repair of a house or the making of a new trail, a buffalo must be sacrificed to the village phi. Likewise, the owner of a house in which a fire originates that destroys part of the village must sacrifice one white and one black buffalo. If there is a non-villager visiting in that house, he also must offer one buffalo as his contribution to the sacrifice. Because the Tau-oi must sacrifice the buffalo and then consume it, the normal procedure is to offer one buffalo per day. Inasmuch as this three-day sacrifice must be preceded by three days of sacrificing chickens, the village is taboo for six days under these circumstances.

When a new Tau-oi village is to be erected at a new site, it is believed that the phi of the new location must be placated through the sacrifice of two buffalo with one being white and the other black. Should a "stranger" enter a Tau-oi village and steal something, and get caught, it is imperative that he sacrifice a buffalo to the village phi in that village where the crime occurred. Likewise, it is taboo to bring into a Tau-oi village the stick with which one has scrapped the wood leeches off himself. Apparently one of the reasons for this is that the phi of the village will see the blood and smell its odor and be frustrated because no sacrifice has been offered to it. The Tau-oi think the appropriate fine for this offense is the sacrifice of a chicken and a pig besides the offering of one brass ring. [50]

Besides the "crisis" sacrifices offered throughout the year according to need, the Tau-oi have at least two important cyclic annual ceremonies. These are those of the harvest and of the village phi, with the former in October and the latter in February or "third month" according to the Tau-oi. The ritual held after the rice harvest is to celebrate the event and to alert the spirits that the villagers are about to begin the clearing of new "ray" (areas of the jungle by slash and burn methods for paddy fields). This ceremony known as "adza" is celebrated with unusual solemnity that requires the Tau-oi to stay in their houses for two days and nights. The "adza" ceremony, lasting three or four additional days, results in numerous poultry, pigs, cattle and buffaloes being slaughtered as sacrifices. As in almost all religious ceremonies, the village is taboo to all non-villagers. The sign of this taboo is the placing in the paths leading to the village, bamboo, star-shaped "leo", signs. [51]

The ceremony honoring the village phi is of ten days duration. During this time numerous chickens and one buffalo are sacrificed. Numerous large jars of rice wine are also consumed as the Tau-oi men sit around the village and smoke their tobacco water pipes.

As previously noted, the village phi ceremony is in February as a "third month ceremony" in spite of the fact that calendar time is almost totally unknown to the Tau-oi. However, during the period of time (October) beginning with the harvest rites through the village phi ceremony, (February), the Tau-oi have taboos against the collection of debts, and the collection of fines for sexual offenses committed against young Tau-oi women; or even the giving of a handful of rice from the family granary to anyone outside the family.

Numerous other religiously-oriented beliefs affect the behavior of the Tau-oi. Since an omen is thought to be the method by which the spirits may warn the tribespeople, repeated ominous omens will cause the Tau-oi village to be relocated. As among the Bru, the Tau-oi do not allow any conversation in the rice fields from the harvesting to the stripping of the grain from the stalk, to avoid offending the rice spirit. Likewise, the placing of taboo signs in front of cultivated fields as signs to stay out is in accord with the belief that the spirits demand this. These signs often are the placing of a leafy branch on a stake in the entrance pathways, and mean "STAY OUT!" The Tau-oi cannot use fertilizer even though its use would increase rice production because of the fear of offending the spirits. The enrichment of the soil through the ashes acquired from the slash and burn method of farming is the only one permitted. In the same spirit, no rice grain must ever be allowed to fall into the fire or deliberately be burned as the spirit of the rice grain and that of the rice paddy would be furious.

Thus the Tau-oi has formulated a set of beliefs and rules that help him to exist in an environment that otherwise would drive him to an utter sense of hopelessness and helplessness. His non-exposure to a scientific understanding of the normal events of life causes him to rely on the manipulation of the "spirits" as a means in which he can avoid the sense of utter despair.

GUIDELINES FOR RAPPORT

The Tau-oi expect that non-villagers in their midst will understand and observe the Tau-oi patterns of behavior. Failure to comply with the expected local etiquette will be considered as offense to the village phi or to the other spirits whose domain is thus violated. Violations of customary Tau-oi patterns of behavior by non-villagers have fines that range from the offering of a brass ring through offering of a chicken, to that of a buffalo. [52] While military personnel may have the might to resist such fines, the results would certainly include tribal fear of the wrath of the phi with Tau-oi resentment, noncooperation and perhaps outright hostility.

When inside of a Tau-oi house, extreme care should be taken to avoid handling any household furnishing not placed in one's hands by his host. This is particularly true of any item that may contain religious significance to the Tau-oi because of the abject fear of the displeasure of supernatural powers.

When approaching a Tau-oi house, it is improper for a visitor to walk under the house for any reason. Should he be a guest in the house and the hearth fire burn low and need replenishment, it is taboo for him to get firewood from that stacked under the house. It is also improper to ever use the back or side door of a Tau-oi house for any reason as the Tau-oi fear that evil spirits might enter such a doorway utilized by non-householders. When sleeping in a Tau-oi house, one must be careful to not point the feet in the direction of the family "altar" and its religious objects. These are normally located on the front wall of the house to the left of the front entranceway.

From time to time the individual Tau-oi house may be taboo and not to be entered by anyone except those who live in that house. The two most common signs of a house that is "off-limits" are: (1) a crudely made ladder, or a log notched as steps which has been withdrawn from its normal place and placed on the porch, and (2) a leafy branch hung on the door or over the doorway. In a similar way, the most common sign that a village is temporarily taboo is a leafy branch hung horizontally from a stake in the middle of the path leading into the village. Except as required by military necessity, these signs ought to be heeded so that needless offense be avoided.

Similar taboos apply to the rice fields in process of being harvested. No stranger is permitted to enter these fields. If this rule is violated, the women harvesters must immediately stop their work for the day. On the following day, the harvest will resume, but if they hear the cry or call of the roe-deer, monkeys or vultures, they must again stop their work for the day. However, the next day the work may continue. [53]

Non-residents of a Tau-oi village are strictly forbidden to bring within the confines of a village perimeter fence any part of a tiger including its skin. This taboo is based upon the concept that the tiger possesses a spirit of its own, and that some tigers can become men on occasion even as some men can transform themselves into tigers. Should a stranger enter a village in taboo because a tiger has been caught in a pit-trap, he is supposed to cover his head with either wood shavings or a piece of red cloth. He is then required to accompany the villagers to the site of the trap where the tiger is caught and join the villagers in dancing, shouting, arm waving and applause. In addition to these acts, he is also required to inform the village phi of the tiger's death and then offer in sacrifice both a chicken and a pig. [54]

92

Likewise forbidden to non-village residents is the bringing of rhinoceros horns or ivory into the village. In a similar manner, the stranger is forbidden to bring either an elephant or a buffalo into the village. If this is done, he must offer a buffalo in sacrifice as his fine to the village phi. [55]

When visiting in a Tau-oi village, the stranger or non-resident must leave the village enclosure to attend to all personal physical needs. Anyone who violates this custom is expected to pay a fine of one brass ring and one pig.

Another custom that may seem quite different than that of the West is the obligation of any guest to inform his host if he has in his possession such items as bars of silver, gongs or jars. It is obligatory that the host take these items down to the stream and wash them to prevent offense to the village phi. Should the visitor neglect to inform his host, or the host fail to wash the items, a fine of one buffalo is extracted. If this procedure is not followed, the Tau-oi believe that rapid death will come to the entire village. [56]

In addition to the foregoing customs of the Tau-oi tribesmen, the Guidelines for Rapport in Chapter One of this study provide a number of basic factors in the wise establishment of American-Tau-oi relationships. Undoubtedly when peace comes to the Tau-oi tribal area in South Vietnam, the Tau-oi, like some of the other Montagnards, will have the opportunity for the establishment of schools, dispensaries, improved farming methods, with sustained attempts to integrate this ethnic group into the nationhood now being established in Vietnam. Limited observation and experience among the Tau-oi by Western personnel indicate that the Tau-oi can quickly learn many of the basic skills of life if offered the opportunity.

FOOT-NOTES

1. Frank M. Lebar, Gerald C. Hickey, John K. Musgrave, Ethnic Groups of Mainland Southeast Asia, New Haven, Conn. Human Relations Area Files Press, 1964, p. 151; Leopold Michael Cadiere, "Notes sur les Mois du Quang-Tri", Bulletin de l'Institut Indochinois pour l'Etude de l'Homme, III, 1940, p. 102

2. George M. Maspero, The Montagnard Tribes of South Vietnam translated from the French monograph Les Traits Characteristiques dans les Moeurs et Costumes des Tribus Montagnards au Su du Vietnam by the Joint Publications Research Service, Washington, D.C. 1962, p. 2.

3. Pastor H. L. Josephsen's 1966 Bru Tape for Navy Personal Response; also see Vietnam Minority Languages List (July 1966) of the Summer Institute of Linguistics, Saigon, Vietnam, "Pacoh".

4. Lebar et al, op. cit. p. 151

5. U.S. Information Service, Montagnards of the South Vietnamese Highlands, Saigon, USIS, July 1961, p. 21

6. LeBar, et al, op. cit. p. 151

7. U.S. Department of State, The Geographer, Office of Research in Economics and Science, Bureau of Intelligence and Research, International Boundary Study No 35: Laos Vietnam Boundary (Washington, D. C. U.S. Dept. of State, June 29 1964) p. 1

8. H.C. Darby (editor) Indo-China, Cambridge, England, Geographical Handbook Series 1943, p. 20.

9. Websters Third International Dictionary, Springfield, Mass, G. and C. Merriam Company, 1961, p. 970.

10. H. C. Darby, Indo-China, pp. 65-84

11. U.S. State Department, op. cit. p. 5

12. Lebar et al, op. cit. p. 151

13. M. Daupley, "Les Kha Tahoi", L'Ethnographie, n.s. (April 15, 1914, p. 44.

14. Bernard Bourotte, "Essai d'histoire des populations montagnards du Sud Indochinois jusqu' a 1945", Bulletin de la Societe des Etudes Indochinoises, n.s. XXX, 1, (1955), p. 30

15. Bourotte, p. 39; Confer Robbin Burling, Hill Farms and Padi Lands, Englewood Cliffs, N.J. Prentice-Hall, Inc, 1965

16. Bourotte, pp. 39 &43; Daupley, op. cit. pp. 43-44.

17. Bourotte, op. cit. p. 43

18. Bourotte, pp. 53 & 73

19. Bourotte, p. 67

20. Daupley, op. cit. p. 43

21. Daupley p. 44

22. Daupley, pp. 110-124

23. Maspero, op. cit. p. 3; Daupley p. 44

24. Maspero, op. cit. p. 3

25. Daupley, op. cit. p. 44 (A similar practice is followed by a remote tribe who live in the Himalayas. This tribe keeps extending the neck spiral until the head no longer rests firmly on the spinal column and the removal of the collar device is to cause the death of the wearer by a broken-neck.)

26. J.H. Hoffet, "Les Mois de la Chaine Annamitique entre Tourane et les Boloven, "Terre, Air, Mer: La Geographie LIX (Janvier 1933, p. 12; Nguyen Van Huyen, Introduction a l'etude de l'habitation sur pilotis dans l'Asie du sud-east, Paris, Librairie Orientaliste Paul Geuthner, 1934, p. 39; Lebar et al, op. cit. p. 151

27. Hoffet, p. 12

28. Charles Robequain, L'Indochine francaise, Paris, Librairie Armand Colin, 1935, pp. 87-88

29. Hoffet, op. cit. p. 34; p. Paris, Decor et construction de maisons Kha entre Lao-Bao et Saravane, Bulletin de l'Ecole Francaise d'Extreme-Orient XIV (1952) p. 567

30. Paris, p. 567

31. Maspero, op. cit. p. 3

32. Daupley, op. cit. p. 49

33. Hoffet, op. cit. p. 12

34. Maspero, op. cit. pp. 5-6

35. Maspero, p. 6

36. Daupley, p. 48

37. Maspero, p. 5

38. Maspero, p. 5

39. Daupley, op. cit. p. 48

40. Daupley, p. 49

41. Daupley, p. 49

42.   Confer with "Death Patterns" of the Bru, Chapter II of this study.

43.   Maspero, op. cit p. 10; Daupley, op. cit p. 46

44.   Maspero, pp. 9-10; Robert L. Mole, 1965-66 Field-notes .

45.   Noel Bernard, "Les Khas; Peuple inculte du Laos francaise - Notes anthropometriques et ethnographiques, "Bulletin de Geographie, Historique et Descriptive (1904) p. 360.

46.   Daupley, p. 46

47.   Lebar, op. cit.   p. 151; Hoffet, op. cit   p. 12; Mole, 1965-6 Field-notes

48.   Daupley, p. 45; Maspero, p. 7, Lebar et al, p. 151

49.   Maspero, p. 7; Mole, 1965-6 Field-notes

50.   Daupley, pp. 47 &50

51.   Maspero, p. 8; Daupley, p. 45, Mole, 1965-66 Field-notes

52.   Daupley, p. 50

53.   Daupley, p. 45

54.   Daupley, p. 47

55.   Daypley, p. 45

56.   Daupley, p. 47

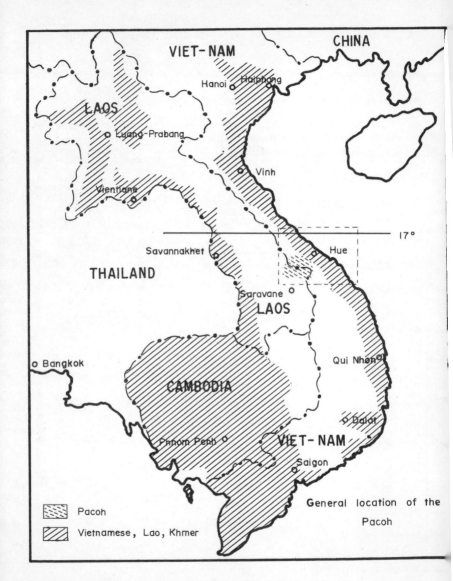

General location of the Pacoh

- ⧄ Pacoh
- ⧄ Vietnamese, Lao, Khmer

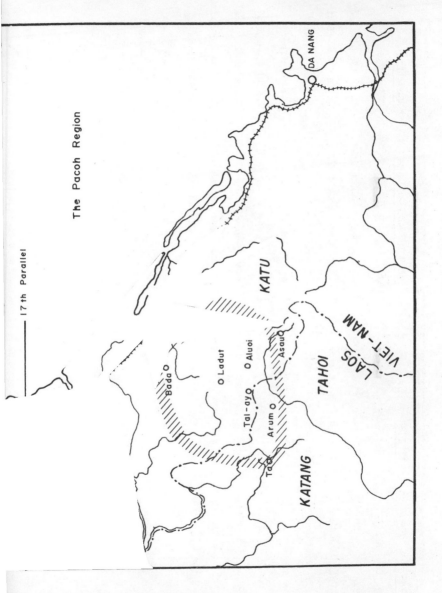

The Pacoh Region

17 th Parallel

DA NANG

KATU

TAHOI

KATANG

LAOS

VIET-NAM

O Bada

O Ladut

O Aluoi

Tai-ay O

Arum O

Asau O

Tao

99

NAVI PERSONAL RESPONSE ELEMENTARY PACOH PHRASE LIST

VIETNAMESE	ENGLISH	PACOH TRIBAL LANGUAGE	PHONETIC
Chào Ông (to a man)	Hello	Bênh xoanh ipe	Bln soan pe
Tôi là bạn	I am your friend	Cừ inh taq yán anửng ipe	Kừ in tấq yấw alửg ipe
Tôi muốn gặp lanh tu bạn	I would like to meet your chief	Cừ inh tumuh arcaih vêl	Kừ in tumuh areaih wẹl
Các bạn là người lãnh	You are good people	Ipe côh ticuar o	Ipe koh tikuei I
Người dân bạn tên là gì?	What is the name of your people?	Amáh nôh ipe?	Anáh nah ipé?
Bạn cần đồ ăn không?	Do you need food?	Ipe inh tanna cáh?	Ipe in tanna kah?
Đồ ăn nầy tốt đối với bạn	This food is good for you	Tanua nnéh o icha	Tanna annáh I Ica
Bạn cần thấy thuốc không?	Do you need a doctor?	Ipe inh do ăn paylah cáh?	Ipe ín da ăn-paylah kăh?
Tôi uống nước được không?	May I have water?	Cừ xeq ngoiq daq, au	Kừ sẹgoip dạ, ăw.
Cám ơn bạn	Thank you	Cam ôn ipe	Kam an ipe
Bạn sẽ bán nỏ không?	Will you sell crossbows?	Ipe bôn tumiang itech cáh?	Ipe bon tumiay itẹc kắt?
Dạ được	Yes	Bôn ừq	Bon, ừ
Không được	No	Cáh	kắh
Bao nhiêu?	How much?	Li mo ê?	Li ammo e?
Xin tha lỗi tôi	Excuse me	Ncừl thét, ipe	aykừl thét, ipe
Xin bạn đi ra	Please come out	xeq ipe ngôt, au	Sẹ ipe yóh, ăw.

THE PACOH

The ethnic group whose very name means "mountain people" are the subject of this chapter. In spite of their proximity to the ancient royal Vietnamese capital, Hué, little has been written of this tribe. Nevertheless, their geographic location now gives an importance in excess of that normally granted them. Insigificant where population is concerned, this small preliterate and semiliterate people have become spectators and unwilling participants in the war and strife of South Vietnam.

The primary authority for this chapter's Pacoh information is the linguist, Mr. Richard L. Watson. Mr. Watson is the current (1968) Director of the Summer Institute of Linguistics (Vietnam) with offices at Number 5, Sường Nguyệt Ánh, Saigon, South Vietnam. He and his wife spent several years working closely with some of the Pacoh in learning the Pacoh speech so that for the first time, it might be a written language. Only as a people learn to speak, read and write, can they qualify themselves to know and utilize twentieth century knowledge.

The successful achievement of the Watsons' feat required intensive study of Pacoh customs, mannerisms and verbal communications. While a few others have written of the Pacoh, their references have been brief and usually even these instances have been generalities. This author has made several brief research visits into the Pacoh tribal area also. Thus, this chapter about the Pacoh is perhaps the best written source of Pacoh information currently available.

NAME: The Pacoh have several other names. These include Pa-koh, Poko, Pokoh, Pocoh, Khas Pakho and River Van Kieu. There is a minor group, largely lowland tribespeople, who speak with a minor dialect and are generally called Pahi. [1] The Pacoh are identified as linguistically belonging to the Bruan subgrouping of the Katuic subgroup of the Mon-Khmer family of languages[2] of the Bru in Quang Tin Province, the Taioh of Laos and Vietnam and the Katu of Quang Nam. [3]

Population Estimates: The estimated numbers for the Pacoh population vary substantially with the extremes being five and fifteen thousand. The Central Vietnamese government's estimate is the lowest one with it being five thousand. [4] If the lower figure is even approximately correct, it would mean that many of the Pacoh have either migrated to Laos or are casualities of the war. Since there are no major population centers in the Pacoh tribal area, there is little hope of obtaining an accurate census for some time.

Location: The Pacoh tribal area is located in Thừa Thiên and Quảng Trị Provinces and in Laos almost directly west of Huế. Their geographical position on the Vietnamese-Laotian map would place their southern boundary just slightly above A Shau in the A Shau valley. This tribal area extends northward until it forms a common border with the Bru. Its eastern boundary extends into the foothills just west of Hue and the coastal cities of Quang Tri and My Thanh. The latter serves as a Pacoh trading market also. The western tribal area adjoins that of the Taioh at the head of the A Shau valley, while further north, it extends into Laos. [5]

Neighbors: Pacoh neighbors in Vietnam are believed to be the Taioh, Bru, Phường and the Katu. [6] The tribal areas are unmarked by western standards or even by governmental procedures, yet the various tribes tend to generally remain in static positions except as outside pressures force migrations. While the Phường are Pacoh neighbors to the south and southeast, very little is known of this ethnic group.

Terrain: The Vietnamese highlands occupied by the Pacoh is wild, rugged and jungle-clad. Where dense heavy forestation does not form an almost continous blanket of green, thick tough tall grass is abundant. Travel, by foot, except in well worn narrow trails is difficult at best. Besides the dense growth of trees, vines, bushes of many varities, the area has many tigers, snakes, wild pigs, some elephants, etc. which add to travel hazards.

The Pacoh tribal area would not be an ideal site to teach jungle-survival to beginners. The heavy clouds, the dense low-lying fogs, the profuse growth and the steep hills and valleys combine to encourage the loss of the sense of direction. Adding to the problems for foreigners in this area are the nearness of the international Laotian-

Vietnamese border and the presence of hostile forces.

The jungle can provide fruits, edible leaves and roots to those who know its secrets. However, few foreigners are capable of existing long in the area without the friendly presence of a Pacoh tribesman or the overwhelming might of organized military forces. Many of the tribespeople seem to possess an almost uncanny sense of direction; of the sources of wild foods and the ability to merge into their environment with almost perfect camouflage.

Characteristics: The Pacoh have a brown skin coloring characteristic of the Mon-Khmer and Malayo-Polynesian peoples. Those who live in tribal villages and spend much time in the sun are a dark brown, almost to blackness. However, the Pacoh who live in the cities tend to become rather light with skin coloring very much like that of the ethnic Vietnamese. The hair coloring and bone features are much like that of other Vietnamese tribespeople.

Generally, the Pacoh are short and stocky with the muscular legs of mountain climbers. While they have excellent endurance in the mountains, the heat and lowland conditions seem to adversely affect those living along the coastal areas. Moreover, psychological conditions may affect the motivational factors of the tribesmen who no longer are true mountain dwellers.

Pacoh men normally wear loin-cloths. This is a fairly long length of cloth about one foot in width. The loin-cloth is wrapped about the waist and then between the legs with the ends tucked over the waist band. The end of the loin-cloth in front is left hanging free from the waist. One indication of wealth among the Pacoh is the length of the free-swinging loin-cloths as the wealthy always wear their cloths with greater lengths than do the poor. [7]

Pacoh women generally wear a wrap-around skirt and a one piece sleeveless blouse. A fair amount of silver bracelets, necklaces, etc. are worn by many women. The women often wear their hair tied into a bun on the back of their heads. Until recently, the men dressed their hair in a similar manner, and most likely still do in the deep mountains. Pacoh men living in the lowlands cut their hair in the same manner as do the Vietnamese.

Both men and women wear earplugs. These vary in size and materials. Many of the Pacoh pluck their eyebrows and tatoo subsititute ones. [8] The removal of the eyebrow hair and the replacement tatooing of the eyebrows seems to be a puberty rite. It is at this time that many have their front four teeth removed also. The teeth are removed by filing, sawing and breaking down to the gums and then painting them with a resin from the forest. While there seems to be no formal requirement for either of these two feats, the Pacoh youth do not accept their peers as mature or consider them to have shown any real strength for their age until they have had these things done. [9]

In resettlement villages, the Pacoh often wear "hand-me-down" clothing provided by foreigners. Many of the lowland Pacoh men wear black pants and white shirts as do the Vietnamese men. Those who are government employees often wear slacks and a white shirt. The women generally stick to their tribal skirts and blouses except for a few who have changed to the black pajamas of the poor ethnic Vietnamese.

The Pacoh seem to be passive, nonaggressive and even reluctant to meet strangers. Fear seems to be a constant feature of their characteristics. Like the Bru, the Pacoh are gentle people who shun fights when possible. Because of their animistic beliefs, they are fearful of war. To them, any violent death leaves its victim without security or position in the "afterworld". In contrast to those who died a "natural" death and are believed to have continuing relations with the living, those of a violent death become displaced and completely separated from their loved ones.

Yet, the Pacoh praise each other for being courageous rather than fearful. Sometimes in spite of an animistic fear of the spirits, a Pacoh is thought brave when he curses a particular spirit. If a spirit has not answered his prayers and sacrifices in spite of the man's sincerity, the adherent is within his rights to curse that spirit and refuse to sacrifice to it anymore. However, sacrifices are continued for other spirits. Thus, the Pacoh may publically denounce a particular spirit without a denial of his supernatural world. Thus his belief is not basically one of groveling fear.

The gentle psychological nature of the Pacoh makes exile the worst punishment one can receive. To be forced to leave the community and seek a place among strangers is thought to be a terrible fate. Sometimes another community may accept an exile. But more often one must live alone in his field or if it is too close to his village, it must also be abandoned. While beatings are sometimes administered as corporal punishment, fear of being ostracized is the more obvious control.

By nature the Pacoh are quite trusting of each other. Thievery is not a major problem among them as they say that not more than one out of a hundred will steal anything. Seldom, if ever, will a Pacoh sneak up and take anything without the owner's knowledge. If in your presence they take something, and you seeing it do not stop them, they consider that you have tacitly given the item to them.

In this regard, the Pacoh appear to trust one another to use each other's possessions and then return them. Often they leave items laying about with considerable disregard for loss by thievery. However, experience has taught them, that this trusting trait cannot be safely exercised toward others. Nevertheless, this tribal openness has and does permit the loss of items to non-Pacoh. While lying is also strongly disapproved, it is not thought to be as bad as stealing. A lier is known as such by the Pacoh and his statements are simply not accepted as valid.

PACOH VILLAGE STRUCTURES

Resettlement villages are much like those of other displaced Vietnamese citizens and constructed of any material available. However, the preferred Pacoh dwelling seems to be the long house. The long house is really a continuing development of a tribal "apartment house" in which related families dwell. Pacoh customs include the practice of adding a room to the long house as each son marries so that he and his bride have a home. Paticularly is this practice followed in the village. Additionally, some Pacoh fields have houses that may contain one or two family units.

When the fields are very close to the village, the field houses may be occupied during the time just preceding harvest and harvest itself. For those Pacoh who live much further away from the villages, their field houses are occupied throughout the year with only occasional trips to the village for special occasions. The amount of time spent in the home community or its isolated field dwellings, varies with the individual family when military and political conditions allow the tribesmen any choices.

The Pacoh usually build their houses and villages below springs or streams of flowing water. Then by utilizing bamboo sections and gravity flow, running water is "piped" into the village or near the door of an isolated dwelling. The individual house is normally built on heavy wood poles well above the ground. Unless, the man is considered wealthy and uses wooden planks for walls and flooring, bamboo is utilized for flooring and walls. Instead of the thatch used by many tribes for roofing, the Pacoh use a strong thorny leaf of a tree. This is utilized more like a shingle than is the more prevalant thatched grass roof of others. [11]

When sacrifice poles are in evidence, they seem to belong to the whole village rather than an individual clan or family. Yet because there is no organized priesthood, the oldest member of each family is responsible for the sacrifices and rituals of spirit worship. Others may perform the essential rites, but the eldest member is primarily liable for fulfillment of such obligations.

SOCIO-POLITICAL STRUCTURE

The Pacoh are primarily oriented to have their closest relationship with the family, then the clan, followed by the village and occasionally the tribe. There is very little sense of tribal unity or cohesiveness except when there is an issue that pits the tribe against another one or the Vietnamese.

The Pacoh are patrilineal with the settlements largely composed around the extended family. Thus, the settlement includes the grandparents, parents, children, unmarried girls and all the married sons with their families. In-laws may be either from the same or other villages.

There are very few inter-tribal activities except for the few tribesmen engaged in trading. Each tribe, including the Pacoh, have a few men who practice this livelihood and travel among the various nearby tribes. However, there are inter-village activities as when one village invites another to join in their feasts or in other major projects. Whereas some villages are quite friendly to each other, some maintain a sense of isolation and won't join with others in various functions of work, feast or play.

Pacoh authority starts within the immediate family with the oldest male. Within the extended family the eldest man is the authority figure even as he is of the clan where the oldest and most respected grandfather has this role. In the larger villages, elders do exist. While rarely formally elected, they are chosen through patterns of respect and reputation. Normally, the man who shows good judgement is called upon for counsel by individuals. As knowledge and appreciation of his wisdom increases, other individuals and groups solicit his advice so that he becomes an important influence in judging matters of the community.

The closeness of the typical community precludes the necessity of formal votes. Speaking contests, judging contests, combined with sound judgment in his family and livelihood, just naturally sift out the community elders. Because of the informality of selection, there is no set number of elders. Convenience seems to determine the number rather than an arbitrary figure.

The only obvious religious qualification for "office" is one of proper relations with the spirits. One who does not maintain good relations with the spirits is thought to be without spirits and not very wise or respected. In fact, he is generally frowned upon by the community. Therefore, an elder would have to have a good religious practice in terms of the spirits if he is to be respected by the community. Moreover, he would have to be able to take leadership roles in religious festivals and community sacrifices.

Marriage: Pacoh seem to prefer cross-cousin marriages; that is, a boy usually is expected to marry his mother's brother's daughter. Normally, she lives in a different village and, being of another clan, has a different name. On rare occasions, some Pacoh villages may have two or three clans so that an intra-village marriage can occur. Upon occasion, a Pacoh male may marry a Taioh or Phương girl, but this is an exception to tribal practice. To the Pacoh, kinship is very important. All the special days seem to be occasions for visiting the in-laws and the grandparents or other kindred. For major sacrifices, festivals, etc., the family participates as a large unit even when a whole clan or village may be involved. For smaller events the individual family operates within the larger unit.

While some of the wealthier Pacoh marry their children before they have the ability to produce offsprings, most Pacoh do not. Most young men and women work out their own selection of mates subject to parental consent and support. The various festivals and holidays provide opportunties for the youthful Pacoh to become acquainted. The male asking a girl for a date must offer her a gift. This may be rather economically insignificant as a spool of thread, a needle, a bit of cloth, etc. While it may be inexpensive, such gifts are deemed to be evidences of sincerity.

Some of the more wealthy families build a small hut high off the ground in plain sight of the family home when a girl is old enough to date. Here the teenage daughter may entertain her girl friends or have dates. If such a place is not provided, she and her date may utilize the little field-huts for the same purpose. If neither of these are available, any cozy place may become their rendevous.

Once the girl has accepted gifts from a suiter, which must be repeated for each date, there are certain courting procedures which are to be followed. On dates, the girl must wear a blouse and skirt that have no rips or holes in them. Even though the clothing may be old, it must have been mended as no torn places are allowed to be in it. In addition to such clothing, she will have her skirt pinned between her legs with a large safty pin. Although the couple may spend the night together and may engage in petting, the preceding precaution and tribal taboos are supposed to prevent physical inter-course. Some tribesmen admit that perhaps one out of ten may violate these "ground" rules. But should this occur and should there be any rips on the blouse or in the skirt when the pin was hooked through, the boy will be ostracized. While this will be primarily by the girl's family, the rest of the village will join them and no parents will allow their daughters to date such a fellow. So perhaps the gifts of thread and needles are not without value after all!

Besides the physical precautions against immorality, tribal beliefs act as strong restraints also. Physical sex relations out-side of marriage are not approved among the Pacoh. In this, they are quite different than the Taioh. The Pacoh have great fear about violating taboos of physical sex as they believe that any immoral relationship by the unmarried will cause the girl's mother to become sick. This is believed to occur whether pregnancy results or not, or whether misconduct is detected or not. Unless the couple confess and make appropriate sacrifices for their error, the sickness will lead to the death of at least one parent. Even for married persons to engage in physical relations outside of their marriage bond is thought to cause sickness and death for the woman so involved.

A girl is under no obligation to accept the gift offered to her by a young man. Normally, she will not date men whom her parents disapprove. However, at the appropriate time, the parents of the young man visits the home of the girl they desire as their son's wife. Particularly is this true when arrangements have not been made when the young couple were infants. During their visit, negotiations as to price, etc., are undertaken. In some the price for a wife is so high that it is difficult for poor men to acquire a wife. Then since the girl is bought by the groom's family, she goes to live with her husband in the family long house. While she and her husband have a room to themselves, she is largely under the jurisdiction of her mother-in-law.

The wedding seems to consist primarily of the marriage agreement and the feasts which accompany the transfer of the girl to her new home. Utilizing one's own possessions and part of the bridal price or other compensations, the girl's family has a large feast. This feast is called aléq-uróq and at this time the bride's father symbolizes the loss of his daughter by dropping the stem of a banana leaf through the hole of the top of the ladder. The food and drink which continues for three days include rice, chickens, birds, pigs and wine of sugar cane or rice. The groom's family usually has to give a sacrifical buffalo besides silver, pots, pans, etc.

Children: Pacoh children are not named until they are several months old since they believe that they have such tender souls that the spirits may carry them away, i.e. cause their death. The excessive infant mortality rate prevent parents contemplating a name for their young infant or to give it too much affection too soon. Incidently, Pacoh names cannot be used again so must not be wasted should the baby die. An additional reason for delaying the naming of a first child is that henceforth the parents will be called by the name of their first child and it would not be appropriate to be called by the name of one who died in infancy. However, when the youngster survives and reaches the age to be named, parents, grandparents, uncles and aunts may suggest names. One name which is most popular will stick while the others will gradually drop off.

The Pacoh are careful not to duplicate names among the living lest the personal or family spirits become confused, jealous or angry. Moreover, names must not be of the recent dead lest this create spirit confusion also. Normally, Pacoh given names are of one syllable with siblings having names that start with the same sound with no obvious distinction of names by sex.

When Pacoh children reach adolescence (when interest in the opposite sex begins according to the Pacoh) their playmates give them nicknames. Some have several nicknames as these do not normally denote a special characteristic. It is about this same time that other physiological-psychological changes take place also. With adolescence, the children begin to learn the facts of life in a conscious manner and must now learn and practice the proper customs of dress and related mores. Now the boys must take their sleeping mats into the communal, or men's room, at the center of the long house. The girls continue to stay in the family room unless the family is wealthy enough to build them a small guest house a short distance from the long house. If this is done, the girls may sleep there; have slumber parties among themselves; or entertain in informal and formal dates.

It does not matter if the first child is male or female insofar as renaming the parents is concerned. For the father, his name becomes that of his child preceded by cŏnh, "male", man, while the mother's name will be that of the child preceded by cán, "female", woman with these generally accepted to mean "father" and "mother". The generic meanings of cŏnh and cán are always "male" and "female" respectively, and can be used of persons or animals regardless of their ages. The meanings "man" and "woman" are more specific in that they require a phrase structure which excludes animals and non-adult humans: ape cŏnh, "the men", ape cán, "the woman", ncŏnh, "a man", ncán, "a woman".

The generic terms for "father" and "mother" are a-ám and a-i, respectively. In the Pahi dialect of Pacoh these terms are used for the parent-titles. The a-, "kin term marker" is dropped leaving the title forms Ám and I, e. g. Ám Dep, "Dep's father, I Dep, "Dep's mother".

The Pacoh have a possessive prefix i- which must be prefixed to all kin terms when they are followed by a possess or the interrogative nnau, "who?", but this prefix has been lost in the Pahi dialect. Examples of the Pacoh are: inhi Cubuat, "Cubuat's uncle", inhi cu, "my uncle", inhi nnau, "whose uncle?". But the possessed forms of "father" and "mother" are not i-ám and i-i, but rather icŏnh and icán. A further development of this dual system is a social one. A Pacoh boy or girl will be asked, "Tŏq mmo icán may?", "Where is your mother?". But the boy or girl, to be proper, must answer with the kin terms using, a-ám cu, "my father", or a-i cu, "my mother".

Since icŏnh and icán are used as possessed forms of "father" and "mother", it is reasonable to assume that cŏnh and cán when followed by a child's name, are title forms of "father" and "mother". The Pacoh terms for using the parent-titles are: doq parcŏnh, "to call father-title", and doq parcán, "to call mother-title".

Some of the social correlates of the parent-titles are: the new social status of parents and the responsibility of parents for their children. Marriage alone does not make the difference in social status because the children of wealthy families are sometimes married before childbearing is possible, and because it is felt that the souls of barren parents are too weak to bear children. Though the young couple will build their own family room to the end of the long house, the bride must spend her time with the mother-in-law as a virtual servant. Once she has a child of her own, though, she can enjoy some independence in her own room and can then look forward to the time when she will be "queen" in her own household. The new father also has a new position in his house and in the village. Grandparents are called by grandparent-titles. The title forms of the kin terms avŏq, "grandfather" and acáq, "grandmother" are used to preface the name of the eldest grandchild, e. g. Vŏq Mua, "Mua's grandfather", and Cáq Mua, "Mua's grandmother".

The Pacoh terms for the grandparent-titles are: parvŏq, "grandfather-title", and parcáq, "grandmother-title". To call by a grandparent-title is doq parvŏq and doq parcáq.

The use of the grandparent titles marks a new position of social respect. In the vocative system avŏq and acáq are extended to terms of respect for persons of wealth, wisdom or official position as well as age. The title of a man to whom the people turn to be judge in their disputes is Avŏq Parchĕn, "the reconciler".[12]

Before a bride is taken into her new home a sacrifice must be observed for her adoption by the groom's ancestor spirits. Since families continue to give daughters to certain families and to take daughters from certain other families, family solidarity is added to the separate families. When there is sickness or trouble, the in-law groups will help to provide food, put in crops or supply other needs. When there is a celebration in a village, the khoi, husband's family group, and cuya, wife's family group, relatives are usually invited to share. At least once a year the cuya group will go to visit their daughters in the khoi group and will take food items to give to the family. The khoi group in turn will give manufactured items, which have been bought or made at home, to the cuya group. This is somewhat of a "Christmas exchange" and since every family is both a cuya and a khoi to at least two other families, the economy has an opportunity to circulate.

In the old days parents almost always chose a cross-cousin or a daughter of the wife's brothers to be their son's wife. Now more men choose their own wives, but continue to make the same preferential choice because they feel very close ties to their cuya and have confidence that the wife will be a good one and that the in-laws will uphold them in any troubles. A further reason for retaining the same marriage groups is the matter of equality - the gift exchange can be kept on an equal basis and bride prices can be met.

There are a number of important factors concerning the special status which women hold in this society. This is in spite of the fact that lineage is patrilineal and that the girls are bought by the parents of the husband-to-be. The mother of the family is the predominate person in production of rice and in serving of meals. The "main" things are often called cán, "female" e. g. the stock of the cross-bow, etc. This can be correlated to the fact that, according to legend, the first human ancestor of the Pacoh was a woman, and that the spirit of the rice is considered to be female. This may also correlate to the fact that parents take food products, including rice, to their married daughters each year.

Totem names: The Pacoh all accept the legend of their origin which tells that following a great flood of the whole earth by the breaking up of the sky which holds the water back, only a woman and a dog were left alive as a result of having been put into a drum. After some time, because of loneliness and the need to repopulate the earth, the spirits permitted the woman and the dog to have eight children. Because of the dog parent, the Pacoh observed the totem taboo of avoiding killing or eating dogs. Whereas the dog taboo was general among all the Pacoh, the totem names and taboos for each family appear to be a later innovation. Furthermore, as separate totems arose, some of the families have in recent years begun to eat dogs occasionally. The Pacoh term for totem is yaq. The totems have no apparent relationship with origin or ancestry, but seem to have been chosen as family jinxes and therefore to be avoided. [13]

Training: Traditionally the young Pacoh have been trained "on-the-job". The girls living in the family room, are usually trained by the mother, grandmother, aunts and other women. The boys, living in the communal room, hear the legends and folklore of the tribe as these are an evening feature there. Here, the old-timers tell their stories and tales so that these are transmitted from generation to generation.

The boys also hear what guests have to say as these sleep in the communal room also. Where there are women guests in the family room, all the men sleep in the communal room. It is also customary that all the men sleep in this room before they go hunting or undertake other dangerous and serious activities. In this way, the boys absorb tribal lore and customs.

Formal education for the Pacoh has been greatly hindered by their geographic location and unwillingness to leave their mountains. They also are reluctant to place their children in lowland communities for the same reasons. Thus, tribal practice and oral transmission of know-ledge is the school for most Pacoh youth. Almost every family will have fields for raising rice and other crops. Besides this, some families will have specialities such as basket-weaving, crossbow making, construction of musical instruments, etc. These crafts are taught to the children routinely. However, a youngster may demonstrate interest and talents for other crafts so that he or she may learn these as primary skills.

While the youthful Pacoh enjoy some kinds of rough recreation, they never rise to the level generally found in American football or boxing. While they have ways of expending their energies for enjoyment and hard work, they do not have the aggressiveness common to Westerners. However, the descriptive terms "indolent" and "slothful" would be improper as they seem to be as industrious as their "world-view" and as circumstances encourage or permit.

Pacoh Justice: The primitive Pacoh have a system of justice that would not be permitted under the Courts-Martial Manual. Nevertheless, for anyone serving in their area, it is well to understand their system. Therefore with minor editing, an explanation by a Pacoh tribesman is given here: "If you know who stole, you speak to him. If he does not repay, you speak to the village; who in turn speak to him. If necessary a hearing may be held in which you debate with the accused and the village decides. If it is a severe crime, the two parties may also be joined by elders of the village and they will decide who loses and what he must pay."

If it is definitely known and determined who should pay, but he refuses to do so, the surrounding villages are told. If he still refuses to settle the penalty, it is decided what should be done to the person. If his family agrees to pay a part, the village will pay the rest; then merely censure and watch the criminal. If he does not have a family, he may have all his possessions taken; be tied; be beaten; or killed by clubbing on the head with a heavy club. This may also happen if he does not listen to his family. If his family is stubborn like him and will not help repay, the village may take all of their belongings also. However, these things rarely have ever happened. Public censure is enough to curb most trouble.

If someone accuses another of a small theft, the two may be tested by tying their index fingers together and putting them gradually into a fire. Whichever one pulls back is guilty and must pay. If neither pulls back so that both are burned, the accuser must pay the accused for having accused him falsely and so tested him.

Four Trials: In cases of a large crime in which the price of ten buffalo may be involved, the entire village and possibly surrounding villages are called together. Each householder must question his own family and then stand responsible for it. Then the householders

114

are stood in a circle and a chicken beheaded in the middle. Whomever the chicken lands on in its fluttering is guilty. If he still does not confess or at least agree to pay part of the payment, he must undergo the next trial.

Two grasshoppers are caught and given to the accuser and accused. They each hold them in the water and cause them to dive under. If one does come to the surface its holder loses. If they both or neither come up and no confession is made, the next test is required.

This test has two candles which are submerged to their tops in water. They are then lighted. They are supposed to burn clear to the bottom in spite of the water, but if one goes out and the other burns, the person lighting the candle that went out loses.

The fourth and last test is the most serious. If neither party gives in, and both parties persist in accusation or non-confession, this test means war. However, the people generally will be on the side of the one who won the various tests. The accuser and accused are yoked together and must put their heads under the water. Then an arrow of hard bamboo is thrown into the water. It is supposed to come up into the nose of the one who is guilty so that he will raise up out of the water.

At any time during these trials the accused person can be humble enough to offer to even pay a part of the fine and the villages will help with the rest. If they do offer to pay, but the accuser insists on receiving every penny for a large crime, the villages will be angry with him. They will get even with him later in some other circumstance.

Before the various tests a sacrifice is made to the spirits and incense is left burning under a long beautiful length of cloth. [14] This is so that the spirits can be present to insure correct results. Because the Pacoh are convinced of the validity of these trials, it is extremely rare that anyone is willing to undergo the full trial procedure. It may also be that the lesser of evils is to confess to a crime of which one is innocent as the penalty may be much less severe.

Sickness: The Pacoh are often confronted with serious sickness. It poses a threat to them just as it does any other peoples without scientific knowledge, medication and equipment. The tribespeople do know of certain herbs that are effective aids in restoring health in some instances. But since sickness is believed to be caused by displeased spirits in most instances, these unseen beings must be placated, appeased and pardon granted. Thus, often after natural remedies are tried and fail, a spirit medium must be utilized.

Interestingly, while the elders of a family, clan or village conduct most rites, those for sickness are by a spirit medium who is often a woman. The spirit medium will go to the house of the sick, burn incense and go into a trance. This medium must ascertain which spirits are creating the illness and what must be done for the restoration of health.

The medium asks each of the ancestral spirits and also the demons, who is the cause of the sickness. Sometimes she then announces that the patient cannot recover no matter what sacrifices are offered and that death is certain! While in trance, the medium converses with the spirits who answer in audible voices according to the Pacoh. As the medium continues in trance with a voice which does not sound like her own, there is an almost continuous chanting and singing. As the medium continues with the strange voice, it will often tell the cause and cure for the patients illness.

Sometimes the Pacoh demand to know for sure that health will be restored before they sacrifice a buffalo or other expensive offerings. They seem to follow the concept of "no cure, no pay!" It is claimed by the Pacoh that when the spirits' requirements are met, the patient will recover. However, there are some instances when the spirits just will not answer the medium's calls, or if they do, they indicate there is no cure so that the victim must die. Even the few Christian Pacoh have strong beliefs about the mediums' power of positive communication with the supernatural world.

Incidently the "office" of spirit medium has no connection with the community leaders who are responsible for the rituals and sacrifices not involving illness. Normally, the spirit medium is a woman who has been visited by the spirits; who have given her dreams or other messages that she has been chosen to be a medium for them. She must therefore give over her life to them and be their channel of communication with the living. If she refuses, she may have serious troubles created by the spirits. Normally, her power is in relation to her response toward the spirit who chooses her. It is also related to the power of the spirit itself. If it is a good spirit which is helpful and gives real cures to the people, she is considered a good medium. If her controlling spirit is very arbitrary and evil, the Pacoh don't expect too much help from that medium.

The spirit mediums are measured by their effectiveness, but must earn a living through normal activities like everyone else in the community. Their fees for consulting the spirits are very meager as in one sense they are genuine slaves of their supernatural spirits. But other than this unusual quality, they have no more community responsibility than does any other woman in the village. [15]

Death: When death occurs in a natural manner, i.e., nonviolently, burial is customary. The poor Pacoh is buried in a cheap or poorly made coffin, with a pig being sacrificed and eaten as a part of the funeral rites. The very poor tribespeople are wrapped in a mat and buried very deeply. For them it is customary to sacrifice a chicken and to light candles, but there is no dancing or the use of alcohol.

While death may be no respecter of persons, the funeral rites by the living are indicative of economic status. The rich Pacoh are placed in a coffin left above ground. The casket, made of a hewed-out tree, is well sealed except for a hole in the bottom from which the liquids drip into a deep hole. Before sealing the coffin the family places the personal belongings of the deceased in it along with gifts for him.

When the rich first die, there is only a small sacrifice directly to him. But on the latter occasion, it may be for other deceased relatives also, as their bones can be then placed together. In a similar manner once every four or five years the entire village will dig up the bones of all its buried deceased. These will be placed in small boxes and then put on top of a large earthen mound inside of a small shed which has walls. The walls are highly decorated and colored in various designs. This reburial ritual is accompanied by the happiest feast of all the burial rituals. [16] This feast may coincide with the third burial of the rich which occurs some three years after the bones have been placed in a small coffin.

Normally, the community graveyard will be marked by the presence of carved images of people. These crude statues are placed about burial sites to keep the spirits away and are not items of worship. Sometimes, they are placed about the village as defense against the spirits also.

Possessions of the dead are disposed of according to tradition. Certain personal items are buried with the dead while some items belong to the deceased's own family. Other items go to parents or brothers and sisters. While these are defined, there is so little according to Western standards that one could scarely realize that there could be any property settlement.

Social and Economic Strata: The Pacoh individual can enhance his social and economic status by his own abilities, hard work and the cooperation of nature. However, upward development is difficult as the whole family works as an economic unit normally. This impediment serves to limit the personal status climb considerably. Factors which strongly affect economic growth and social status include family size, thrift, the interaction within the tribal community, and external conditions.

Wealthy Pacoh are usually able to hire help for clearing, planting and harvesting their larger fields. They may also hire others to perform any of their essential tasks which can include some trading with other tribes or ethnic Vietnamese. The wealth of some Pacoh men allow them to marry more than one wife at a time. Having more wives, permits a larger number of children who can be economic assets in clearing, planting and harvesting the fields. Some of the wealthier Pacoh have slaves also. These are comparatively rare at the present time. Such slaves seem to be treated much as a member of the family and are rarely mistreated as they are a valuable economic and social asset. When both Pacoh and slave are of "good quality", there seems to be little awareness of bondage. Strange as it may seem, these endentured servants may be of ethnic Vietnamese origin. It appears that ethnic Vietnamese, from time to time, sell and deliver their children to the mountain dwelling Pacoh. This is apparently done in order for the parents to have food for themselves and to also increase their children's opportunities to live. More than one desperate parent has tried to sell or give his or her child to someone else so that the youngster will not starve. It may be wise to stand in another's shoes before we judge them too harshly for actions with motives we do not understand.

Currently there are less than a hundred Pacoh resettled and under government control and safety. Previously, others lived in resettlement villages, but these have been overrun by the communists or abandoned by the tribespeople.

Perhaps the greatest emotional problem with social overtones is the resettlement endeavor. The Pacoh seem bewildered when things don't work in the lowlands that succeeded in the mountains. Consequently they suffer in their personal wants and in employment which is congenial to them. They cannot raise their favorite crops in the accustomed manner due to factors which they cannot control. Moreover, the various administrative functions of the family, clan, settlement, have been removed from them. Generally, the Vietnamese district cadre has these duties and seems to treat the Pacoh as uncivilized savage children. Thus, the Pacoh are not allowed to make their own decisions or to live their kind of life. In many respects, the situation is similar to the American Indians in the last half of the past century and well into the twentieth. This Pacoh emotional upheaval preempts emotional reactions which might be otherwise quite obvious.

In those rare situations and projects where the Pacoh has freedom of choice and action, their leaders do show initiative. The Pacoh can and do work together with teamwork when permitted to do so without constant outside interference and supervision. After all, their tribal method of clearing, planting and harvesting fields, building a house or community feasts are all group activities.

Incidentally, the religious beliefs of the Pacoh affect both social and economic development patterns. Their beliefs affect cultural expansion, interchanges with other peoples and migration. Generally the Pacoh are afraid to leave their familiar areas in which they are acquainted with the spirits. They fear the unknown spirits of a new and unfamiliar place. This fear tends to keep them close to home communities while thereby providing family solidarity. Like other peoples, the Pacoh also have taboos and fears about digging up the earth so that at times progress is delayed.

The effects are not all negative however. They do tend to retard immorality, thievery, dishonesty and other possible social ills. Additionally, their beliefs toward violence affects tribal conduct. This fear seems to be directed toward the spirits more than toward physical injury. They fear disrespect of both their personal and family spirits and angering the spirits of others. These fears seem to create a basic desire to live in harmony with their fellow man and with nature in order not to wrong any spirit.

Incidentally, while the Pacoh think that most ills are spirit created, some diseases are recognized as contagious. Smallpox has killed many Pacoh through the years. Now they practice semi-quarantine in that the family of the ill do not leave the house. Even when family members must leave the home, the patient is not allowed to move about in the community.

<u>Defense</u>: Normally, the Pacoh have for their weapons, spears, crossbows, long knives and short blade knives also. These are used defensively as the Pacoh are unwarlike.

The Pacoh use various poisons to increase the effectiveness of their weapons in hunting. Their three grades of poison are distinguished by the speed with which they cause death. While apparently not used against people, poison may be placed on spear blades or arrow tips for use against either large or small game and tigers.

An additional defense is sometimes used to protect the village against spirits. When the village is taboo for foreigners to enter or even villagers to depart, sticks may be placed in certain patterns in entrance-ways. Sometimes spears are placed in threatening position to frighten away the spirits. The Pacoh beliefs about the spirits do not require elaborate physical defenses and symbolic aids appear sufficient.

LIVELIHOOD

Farming is the major means of livelihood. Every Pacoh family will have one or more fields. This will be mountain or dry rice rather than paddy-rice. Rice is the Pacoh staple. If they are short of rice, they feel that they are hungry and almost starving even though they may have other things available to them.

120

The technique for planting rice is the dibble stick. After the land has been cleared of vegetation by cutting and then burning the dried growth, a sharp pointed stick, held in either or both hands, is used to punch holes into the ashes and soil. The seeds are dropped into these holes by the women and then covered by a tap with the heels. Harvesting is done by using the hands to strip the grain from the stalk into the baskets worn about the waist. This is different than the use of a sickle and collection of straw as practiced by most lowland rice farmers.

Generally, the Pacoh women are responsible for harvesting the rice from the stalks as the spirit of the rice is thought to be a female, and the seeds for the next crop is always handled by the women. Thus, harvesting is always handled and supervised by the women. Young men may have to help with the harvest, but generally their role is carrying the filled baskets from the fields to the storage barns.

Incidentally, the women also conduct the sacrifices to the rice-spirit. These include the sacrifice for opening the storage bins and also for closing them. Moreover, the people involved in harvesting the rice are not allowed to bathe during the entire harvest. This taboo is based on the fear that the water of the river may carry away the rice chaff from the harvester. In doing this, the spirit of the river may also carry away the rice-spirit. Were this to happen, the yield of rice would diminish rapidly. Even were there a good harvest, it would dwindle rapidly rather than lasting through the year.

Next to rice as a crop would be sweet potatoes and corn. These are accompanied by squash, green beans, cucumbers, and other edible vegetables. The Pacoh seem to like corn for several reasons. These include not only the use of corn as a food, but also for the reason that corn attracts birds, squirrels and deer. Sometimes the Pacoh make a rich meat sauce into which they dip the roasted or boiled corn. Some Pacoh think this to be very delicious and it does seem to give them additional weight.

As with the rice, so only women pick the ears of corn. The men carry the corn from the fields to the houses and storage bins. The thought of an abundant corn yield makes this harvest a happy one with lots of fun and laughter and much talk. In the evenings, after supper the corn is shelled by pounding it loose from the cob. The shelled corn is used as gifts to one's sister's family and for feeding one's own family.

121

In one area, the tribal corn fields attracted the deer who came to eat the tender plants. The deer attracted the tigers who came to eat the deer. When the dogs of the tribespeople interferred, the tigers ate them instead. The mountain people then requested Americans to come and shoot the tigers, but the presence of those who would shoot the Americans left the tigers free to roam the fields.

Perhaps next to farming for a livelihood would be gathering from the forests and jungles. During the off-seasons when the rice and corn are in limited supply, the women spent most of their time in the hills gathering edible roots, leaves and fruit which grow wild. While the women go about their duties, the men utilize a consider-able amount of their time in hunting and fishing. Much of this is on an individual basis or in pairs. Occasionally, large groups may work together in hunting deer, wild pigs or in building a temporary dam or nets to catch fish.

Formerly trading was important, but current conditions have largely eliminated this as a mode of life. The hazardous nature of this occupation permits only the few who are willing to take danger-ous chances to act as tradesmen. They must have assets with which to purchase items for resale, be able to speak Vietnamese and run the risks involved in traveling under various dangerous conditions. Another factor retarding trade by the Pacoh has been the harsh treatment received from time to time by officials who did not always appreciate the tribesmen's efforts.

While the Pacoh make crossbows, musical instruments, etc., these are for barter rather than direct sale. They also make and give things to one another within their family and clan. At least once a year, the Pacoh practice giving purchased manfactured items to their parents-in-laws while homemade items are given to married daughters.

In all instances, however, the cycle of livelihood activities follow the clearing, planting and harvesting of rice. This is true in spite of numerous activities of the settlement. Normally, a family settles its debts to another by giving so many baskets of rice at harvest time. Truly among the Pacoh, rice has the ruling role.

RELIGION

The Pacoh are almost totally animistic with extremely little outside religious influence to be seen. Their spirits are local ones with primary interest given to those who represent a particular need at a given time. They do believe the Spirit of the Sky is most important. However, they don't know much about him nor do they give much attention to him.

The Pacoh reason for this neglect is that the Sky Spirit is too far above them so that they have no access to him. However, in times of serious trouble, such as an extended drought, and when other spirits have not provided help, the Pacoh will offer a special sacrifice to the Sky Spirit. This sacrifice is too special for the use of chickens or pigs. Only a buffalo will suffice. However, an additional offering which precedes that of the sacrifical buffalo is one of seven white and seven black goats being slain in ritual rites. This special feature is only to the Spirit of the Sky.

The Pacoh, generally, feel they are dependent on spirits closer to them than the one of the sky. These closer spirits tend to govern their immediate lives. Of these spirits, they sometimes claim the spirit of the highest mountain is most important. But even this one would be under the jurisdiction of the earth spirit in some manner. Normally, offerings are made to the earth spirit, in a rather perfunctionary manner, during their large festivals. But little is said about the spirit of the mountain as silence seems best.

The rice spirit is very important to the Pacoh as is that of the village. Other spirits include personal spirits, ancestral spirits, house spirits, spirits of rocks and groves of trees.

The spirits of the rocks and groves of trees are believed to be troublesome. The Pacoh attempt to stay away from these. If necessity forces them to go through these haunted places, the Pacoh will leave various sacrifices for the spirits. The Pacoh fear to have uncorrected wrongs in their life if they must leave the village for a trip. They believe that serious guilt on a journey will result in a tiger or bear killing them. Even small wrongs make them fearful so that sacrifices are frequent before leaving the village.

When the Pacoh seeks to establish a new field, sacrifices are offered to the spirit who may reside in that particular place which they hope to farm. Often an egg, etc. will be left at the site. Then they wait for the spirit to give them a dream within the next few nights. A good dream is accepted as permission by the spirit whereas a bad dream is a denial of the request. Other methods of supernatural communication may be the cry of a certain bird, the call of the barking deer, etc., which, when heard at the wrong time means the Pacoh cannot leave his village, go to his field, or engage in other planned activities.

The Pacoh have numerous ghosts. These may include the spirits of all who die violently. Such are always feared. These are offered sacrifices when the Pacoh first dies so that they will not kidnap the spirit of the newly deceased. Otherwise the deceased's spirit cannot be reunited with the ancestral spirit. The Pacoh are not clear on just what happens to the spirit as it appears to retain some type of individualism even as it is absorbed into the family spirit.

The soul, which is classified differently, returns to the place where souls are kept in storage. From there, it will become part of someone yet to be born. This transmigration is sufficently positive that the Pacoh believe it is possible to recognize traits in the newly born which belonged to the deceased. Thus, great care must be exercised not to misname someone with the name of another person lest there be antagonism and jealousy between the souls. However, Pacohs do not consider "souls" to be as important as "spirits". The fact that one's soul may be reborn in another creates no concern as this refers only to traits and personality. The spirit, however, wants to live in the afterworld by rejoining the ancestral spirit. There is no desire to be a wandering spirit, to be destroyed, captured or made a slave to a more powerful spirit.

This belief of spirits is well illustrated by the Pacoh beliefs about the rainbow, or "YANG PIRENG" in Pacoh.

Pireng means "killed", in contrast to "cumuiq" which means "died". Yang means "spirit"; so yang pireng means "spirit of one who has been killed", and yang cumuiq means "spirit of one who has died of natural causes".

Deaths which are in the category of pireng are: murders,

suicide, drowning, death by poison, by falling, by injuries or in childbirth. All sicknesses are considered as natural causes.

The Pacoh fear unnatural deaths very much because the spirit of
one who so dies, yang pireng, has no position or authority in the spirit
life, but can only wander aimlessly with other low-class demons. The
body of one who so dies is not taken back to the village or home. No
funeral involving sacrifice, dancing, beating of the drums and placing
gifts and belongings in the casket is held. The body is buried unceremo-
niously without a casket in a plain grave in a separate graveyard beyond
the regular graveyard and usually across a stream. During feast times
when other spirits are honoured and sacrificed to, the yang pireng is
never considered. At intervals of four to six years when the celebration
of the tombs (ariau ping) is observed and the bodies of the dead are dug
up to have their bones washed and placed in smaller caskets in artisti-
cally painted tombs above the ground the pireng are left untouched.

The rainbow is the visible manifestation of a yang pireng as it
reaches from the grave to water for a drink. The Pacoh say that they
have seen rainbows that reach exactly from the graves of yang pireng
to water, and that they believe that this is true whenever a rainbow is
seen. The rainbow spirits are usually only seen when they allow themselves to be seen, but there are persons gifted with the magic cun pireng
to see the rainbow spirits at any time and to enable others to see them
at the graves of such spirits.

So rainbows are not seen as phenomona of beauty or of promised
sunshine. Rather, the vivid coloring depicts the violent deaths of the
spirits of the lost and are sinister warnings to live carefully in fear of
such a death. [17]

Myth of Creation and Flood: The Pacoh story of the flood is of a
general destruction of the earth by water. Just how the earth was made
or how people first originated is still vague. But the flood story involves
a spirit woman who weaves the sky. The Pacoh think of the sky as being
solid and woven as a huge blanket. The woman lives at one corner where
the heaven and earth meet and spends her time ever weaving this sky
covering.

Somehow each time the sky gets completely woven it is destroyed
and started again. The mystical woman uses the hair of the dead for

her weaving. Just how the sky and earth mix in the flood, the Pacoh don't know as this last happened a long time ago. At any rate, only this woman and a dog were saved in the last calamity. These mated and had children. The Pacoh, like the Hrey, believe they are descended from a woman and a dog. For this reason, dog meat is taboo to them. In some vague way, the woman and dog still live together as she weaves the sky. Occasionally the Pacoh believe they hear the dog barking across the sky. Incidently the Pacoh expect another destruction when the woman completes the weaving of the sky.

The Pacoh have a number of myths. One is about a Poor Orphan Boy who the spirits favor. Therefore, he always wins the victory over the rich man. He acquires the most beautiful wife and the most possessions while his rich opponent is destroyed.

Many of the Pacoh tales personify animals. Even in myths involving people, they often can communicate with animals and animals with them. To the Pacoh, this relates back to their original parent being a dog. They seem convinced there was a time when animals spoke and acted as intelligiently as people. For typical of most preliterate peoples, the divisions between animate and inanimate, natural, mental and spiritual are blurred and indistinct when any differences are made.

The religious practices of the Pacoh are transmitted from father to son through the family without the need of a special clergy. Often the prompting of a sacrifice seems to be fear or even desires for greater gain from arbitrary spirits. If spirits are angered, destruction may occur, while pleased spirits can give blessing and abundance.

Religious beliefs affect almost every Pacoh activity. Building a house, clearing a field, planting, harvesting, etc. all involve sacrifices. All life crises also have their rituals and sacrifical rites. The biggest Pacoh rite is the yearly festival following harvest. This always involves sacrifices of various animals including the buffalo. Other than sacrificial animals, the rites usually includes incense burning, prayers and chants.

GUIDELINES FOR RAPPORT

The Pacoh seem capable of learning when given an opportunity.
Some seem exceptionally quick to learn when explanations and demon-
strations are on their levels of previously limited opportunity to learn.

The Pacoh have some people known for their abilities as story
tellers. These would make excellent communicators as they already
have the techniques of transmitting ideas. Moreover, they are accepted
by the tribespeople more readily than outside sources of information.
Since most Pacoh cannot read, printed materials are not practical.
Radios are rare among the tribespeople. Moreover, their value would
not be too high unless Pacoh speech were utilized at fixed intervals.

While opinion leaders might be divided among the village elders
and those with "outside experience", the younger generation seems
anxious to learn of life beyond the village. Skillful use of persuasion
may reduce opposition from the traditional leaders and even win their
tacit consent or full support.

The Pacoh do not react with violence among themselves or toward
others. Normally, they do not even want to meet strangers. Should
these be unavoidable, it is doubtful that the Pacoh would resort to
violence through his own choice. Generally, the tendency of the Pacoh
would be to flee from strangers and avoid all contact. This is due to
fear rather than hostility.

In fact, when the Pacoh starts to leave the village on his way to
work, fish or hunt, others are not to speak to him. Such would be
taboo as they think that once they leave their house they must not be
spoken too lest the spirits be angered. While carrying his implements,
if anyone does speak to him, his venture will not be successful.

Undoubtedly the Pacoh have ways of friendship and communication
between those who travel together, when another can talk or not, but
these are unknown at present.

It is imperative that non-tribesmen respect the property rights of
this primitive people. To pick or destroy their crops and fruits can
only create hardship and bad relations. It would be better to leave
small inexpensive but practical gifts for them than to take their food
from them. These could be small packages of salt, matches, lighters,

etc.

To the degree that the Pacoh believes you are interested in him, he will be cooperative and helpful. They do resent the treatment which has been too often melted out to them without cause.

Ideally, there should be Pacoh trained as translators in Vietnamese and English. Only in this manner can the full story and emotions of the Pacoh ever be meaningfully related to non-tribespeople. This would help achieve our mission while enabling the Pacoh to more easily make the necessary adjustments to the twentieth century of which they are a part.

CHAPTER IV

PACOH

FOOTNOTES

1. Frank M. LeBar, et al, Ethnic Groups of Mainland Southeast Asia, Human Relations Area Files Press, 1964, p. 145; E. H. Adkins, A Study of Montagnard Names in Vietnam, R. Ziemer, "Tribes of South Vietnam" Lecture at Ban Me Thout, Vietnam, August 1964, p. 1; Richard Watson, Director, Summer Institute of Linguistics (Vietnam), April 1968 tape for Navy Personal Response; "Pacoh" in Vietnam Minority Languages, July 1966, Summer Institute of Linguistics.

2. LeBar, et al, op. cit., p. 145; Leopold Michel Cadiere, "Notes sur les Mois du Quang-tri", Bulletin de L Institute Indochine pour L'Etude de l'Homme, Vol. III, 1940, p. 102.

3. Richard Watson, April 1968 Transcribed Tape about the Pacoh for Navy Personal Response. Hereafter this excellent source will be referred to as Watson, op. cit. (The original tape is a part of the research files of Navy Personal Response.)

4. Ziemer, op. cit., p. 1; Adkins, op. cit., p. 6; U.S. Information Service, Montagnards of the South Vietnam Highlands, (Saigon, U.S.I.S. July 1962), p. 20; Watson, op. cit.; Summer Institute of Linguistics, Minority Languages, "Pacoh", July 1966.

5. LeBar, et al, op. cit., p. 145; Watson, op. cit.; Mole, 1965-66 and 1967-68, Fieldnotes; Vietnam Minority Languages, "Pacoh", Summer Institute of Linguistics (Vietnam), July 1966.

6. U.S. Information Service, op. cit., p. 20; Summer Institute of Linguistics (Vietnam) Map of Ethnic Minorities in South Vietnam, July 1966; Watson, op. cit.

7. Watson, op. cit.

8. U. S. Information Service, op. cit., p. 20; Watson, op. cit.

9. Watson, op. cit.

10. _Ibid_

11. _Ibid_

12. Watson, _op. cit_. "Pacoh names".

13. _Ibid_

14. _Ibid_

15. _Ibid_

16. Watson, _op. cit_.

17. _Ibid_

1. Nno lxam (lixam)**	mua lanh	winter (Nov.-Jan.)
2. Nno tahiang (tanghiang)**	mũa xuân	spring (Feb.-April)
3. Nno culung (nam)	mũa hẽ	summer (May-July)
4. Nno nhanhom	mua thu	fall (Oct.-(rice and corn)

* According to crops, not weather

** Pacoh Pahi words are in parenthesis

1. ntôm tacoi	16. tanorang
2. rôiq tacoi	17. tarleang
3. ntôm ilau	18. ntôm camuiq
4. rôiq ilau	19. rôiq camuiq
5. ntôm calang	20. ntôm palnoang
6. rôiq calang	21. rôiq palnoang
7. ntôm phũng	22. ntôm pv̉ng
8. rôiq pũng	23. rôiq páng
9. ntôm palnoang	24. ntôm calang
10. rôiq palnoang	25. rôiq calang
11. ntôm camuiq	26. ntôm ilau
12. rôiq camuiq	27. rôiq ilau
13. tarleang	28. ntôm tacoi
*14. truq (full moon)	29. rôiq tacoi
*15. tarcoal (full moon)	30. nhil nha (no moon)

"ntôm" - tree
"rôiq" - intestines

* If number from tacoi, truq is half month; if number from nhil nha, tarcoal is half month.

PACOH WORD LIST

Underlining added to indicate the presyllables - a nasal must conform to the point of articulation of the main-syllable-initial consonant. The accent marks short vowels, the circumflex marks close vowels, the breve marks tense vowels, a is short o, c is k, except before i.e; x is similar to s; - marks glottal stop between syllables, q marks glottal stop word final.

#	Word	Pacoh	#	Word	Pacoh
1.	all	ngéq	31.	drink	ngoiq
2.	and	moi, anha	32.	dry	preng
3.	animal	a-át	33.	dull	nxil
4.	ashes	abóh	34.	dust	tarkénh
5.	at	dáng, déq	35.	ear	cutór, ngeang
6.	back	crong, kíc	36.	earth	cuteac, cuteq
7.	bad	nnhóp	37.	eat	cha
8.	bark	ncár along	38.	egg	tireal
9.	because	cò	39.	eye	mat
10.	belly	pallung	40.	fall	ntóh, prúp
11.	big	pít, púq	41.	far	yong
12.	bird	achéq	42.	fat-grease	nxeng
13.	bite	cáp	43.	father	a-ám, icónh
14.	black	cóm, tuq	44.	fear	adáh, axéu
15.	blood	aham	45.	feather	xóc, achéq
16.	blow	pru	46.	few	beaq
17.	bone	nghang	47.	fight	taq
18.	breathe	tanguh	48.	fire	uth
19.	burn	chóng, ncat	49.	fish	boaiq, xeaiq
20.	child	acay	50.	five	xóng
21.	cloud	aluat	51.	float	dól
22.	cold	nngéat, tangan	52.	flow	hoal
23.	come-go	póc, róp	53.	flower	piar
24.	count	ngiaih	54.	fly	par
25.	cut	cut	55.	fog	tulúc
26.	day	ingay	56.	foot	adyúng
27.	die	cuchet	57.	four	poan
28.	dig	píq	58.	fruit	culay
29.	dirty	a-áyh	59.	give	dyón
30.	dog	acho	60.	good	o

61.	grass	xac
62.	green-blue	xeng
63.	guts	roiq
64.	hair	xŏc
65.	hand	ati
66.	he	do
67.	head	plô
68.	hear	xang
69.	heart	aneal, acheal
70.	heavy	ntáng
71.	here	mnéh, nnâh
72.	hit	pŭh
73.	hold	cadyiq
74.	how	imo
75.	hunt	taveng, patáq, papênh
76.	husband	cayâq
77.	I	cu
78.	if	nam, láh
79.	in	calling
80.	kill	cachêt
81.	know	chom
82.	lake-pool	tarlŏng
83.	laugh	cachang
84.	leaf	ula, ila
85.	leftside	svear
86.	leg-upper	pilau, pulau, adyŭng
87.	lie	big,
88.	live	tumŏng
89.	liver	lom
90.	long	tolq
91.	louse	nchên, nchih

92.	man-male	conh
93.	many	clung, e, ap
94.	meat-flesh	xech
95.	mother	a-1, ican
96.	mountain	coh
97.	mouth	hong ncang
98.	name	noh
99.	narrow	hep, kitat
100.	near	tuman, tubol
101.	neck	ticong, tancong
102.	new	tamme
103.	night	idau
104.	nose	moh
105.	not	layq, cah, avaih
106.	old	buih, ih
107.	one	tiaq, iauq
108.	other	moi, muai
109.	person	cannot
110.	play	ticuai, naq
111.	pull	clon, anhoi
112.	push	luq
113.	rain	kituh
114.	red	bo
115.	right-correct	cuxo
116.	right-side	cray
117.	river	atam
118.	road	daq put
119.	root	carna, na
120.	rope-strap	reaih, rib
121.	round	ntar
122.	scrub	nxoh, xah

#	English		#	English	
123.	salt	boi	159.	there-further	ntih, ntuh
124.	sand	choah	160.	they	ngaum Jape
125.	say	tônɡ, pl	161.	thick	ticĭc, crih
126.	scratch	cavat	162.	thin	pĭnhɛ, oĭq
127.	sea	bĭan (VN)	163.	think	rnɡĭh
128.	see	hôm	164.	this	nnâh, nnéh
	look	nhồng	165.	thou	may
129.	seed	mma	166.	three	pe,
130.	sew	ểh, hêng	167.	throw	aduh
131.	sharp	ng-ệp̂	168.	tie	tônɡ
132.	short	chachâp̂	169.	tongue	ntag
133.	sing	ticu	170.	tooth	kineng
134.	sit	ncar	171.	tree	tôm, along, nlong
135.	skin		172.	turn	plĭt
136.	sky	rbang, parbang	173.	two	bar
		pĭlónɡ	174.	vomit	ti-ôq, ta-ôq
137.	sleep	(bĭg) nɡear	175.	walk	pôc, ticaq (step)
138.	small	két	176.	warm	kitau, catau
139.	smell	xáng, ahét	177.	wash	rao, boăiq, pĭah
140.	smoke	cuyâq, cuyĭaq	178.	water	daq
	to smoke	areac, ngoiq	179.	we	he,
141.	smooth	cutear, bôq	180.	wet	dyĭp
142.	snake	cuxênh, tulan	181.	wnat?	amâh? mbár lla
143.	some	beaq, cleap	182.	wher	ndônɡ mĭmo,
144.	spit	cuchéh	183.	where	Tôq mmo, dang mmo
145.	splip	Trec, cláh	184.	white	cloq, plai
146.	squeeze	diq	185.	who	nnau
147.	stab-pierce	chât,	186.	wide	pôh
148.	stand	taying	187.	wife	campay, capay
149.	star	pantor	188.	wind	xeang
150.	stick, a	nnam	189.	wing	nnár
151.	stone	bŭl	190.	wipe	chut
152.	straiɡht	tinâng, tanâng	191.	with	alŭng
153.	such	dyểoq, uq (nurse)	192.	woman	can,
154.	sun	mát-rbang, parbang	193.	woods	raving, mbut,
155.	swell	ayh,	194.	worm	tŭloi, talĭiu
156.	swim	pong daq	195.	ye	ĭpe

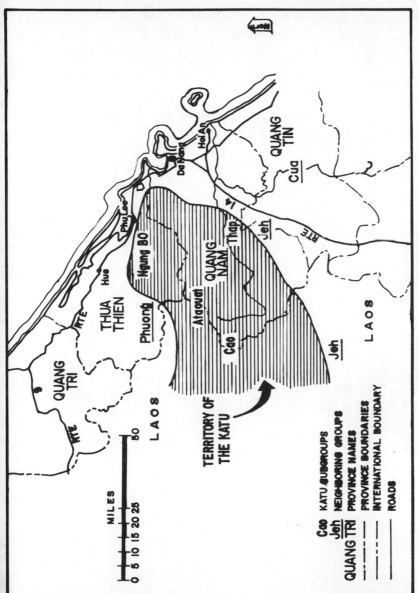

NORTH

MILES
0 5 10 15 20 25 50

Coo KATU SUBGROUPS
Jeh NEIGHBORING GROUPS
QUANG TRI PROVINCE NAMES
——————— PROVINCE BOUNDARIES
—·—·— INTERNATIONAL BOUNDARY
————— ROADS

TERRITORY OF THE KATU

QUANG TRI

THUA THIEN

QUANG NAM

QUANG TIN

LAOS

LAOS

Hue

Phu Loc

Da Nang

Hoi An

Cua

Phuong

Ngung BO

A'ouat

Coo

Thap

Jeh

Jeh

RTE

RTE

RTE

14

RTE

THE KATU SUBGROUPS   MAP FROM/CRESS/CINFAC R – 0426

135

English	Katu
Hello	ve mâi
I am your friend	ku nhôr mâi
What is your name?	hau rau achak mâi?
Are you sick?	mâi ka-aai kah?
No.	kah, yauq
Are you well?	mâi karð kah?
Yes. I am well.	hu'an. karõ'
My name is Kimet (father of Met)	pakonh ku Kimeet
My name is Jo	achak ku Jo
Where do you live? (Where is your village?)	nleq krnóon mâim
What village are you from? Is your family well?	hau mâi dóók krnóon mâi? danong mâi yuaq rau ka-aai kah?
mother	amêêq
father	ama
child	akóón
wife	kadial
husband	kayiik
Where is the chief's house?	daleq dong takóh krnóon pe?
point it out for me	cha leq dóng ku lâi
where is the chief?	daleq takóh krnóon pe?
I want to take your photo	vôiq nôq leq dóng ku chup bong mât
will you let me buy?	ve mâi dóng ku ko'l kah?
how much money do you want?	mð mâi kiang jêên?
what are you doing?	hau rau mâi têêng?
what is that?	hau rau adek?
that is right, OK	dalam, â-â
I do not know	ku kah nal

English	Katu
where are you going?	nleq mâi vôiq?
wait for me here	mâi tðót nôk diq, dóng ku vôiq, óóq mâi ting vôiq
I want to see your village	ku kieng lâi krnóon mâi
sell me meat	nôq pe ve adah, dóng ku kôl
chicken	atûdch
eggs(chicken)	karaau atûlch
eggs(duck)	karaau ada
fish	kadóóng
vegetables	kruung
bananas	priiq
papaya	rudu
manioc	buar
potato	agô
manioc leaves	soq buar
beans	atuang
corn	adóóng
squash	kadók
sunrise	blo mat
early morning (6-10 am)	yayong
late morning	jaiïa
noon	dông
early afternoon	brvïh
later afternoon(4-6 pm)	habu
sunset	mat sariap
dark	blót, kanam
light	bruang
from morning till night	tâáq yayong tuaih blót
yesterday	manua
month (moon)	kase
this month	kase dók
before (of time)	balek

CHAPTER V

THE KATU

Names: The Montagnard tribe of Katu has numerous synonyms: Teu, Attouat, Kao, Khat, Thap, Nguon Ta, Ta River Van Kieu, Phuong Katu, Kato, Cao and Ka-Tu.[1] Individuals of this ethnic group, similar to numerous other minority groups of preliterate and semiliterate peoples, tend to identify themselves as members of a specific village rather than as members of a tribe. This procedure of identifying oneself is a common practice in those societies where villages are largely self-sufficient, and in which little or no higher cohesive centralized political structures exist. The Katu do this through the use of "people", monui, and the village name so that people who are not aware of this custom may be confused as to just what tribe is involved. This method of identification is used by this tribal people rather than the appellative "Katu" which has been applied to them by the surrounding ethnic groups inasmuch as Katu means "savage".[2]

Language: The language of the Katu is that of a sub-group of the Mon-Khmer with the latter being a member of the Austroasiatic family of languages.[3] Basically, Katuic speech is composed of monosyllabic words supplemented by borrowed polysyllabic terms. Each of the Katu subgroups, and the tribe has several of these, has its own dialect. However, these dialects possess sufficient similarities to permit mutually intelligible conversation.[4] The Katuic language base is also quite closely related to that of the Phuong tribe who share a contiguous border with the Katu on the Katuic northern border.[5]

Until quite recently, Katuic was only spoken. Now through the strenuous efforts of the Summer Institute of Linguistics, with headquarters in Saigon, the Katu language has been reduced to writing. The communists of North Vietnam have also been working at this task and some of their literature is now being utilized among the Katu.[6] However, the opportunities for American and South Vietnamese contacts with the Katu peoples have been limited for a number of years. When the opportunity is presented, reading and writing in both Katu and Vietnamese will be taught. This undoubtedly will provide opportunties for the development and expansion of Katu mental horizons, which at present are limited by the lack of adequate tools of communication.

The Katu speak no other language than their own, except for those tribesmen who have been taken to North Vietnam and have been indoctrinated, trained and returned to work among their own people. Very few Vietnamese know enough Katuic to effectively communicate with this tribal group.[7]

Population Estimates: Only an educated guess can be made on the Katuic population due to geographic location, linguistic barriers, (inadequate communication methods), the International South Vietnamese-Laotian Border, and the current conflict. Therefore, population estimates range all the way from 20,000 to over 50,000.[8]

The origin of the Katu is unknown. This ethnic group may have originated among the peoples who once inhabited the upper reaches of the Mekong. The Mekong has some of its tributaries in what is now known as Yunnan Province of South China. Without a written history or other materials beside Katu oral traditions, there is little evidence to either prove or disprove the traditions of the origin of this tribe. On the other hand, if the oral traditions have any validity, the Katu may have reached their present location either by migrating down the Mekong Valley and the n moving into the mountains, or may have come down the coast of the China Sea and then been forced back into the mountains.

Location: The Katu are found in three of the five provinces; Thua Thien, Quang Nam and Quang Tin, of I Corps, South Vietnam and across the Vietnamese-Laotian border is Laos.[9] Located in the highlands of South Vietnam, the southern tribal boundary would be inland about fifteen to twenty miles on the level of Hoi An. From this point, the southern boundary moves southwestward through northern Quang Tin province into Laos. The eastern tribal border is within ten miles of Danang as it extends northward almost to Dam Cau Hai (Bay) and Phu Loc Hung. Here the northeast corner of the tribal area is about five miles off the coast. The northern boundary goes almost due west until it reaches the Phuong tribal area some twenty-five miles west of Phu Loc. It then dips down below the Phuong area and continues westward more than forty miles into Laos on a line about even with the city of Danang and just south of the former Special Forces outpost in the A Shau Valley.

The major subgroups of Katu (Lower and Higher Katu as well as those subgroups known as Cao, Thap, Ataouat, and Ngung Bo) live on the slopes of the mountains which are transversed by the Song Boung, Song Cai and Song Giang rivers, with "Song" being the Vietnamese term for river. [10] The tribal area ranges from the foothills near the coast of Vietnam, through the rugged mountains with steep gorges and peaks up to 8,200 feet, and is affected by the May-October summer, and the November-January winter monsoons. Rainfall in the higher elevations average more than 150 inches, while the lower levels receive more than 80 inches per year. This evenly distributed rainfall through most of the year, combined with tropical temperatures promotes a rain forest in much of the region. In such forests, trees average 75 to 90 feet tall and form an almost continuous canopy. Smaller trees of 45 to 60 feet high form a second layer of foliage, and below these can be found an abundance of saplings and seedlings. Because little sunlight penetrates to the ground level, not much ground cover exists. However, clinging to and suspended from the trees is an abundance of woody climbing plants known as lianas, epiphytes, orchids and other herbaceous plants.

Where the foregoing primary rain forest has been cleared and then left uncultivated, the forest growth is smaller with an abundance of heavy ground growth of tall grass (tranh in Vietnamese), lianas, and other herbaceous climbers. The heavy, dense grass may grow to a height of more than twenty feet so that penetration through such jungle is difficult and requires the almost constant use of a machete, or bush knife if one does not use the well-worn paths. Travel is largely by foot or pack animal along previously made trails, with these being well-sheltered by the forest canopy. Due to heavy rains jungle growth, and communist activities, there are no major roads at this time in the Katu tribal regions. The French built dryweather, unsurfaced roads that once ran from Danang to Kontum via the Song Thu Bon (River).

Among the high mountains of the Katu area there is one named Ban-Nam. This mountain is twenty to thirty kilometers west of Danang, and in the time of French rule was used as a resort by the peoples of Danang, Hue, and other coastal cities of central Vietnam. The route into the Katu area runs through the valley which extends from Hoi An, previously known as Faifo, some fifty kilometers where the valley divides into north and south. The southern division leads to Kontum and Pleiku, while the northern division leads to the village towns of

Dai My and An Diem.[11]

Formerly at least three Katu villages were open to direct
American influences through the presence of language technicians,
Missionaries and Special Forces personnel. These were Nam Dong,
north of Danang; Thuong Duc, some sixty kilometers west by south
of Danang almost due west of Hoi An; and An Diem. Only a small
number of Katu who live near the Special Forces camp at Thuong
Duc are now accessible. The vast proportion of the Katu tribal area
is much more subject to Viet Cong influence than it is to that of the
South Vietnamese governmental structure.

Neighbors: The neighbors of the Katu vary in language and
ethnography. The Laotian tribes are the Katu neighbors in Laos.
The Jeh ethnic group is the southern tribal contiguous to the Katu
in Vietnam from the Laotian border eastward to the area of the
Takua. The Takua, as a small tribal group living in the Tra My
area of Quang Tin province share common borders with the Jeh
and the Katu on the southeast corner of the Katu tribal area. The
ethnic Vietnamese are the eastern neighbors of the Katu as well
as the northern neighbors from the coastal area inland to the Phuong
tribe on the northwest Katu tribal border. The Katu neighbors have
been unsuccessful in promoting friendly interchanges with the Katu
inasmuch as the appelative name of these people denotes the attitude
which the Katu have created among other peoples.

INDIVIDUAL AND GROUP CHARACTERISTICS

The individual Katu male varies in height from about five feet
two inches to five feet six inches. Similar to the American Apache
Indian or the Indonesians, the Katu have dark brown skin, black
and sometimes brownish-black hair, with sparse beards, and little
body hair. Muscular and stocky in build, the Katu are capable of
sustained endurance in mountain climbing and walking. Katu
people have difficulty in carrying heavy loads or in running. A
distinguishing feature of the Katu is their teeth which are filed or
broken down to the gums and covered with a black tree sap which
must be reapplied every month. The sawing or breaking of the
teeth is a "rite du passage" or initiation into adulthood. This
ceremony is performed when a youth is about twelve years old,
and is exceedingly painful as a bush knife is the instrument used

for sawing the teeth. [12]

Many of the Katu - both male and female - have tattoos about the face, forehead, chest, arms and wrists, and on the legs own to the knees. The most popular tattoo motif seems to be that of a dancing girl on the forehead or arms; triangles composed of three dots; sometimes a Buddhist Chu Van, (swastaka), within a circle, or other geometric figures and shapes. [13]

The Katu men wear a loin cloth which may occasionally be decorated with small lead rings. Because many of the Katu live in the higher mountains where it may be rather cool, the men may also wear long blankets of blue cotton about their shoulders and chests. This apparel was previously made largely by a Katuic subgroup, the Ataouat, but now much of it is obtained by barter with ethnic Vietnamese. Some of the Katu men occasionally wear a garment that resembles the Middle Ages', "European coat of mail", in that it is made up of cloth and covered with small iron rings interlaced through the cloth as protective devices.

The high Katu women wear a tribal skirt which extends from just below the breasts to the knees. These skirts are normally made of black cloth with red stripes as black and red seem to be the only colors which the Katu have. The low Katu women also wear a V-shaped neck, short or long sleeved over-blouse. [14] Most Katu girls wear this short blouse until they marry, after which the blouse may be discarded when the weather is hot, humid and sticky. However, when strangers are in the village, many of the women will wear their blouses or hold them in front of them due to some exposure to Western concepts of modesty. [15] Like nearly all tribal peoples the Katu men and women go barefooted so that they have thick tough calouses on their feet.

Katu women are readily identifiable by the long gold or brass bracelets which they wear and which are composed of one piece of coiled brass that reaches from the elbow to the wrist. [16] Anything that glitters may serve as adornment or jewelry for the Katu. Therefore beads seem to form an essential part of their apparel, and both men and women wear them! [17] The chokers worn by the men may be composed of white, yellow, or reddish-orange beads, as well as necklaces composed of large white and black beads interspersed with tiger teeth or the claws and beaks of the hornbill bird. Women may also wear such chokers or necklaces composed of three or four strings of beads at one time.[18]

The Katu have varied hair styles. Some wear bangs while others utilize a chignon, or bun, that may be held in place by a comb. Combs are made of copper or the tusk of a hog, which is five to six inches long. Le Pichon has observed that the Katu will carefully feed a hog six or seven years in order for their teeth to be used as hair ornaments. Also, the Katu may wear bamboo sprays or bamboo rings with attached buttons to enhance their hair styles.[19]

Long considered to be one of the most warlike tribes of South Vietnam, the Katu have a history of violence among themselves, against other tribes and toward foreign peoples. They have resisted "pacification" by the Khmer, Chams, French and ethnic Vietnamese. Not only are they geographically inaccessible, but also are known as a very unfriendly group. Their name Katu "savage", acclaimed by their neighboring tribes is indicative of an attitude which the Katu have earned by tribal action through the centuries.

Their diet, which lacks salt and vitamins, permits numerous eye and skin diseases. It has not yet been determined how much this may affect their dispositions. As a people they are believed to be sullen, hostile, and easily stirred to violence. Their fears and superstitions do not hinder their ability to fight well or persistently. The Katu definitely dislike non-tribal peoples and have a distinct distrust for the ethnic Vietnamese, who generally respond in a reciprocal manner. In a few Katu areas the tribesmen will accept food from Americans, or will accept medical aid when they are convinced of its beneficial results. Some tribesmen, their friendships once won, are friendly, helpful and cooperative to degrees allowed by social pressures of the tribal community. Nevertheless, even those who may be both hospitable and generous, often tend to be boastful and vain.

THE VILLAGE AND ITS STRUCTURES

The Katu appear to be very emotionally attached to their villages and demonstrate a reluctance to leave them even for a short time. Yet when these communities are attacked by a superior expedition, the Katu will abandon their village, bury their valuables, and flee into the surrounding jungles. [21]

The Katu villages are generally located on hillsides. This may be an attempt to avoid the high humidity of the valley floors, and yet not be too far from a permanent source of water be it brook, stream, river or spring. The typical village is surrounded by a perimeter stockade, and contains anywhere from five to fifty houses. The houses are generally built in a circle or circles with a large open space that forms the center of the village and may contain a carved wooden post. This rather substantial post serves as the sacrifical post to which larger animals are tied for the sacrificial rites of the community. [22] In the larger Katu settlements, a communal house may also be located in the central "square" or on its inner circle. The fencing that surrounds the Katu village serves as protection against wild animals including tigers and elephants; attacks by villages, or supernatural powers envisioned as "spirits". This fencing may be of bamboo or wooden posts planted in the ground close together with sharpened ends protruding outward at an angle to prevent enraged elephants or men from rushing the fence and destroying it. In addition to the fence, there may be a complex of barriers that include concealed animal traps, punji sticks, hidden tribal "booby-traps" of spears or arrows. The latter are released by touching an "innocent looking" line or vine attached to the weapon's trigger. Moreover, there may be devices to lure evil spirits aside or to frighten them away from the village entrance.

Naturally, there are some exceptions to the foregoing description of the Katu village. Vietnamese government resettlement villages may be composed of individual houses for the nuclear family, or long houses in which the single family might have two or three rooms depending on family size. Generally, the relocated villages are in the form of a horseshoe with the open end facing a river. The open end of each relocated village provides either a permanent sacrificial post or space for erection of a temporary post as the need arises. Some of the Cao subgroups vary their village style by placing their communal house in the outer circle of the village homes rather than in the center. Others may erect their houses on short wooden poles or even on raised mounds of earth. Some of the Katu deviate from the normal pattern by building their long houses in even-numbered clusters rather than in a circle.

<u>Houses</u>: Typical Katu houses are constructed of either bamboo or wood. These may be erected on one to two feet high piles, or placed directly on raised earthen mounds. They are either rectangular or semi-circular in shape, and have thatched roofs which slope from a center ridgepole down over short side walls. ' Because the sidewalls are only three to four and a half feet in height, and the roof extends down over them, it is necessary for tribesmen to stoop quite low in order to gain entrance. Entrance is made through a sliding door on the front of the house, which may or may not have a front porch. The floors of these houses are made of bamboo poles or sections of poles which have been split and reinforced.

The home of the more wealthy Katuic peoples, which includes the village chief, are generally more ornate in construction. These houses are built without interior partitions and may measure fifteen by thirty feet in size. The larger the house, the larger the size of the tanol (center post). The ridgepole of the larger houses is supported by this post. The crossbeams (rafters) may have their upper ends attached to the center post or to the ridge-pole depending on the house size. The lower ends of the rafters rest upon the vertical posts that serve as supports for the low exterior walls.

The center post, the ridgepole, the rafters, and the vertical wall posts, are often painted or carved with hunting or fishing scenes, animals, man, or phallic symbols. The latter, commonly seen among the animistic peoples, is of significance due to Katu fertility concepts. The walls may be of rattan, plaited bamboo, palm fonds, or pandanus leaves plaited or woven into solid walls. The roof may be of the same materials or thatch, held into place by long slender logs placed as weights and tied into place.

The Katu house has no partitions, nor do they generally have such items as tables, chairs, beds, etc. The Katu houses do have rattan hammocks which are used for babies and children to sleep in . Adults may also use them for sleeping or relaxation. While no chairs are usually seen, the Katu do have small wooden stools. The living and storage spaces of the house are intermixed. The house will contain large jars of rice grain, jars of fermenting rice-wine, clay bowls, trays and baskets. Attached to the walls or suspended from the thatched roof ceiling may be found such items as: fresh game, ears of corn, green bamboo tubes filled with meat, animal traps, fish nets, gongs, drums, crossbows and quivers of arrows, long iron or steel pointed spears, mountain axes and tribal knives.

Individual Katu families have an earthen hearth holding a fire which must not be permitted to go out. The Katu house has a fire place for each family in the house. Since many households consists of the male clan composed of father and sons with their families, there may be a number of fire-boxes located at one or both ends of the house. Fire-boxes are always at the ends of the house rather than at its center. The embers are carefully banked in ashes when not in use. The smoke of the cooking or warming fires must find its own way out of the house since there are no chimmeys or smoke-stacks. Consequently, the escaping smoke darkens the ceilings and walls giving them a dark sheen. It also serves to dry out moisture and aids in preventing the lightweight building materials from rotting.[23] The floor serves as the Katu bed, their table for eating, lounging area during heavy rains, or during enforced inactivity created by tribal taboos.

Communal House: The communal house, "gual", of the larger Katu villages, is quite similar to other village houses except that it is larger and more elaborate. It is the largest structure in the village; its roof may soar thirty-five or more feet into the air. Since the communal house is built as a community project, its cost is borne by all villagers. Every male is expected to participate in its construction.

Often the communal house walls are decorated with the heads of wild goats, deer, buffaloes, carved masks of human faces, and birds. The masks, which must always be hung in even numbers, are blackened by the smoke that rises from the open fires within the communal house. The toucan or hornbill, which is sometimes hung on the communal house walls, is a tropical bird or the Ramphastidae family that is found in Central and South America as well as in Southeast Asia. It is one of the numerous fruit-eating birds with a very large, but light-weight, thin-walled beak, (nearly as long as its body). The beak as well as the plumage is brilliantly colored in a striking red, yellow, white and black contrast.[24]

The communal house is the village social center for all males.

145

It is the sleeping place for all unmarried men, (and boys who have undergone initiation), a meeting place for the men of the village, and the site of the village council. It is also used as a sanctuary from intra-village quarrels and fights, (as these are not allowed within its walls), an asylum for strangers in the village, and the residence of the village spirit. Because of its importance to the Katu males, no women may be admitted to it under any circumstances.

Sacrificial Pole: The sacrificial pole is a feature of most Katu villages. It is normally found in the center of the circular village, or in the open end of the "horseshoe-shaped" village, and may be a permanent structure of the community. The sacrificial pole is generally sculptured or painted with designs including the sun, stars, the cross, geometric figures, sacred animals as the cock, toucan, iguana, tortoise, snake and fish. The Katu paint their designs in three basic colors which are made from lime, betel leaves and soot. The lime produces the color white, the betel leaves produce red and soot mixed with water or natural oils of the jungle gives them their black color.

When sacrifices are offered, customarily, the sacrificial poles will have additional decorations. These decorations include two long highly ornamental bamboo poles which are tied to the sacrifice post, and which soar over it to form armlike wings. These traditional decorations are believed to make the spirits happy. A French student of Katu culture suggests that the sacrificial posts were used for Katuic human sacrifice before these public rites were suppressed[25] and subsequently became secretive acts of the jungle.[26]

Family Burial Vaults: Although death is discussed in the religion section of this chapter, the family burial vault is a structure of the Katu community worthy of mention. This small house-like structure is the permanent place for the second and more elaborate coffin of the deceased. The family "vault" is open on all sides, and is normally constructed of heavy lumber and supported by a minimum of four posts. These usually contain carvings of significance to the Katu. These four posts support the roof of the vault. In regard to the vault, it ought to be remembered that only those who die of natural causes - have the "honor" of a second "burial" in the family vault. Because

of the Katuic concept of the spirit-world, the family vault is an important structure and not one to be lightly dismissed by an non-Katu in
the tribal area. [27]

SOCIAL STRUCTURE

Katu social structure is based upon the patrilineal concept. The
clan is of greater importance than are the individual families or the
village. People have many responsibilities to the clan so that it takes
precedence over the village. With the exception of a few Montagnard
tribes, this is the pattern of most of the South Vietnamese mountain-
dwelling ethnic groups. Le Pichon calls the Katu a "regime patriarchat"[28]
by which is inferred that the family or household is headed by its eldest
male. As the patriarch of the family or household is headed by its
eldest, he owns all of its property, and is the family authority on all
internal matters. He represents the family in village affairs.

In Katu communities, residence is patrilocal. This means that
the immediate kin-groups composed of married sons and their families
live in the house of their father. Where dwellings are for nuclear
(man, wife and children) families, the modified patrilocal system
has the sons still living near their father and subject to his regulations
in most of life's daily affairs. The basic economic unit is the household, inasmuch as all its members cultivate the fields and share the
crops in common. The Katu village, with rare exception, is composed
of extended families, and forms the highest sustained effective social
and political unit of Katu society.

The Katu village is governed by its chief and a village council of
elders. The village chief, "ta-ka" who is chosen by the village council,
is considered to be the most clever elder of the village. He has either
led a successful blood hunt, or has favorably negotiated economic
matters for the village. When Katu villages suffer epidemics, poor
crops, or other serious calamities, the chief quietly and quickly
resigns his post and even helps to pick his successor. This is believed
to be the proper procedure and receives the approval of the ancestral
spirits. [29]

The village chief and council have jurisdiction over disputes
between families, intra-family, (arguments which the family head
cannot solve), and affairs which involve other villages. These may

be quarrels, adultery, marriage conflicts, thievery, or murder and war. When other communities are involved, the council and the chief decide the appropriate action to be taken by the village to obtain vengence for any crimes which have been committed.

The village chief handles the situation with the advice of the village council , when family problems cannot be settled by the family head, or the problem is not of intra-family nature. If the plaintiff does not accept the decision of the chief and his council, his only recourse will be to abandon his house, leave the village, move to another that will accept him, and start a new life. This procedure is possible only when the unfavorable and unacceptable verdicts are not the results of serious crimes.

Judicial verdicts for intra-village justice normally include the payment of indemnities for the victim to his family, and village fines that include the sacrifice of a rooster, pig, or buffalo. When the Katu tribesman accused of murder cannot prove himself to be innocent, he may be required to pay the enormous indemnity of ten to twenty buffaloes. If he does not pay this indemnity, or some-one else does not pay it for him, the family of the murdered victim has the authority and obligation to kill the condemned man by repeated thrusts of their long-handle spears. If the condemned murderer is of another community, the responsibility is upon the entire village to obtain justice for the victim. Since there is a taboo against appearing in public, or eating the sacrificed buffalo until the dishonor has been erased, the result is village-organized war. Otherwise the village would be both dishonored and disgraced. [30]

The Vietnamese government is the nominal authority of the Katu tribal area. Currently it has only limited control and func-tions among this people. Officially, the government controls intra-village Katu relations through appointed officials. These officials are responsible to the district and province chiefs. Thus, the central government is organized to govern the tribal area as it gains de facto control. [31] However, even before the present conflict, the isolated and difficult terrain and psychological atti-tudes of the Katu, provided only minimal contacts. [32]

The Vietnamese government re-established the legal status of the tribal laws and court system with tribunals at the village, district, and province levels under the March 1965 Decree. These courts are set up to judicate both civil and criminal matters when all involved parties are Montagnards. In one sense, the Decree restored the earlier French-established system of justice for the tribesmen. However, it is only in those areas under the actual control of the Vietnamese government that this system can be effectively operated. Under the Decree, the village court which consists of the chief of the village and two Montagnard assistants, hear all village cases brought before it, and make appropriate judicial decisions. Upon rendering a decision, if all involved parties sign the decision, the right of appeal to higher court is eliminated. If the case is not settled at this time, it can be appealed to the next higher court, which is that of the district. [33] District courts, composed of the district chief and two Montagnard assistants, hear all cases which are appealed and those matters deemed serious according to tribal customs. At the province level, the court is a section of the National Court with all Montagnard cases heard by a Montagnard presiding judge and his assistants. They hear all appeal cases from the district courts or other matters too broad for the village or district courts to have first jurisdiction. But as noted earlier, most Katu matters are still handled according to Katu tribal customs inasmuch as the Vietnamese government's de facto control is limited.

Katu society is thought to have four classes: free men, foreigners, (non-tribesmen living in the tribal area), debtors or servants, and slaves. The latter may be prisoners of war, etc., and depending upon prevailing circumstances can aspire to eventual freedom. The other classes can sometimes be distinguished by visible symbols of wealth as the size of the house, personal ornamentation, numbers of jars and brass gongs, buffaloes or wives.

The "wealthy" may have servants. The first type of servant is that of "orphans" who may, or may not be relatives. In the closed society of the tribal community, these must be "adopted" by relatives with a fate similar to slavery, or else accepted as bonds-servants by non-relatives. Orphans who reach adulthood are sponsored in marriage by their " owners ". At this time, they may choose either to continue living with the same family and receive their food and a portion of the rice harvest, or establish their own home as free persons. The second class of servants is composed of men or women, individual or family, who through circumstance and bad choice became hopelessly in debt. These, by means of a verbal contract enter into servantship and live in the house of their master. They are given their sustenance, a portion of the yearly rice crop, and one buffalo per year. Should differences of opinion create the need for separation between them, the master pays the servants one-half of the agreed wage and releases them to form a life of their own choosing.[35]

As in most strongly primitive patriarchal societies, Katu women have a decidedly lower status than men. This status is graphically symbolized by the women walking behind their husbands, while he saunters along with his crossbow. As the undisputed head of the family, he awards all punishment, and through his sons, forms channels of inheritance so that family goods are passed down from male to male according to seniority. The eldest son receives the bulk of the inherited goods, while the other sons divide the balance of the inheritance which is generally meager. The goods may consist of a rice paddy, brass gongs, jars, and a buffalo or two.[36]

Marriage: The Katu young man seems to be able to select his own wife subject to economic, social and religious conditions. She may be either from his village or from neighboring ones. Once he has made this selection, and the girl tentatively agrees, he communicates his desire to his father. He normally chooses an intermediary to negotiate all the complicated arrangements to prevent loss of "face". Girls are not generally forced into marriage. Once the selection has been agreed upon by the young man's family, the father has an intermediary arrange for the respective families to meet and a feast is shared by them at the time of a full moon. At this time, the families discuss the amount of cloth, gongs, pots, jars, and buffaloes which must be given as a "bride price". The "engagement feast" includes one slaughtered buffalo, the playing of gongs, and dancing.

Once the economic arrangements are settled, the spirits must be consulted for their approval or disapproval of the proposed marriage. The prospective groom must produce a rooster; an old man or a sorcerer cuts off the right foot of the living rooster inasmuch as each outer claw symbolizes the boy and girl. If the two claws match in certain ways, or if they contract in a certain manner, it is concluded the spirits believe this will be a good marriage. If the middle claw keeps the end claws from meeting, it is believed the spirits may be in disagreement over the proposed marriage.[37]

The bridal price is normally set according to the wealth of the families. If a young man is poor, or if he cannot raise a sufficient dowry, his only hope for marriage is to an old woman. This is considered to be a disgrace by the Katu inasmuch as they desire a young wife. The qualities most desired in a prospective wife are good health, (strong enough to be a good worker), good temperament and good looks.[38]

Normally, the Katu men do not marry too far out of their own village. In fact, according to their clan system, the best girl for a young man to marry is his uncle's daughter, that is, his first cousin by his mother's brother. In fact, if he does not want to marry one of his available first cousins, he is required to pay her family a number of crocks and other items.

Katu engagements may last for periods of two years or more. During this time, either of the prospective marriage partners may have sexual relations with other persons provided pregnancy does not occur. The engaged couple may participate in premarital sexual relations with each other without criticism unless the woman becomes pregnant. If this occurs, the couple are banished from the village for one year. To a people who live closely together in long houses, exile or banishment is the worse punishment possible short of death. [39]

Since polygamy is accepted by the Katu, the wealthy man may have two or more wives. However, comparatively few can afford three or four wives. Thus, economics is the major barrier to plural marriages rather than social or moral concepts. [40] When plural marriages do exist, all the wives may live in the same house, but have their own hearths, and separate living areas which they share with their respective children.

Birth: The pregnant Katu woman continues her routine work until labor begins. She is expected to deliver the baby herself although other women may watch. Having delivered the baby in the brush outside the house, she buries the placenta, bathes the baby and then returns to the house. There she will stay in the "gaving", which is a portion of the house sectioned off for her for three days.

It is customary for the new mother to resume her house-hold duties three days after delivery, and field work shortly thereafter. She nurses her baby as long as her milk lasts. The baby is gradually introduced to such foods as rice, cooked herbs, corn and manoic. (Manoic is a starchy root which can be used much like potatoes.) If the baby lives and the mother dies, attempts are made to acquire a "wet" nurse. When this cannot be done, rice-water is provided. However, it is a poor substitute. If the baby perishs after living seven days, its death will be viewed as an "evil death", and will require offerings to the spirits.[42]

Childhood: The Katu love their children and show this in many ways. The mothers carry their off-springs on their backs until they are able to walk, and are then left in the care of older brothers and sisters. Before long, the lad is charged with watching the family buffaloes, and allowed to visit the communal house where he is informally instructed in tribal legends, songs, arts, etc. At age seventeen he is allowed to move permanently into the communal house and is considered a man. Girls tend to lead more restricted lives, and remain in their parent's house until marriage. Because the girls maintain a lower status than boys they soon participate in the same strenous tasks as do their mothers.[43] Katu children appear to be disciplined by voice without the necessity of physical punishment. Katu youth learn by precept and example as no formal schools yet exist among this tribal group.

Divorce: Divorce may be secured in Katu society by either the husband or wife. However, the Katu patrilineal system requires that children remain with the father and his family.[44] A major cause of Katu divorce is adultery. A wife who has committed adultery usually cannot return to her family because they do not want her. Therefore, she must live alone. Her offending male partner is punished by a fine of one buffalo to the husband and one buffalo, which is offered in sacrifice, to the village. The guilty man is futher punished by being struck on the head by the husband in public for everyone to see. Should the guilty couple desire to become life-time mates, this can be achieved by securing the husband's consent and repayment of the original bride price.

If the husband is guilty of adultery and this results in divorce, he must pay the departing wife one-half of her original bride price or dowry. Should the offending male partner reside within the same extended family - brother-in-law, uncle, cousin - he is fined a pig which is slaughtered and consumed by the entire family. Some

Katu offenses warrant banishment or death, yet incest and sex deviates are treated with leniency. [45]

Death: The Katu believe that there are two types of death. These are good or natural death, versus evil or accidental violent death. The Katu are convinced that the way in which the deceased perishes is more important than the way in which he lived. The fate of one's spirit is determined more by the manner of death than by the mode of one's life. [46]

This attitude toward death is predicated upon Katuic belief that each person has a good and a bad soul. The method by which the individual dies determines which of the two souls will survive. Thus a natural death is believed to be "good" as it promotes the status of the good "spirit", while an evil death through accident, childbirth, murder, suicide, etc. perpetuates the evil "spirit". [47] Moreover the Katu believe that the good spirit watches over living descendants of the deceased, and protects them through warnings and intervention in the supernatural world which surrounds the Katu peoples. This protective effort extends to giving omens or visible signs that evil spirits lurk close by. Some omens include: a large tree which has fallen across a path, the sound of a bird in its nest on the left side of a path being traveled, peacock eggs found in a path, roosters crowing at midnight, sighting a python, the sight of toucans flying toward the sun, the sudden, unexpected sight of certain plants in the forest, and sneezing just as one is preparing to undertake important business. [48] Evil spirits also have visible forms that include the sight of a tiger, the sight and sound of a cobra hissing in the afternoon, or the flood waters that cause persons to drown, etc. [49]

When the Katu die, the body is kept in the house for two days during which mourners come, wail loudly, while both gongs and drums are beaten with a slower cadence than usual. [50] If the death has been a natural one, the body is placed in a coffin made from a tree section which has been split and hollowed out. The chippings of the tree-casket are considered taboo, and, therefore, are unuseable by the Katu. The coffins are carefully prepared in advance, so that the half sections fit tightly together. The coffins are never brought into the village until a death has occured. Instead, they are stored in natural caves so that their presence in the village will not give the lurking evil spirits a desire to create more death.

The first of two distinct burials takes place when a deep hole of about nine feet is dug in the forest and the tree-coffin, containing the deceased and his personal possessions such as: clothing, pipes, crossbow, personal wine or water jug, etc., are placed in the deep hole. If all the personal possessions cannot be fitted into the coffin, they are placed on the lid of the coffin after it is placed in the ground. The coffin is partially covered with dirt so that the spirit of the deceased may escape, and return home as the protector of the surviving relatives.[51] When death occurs, the Katu on the same day, generally sacrifice a buffalo at the village sacrificial pole. If the deceased was very "wealthy", several buffaloes may be sacrificed on succesive days at the rate of one per day. During the nights of such sacrifices, the beating of drums and the sounding of gongs accompany the extended "wake" to inform all relevant spirits that the appropriate sacrifices are taking place.

About seven months to two years later,[52] after the initial burial, the coffin is opened and the remains of the deceased are transferred to a highly decorated and sculptured coffin. This is done in the presence of relatives and friends and is accompanied by the chant of traditional tribal prayers, the sounding of gongs, and the beating of drums. The new coffin is then placed in the family vault which was previously described under the Katu village structures.

At the time of the second burial, alcoholic libations and prayers are offered for the soul or spirit to rejoice in the company of its ancestors. Such petitions are believed to cause the spirit to regard the family with benevolence when they are accompanied by sacrifices. The Katu feel that these rites are a necessity, for in this manner the spirit is placated and propitiated so that he will not be angered and cause the family to have nightmares.[53] From time to time the family members remember the deceased with additional sacrifices offered to his spirit, so that they will continue to benefit from its kindness. This Katuic practice is quite different than that of the Bahnar ethnic group, who ignore and seem to utterly forget their dead after an "abandoning the grave ceremony" which takes place in the spring following one's death. In some of the Katu second burials, the deceased may be buried in a graveyard rather than in the vault, and in such cases, the graveyards are as nice as could be anticipated under primitive conditions.

If a death is "bad", the family is required to bury the corpse in a remote area of the jungle some distance from the village. Also, they are required to kill all animals which were the property of the deceased, abandon their home and fields, and take temporary residence in the forest.

Formerly, if death came by being devoured by a tiger, stringent taboos required the permanent abandonment of the village and all animals, including dogs, were killed. Currently, the Katu villagers do not permanently abandon their village, but live in the forest for as long as the taboo may last. During this period which lasts up to six months, they may neither build a house or eat the meat of buffaloes. Since the spirit of the unburied dead are transformed into wandering, troublesome spirits, great effort is made to secure the bodies and bury them to prevent added dangers to the family and village. The victims of evil deaths are placed in quickly-dug graves. The bereaved rush from the vicinity of such graves back to the environment of their village as they greatly fear the angry, or evil spirits will also seize them. It is imperative that no one linger near the grave.

If it becomes necessary to construct a new village as the result of one or more "evil deaths", the Katu construct and erect statues which are placed at the doors of new houses, around the communal house, and on the paths leading into the village. These devices are displayed to frighten away the evil spirits which were created because of evil deaths. These wooden statues are grotesque figures of human beings with large misshaped heads and faces, and may be that of pipe smokers, or even dancing girls.[54] These figures are used for snaring the attention of the spirit and causing it to forget its evil designs. Sometimes small tables with food, and even chairs, are set out for the convenience of the spirits. Occasionally, steps are cut into the hillside, or a ladder is provided, so that the spirits may easily climb to these tempting refreshments.

KATU ECONOMICS

Farming: The Katu have no concept of land ownership; the first cultivator of a jungle cleared field has its use until he abandons the site. Moreover, the crop of a field belongs to the family who cultivated the land. In spite of the fact that new village sites, and plots for fields, are chosen by the village chief in consultation with the elders and the sorcerer, there are no communal lands held or administered by the village. [55]

The subsistence economy of the Katu is primarily based upon the slash/burn (swidden/ray) method of farming. Their major crops are dry upland rice, maize (corn) and manioc. Manioc or cassava is a tropical plant that has edible starchy roots, which may be used in making either bread or tapioca. The Katu also have small gardens near the village in which they may grow vegetables and other leafy edible plants as well as tobacco.

Choosing a new site for a field, involves the participation of the village chief, the elders, the sorcerer and the head of the family using the site. These must follow the rules and interpretation of Katu tradition. They check the soil condition by careful examination of the vegetation growing there. They also follow the rules of divination to determine if the spirits view this as an acceptable site.

The site of the new field having been chosen, the Katu men of the family begin to cut the brush and fell all but the quite large trees late in the rainy season or early in the "dry" season. The cuttings are allowed to sun dry where they fall until burning time which is about a month before the rainy season starts anew. Then on a day chosen by the sorcerer, and after offering a sacrifice, the area is carefully burned so that the fire does not spread to the jungle. When the area has cooled down, all the remaining trash and boulders and moveable unburned logs are moved to the edges of the field to make room for planting and to act as barriers to the wild animals who may destroy the new crop. The thick layer of ashes is left on the ground to act as the field's only fertilizer.

When the first rains of the new season have softened the soil, the men and boys with sharpened "dibble-sticks" make holes either in rows or in a random pattern throughout the field. The women and older girls follow the men dropping several grains of rice or other seed in the individual holes and cover these by using their heels to press dirt over the seed. From this time until harvest, the only strenuous attention given to the field may be weeding as it becomes necessary and attempts to keep wild deer, etc. from devouring the various crops.

Fields are used for three or four years and then allowed to lie
fallow by gradually returning to the jungle. This may continue for twenty
years as the Katu allow the soil to regain its nutrients. The long fallow-
ing period and the lack of fertilizer may cause the Katu fields to be a
full day's walk from the village.

Gathering: The Katu, like other Montagnard peoples, farm the
jungles by gathering and using its products in many ways. From it, the
women and girls collect shoots, roots, edible leaves, fruits and herbs.
The only natural medicines, which the Katu have for their use, are the
leaves and roots of the jungle which they cook and use as medicine in
such forms as liquid, poultices or as external rubbing compounds. Also,
the women gather birds, squirrels, snakes and lizards for food with the
help of various homemade devices and their dogs.

Domesticated Animals: Besides the elephant and the buffalo, the
Katu raise pigs, chickens, dogs and occasionally a few goats. However,
all of these with the exception of the elephant, are used as meat only
after being offered to the spirits. Through sacrificial animals are used
as meat, the major source of flesh food must still come from the jungles.

Hunting: The Katu men are quite adept hunters as they use traps,
the crossbow with and without poisoned arrows, and spears. They catch
fish in fish-traps, by gigs, hooks, nets and by poisoning still pools of
water. With poison the fish are paralyzed and float to the surface.
Fish may be caught by daming water courses and sipping out the excess
water also. The poison used on the fish does not spoil the fish for food.
Likewise, poison is used to kill various jungle game so that the meat
can be used as food. However, if this poison enters a man's blood
stream through a cut in the skin, it will bring death quite quickly. Water
which has been poisoned will bring death to all those who drink from it
as it paralyzes the autonomic system.

The Katu spear is of better workmanship than that of the Bru
peoples north of the Katu tribal area. The Bru spear is more strongly
constructed and is rugged and sturdy in steel point and wooden handle.
However, the Bru do not demonstrate the finer workmanship of the Katu.
The reason for the more rugged Bru spear is that almost all of Bru
area is tiger infested while only part of the Katu area is so bothered. [56]

157

Crafts and Arts: In every Katu village, Basketmaking is a skill. Their baskets, made of thin strips of rattan, are both well designed and executed for the purpose which the baskets are to be used. The rattan, which the Katu use, may be any one of a number of long slender tough stems of climbing palm which grow abundantly in the tribal area. In addition, the tribesmen use bamboo, palm leaves and wood for the making of mats, light wall materials, nets, traps, containers of all types, weapons, etc. Green bamboo sections may be used to store excess meats or as cooking utensils. Food will cook in the green tubes by boiling before the fire dries the tube enough to burn. The dried sections are also excellent containers for salt, water, tobacco or other small food items.

Katu women weave coarse colorful pieces of cotton cloth using home made looms. While the Katu previously grew their own cotton for thread, they secure the necessary thread by trade with ethnic Vietnamese merchants now. One subgroup, the Ngung-Bo, has skill in tanning hides, while the Ataouat are noted for their skills in making blankets, jewelry, pottery and metal spear points. [57]

Trade: Some Katu earn money as wage earners. But the vast majority of the Katu depend upon barter for their economic interchange with the Vietnamese, other tribes and foreigners. The Katu trade or sell wood, betel leaves, tropical laurel treebark (cinnamon), medicinal roots and leaves, rice, corn, fruits, spear tips, jewelry, blankets, etc. [58] In exchange, the Katu secure salt, sugar, cotton goods, iron for essential needs, and metal pots, blankets, beads, necklaces, etc. Some of the Katu like the Ngung Bo specialize in selling both live buffalo and buffalo hides to the ethnic Vietnamese merchants in much the same manner that the Thap subgroup specialize in disposing of betel leaves.

RELIGION

Religion, whatever its name, has among its purposes, the integration of the individual's behavior with his society. It gives confidence for meeting crises which life inescapably brings. Moreover it introduces into the individual's existence, a stable central core by which values may be assigned to ideas, events and proposed courses of action.

The life of the average Katu is overshadowed by the fear of the many spirits believed to affect or control all parts of his life. His birth, childhood, marriage, economic life, death and all other phases of existence are governed by taboos created to avoid offending the spirits. Broken taboos anger the spirits who may cause grievous sickness or death unless the offender quickly makes amends by offering a satisfactory sacrifice. The Katu, arising from a night's sleep, rubs a prepared medication all over himself or herself, and then asks the spirits for protection from sickness for the day. Likewise, before the rice is planted, the spirit's favor is sought. If a poor harvest occurs, the obvious reason is the spirits were angry and caused the bad crop. [59]

The communal house and the sacrificial pole form the religious center of the Katu village. This privilege belongs to these structures inasmuch as the communal house holds the distinction of being the residence of the spirits of all the deceased ancestors who died a "natural" death. The cult of the dead is basic to the Katu religious system due to the concept of each person possesses a good and bad spirit with the type of death determining which soul continues to exist. [60]

The Katu have a pantheon of spirits that intervene in daily life. The tribesmen try to avoid any action that may anger the spirits as these must be then appeased by the various sacrifices that may even include human sacrifice. The Katu are thought to be the only Montagnard group in South Vietnam still practicing this rite.

The Katu use numerous devices to protect themselves against the spirits that may be bent on creating havoc. These include the wearing of armbands, amulets, charms, etc. The Katu tattoos have significant religious value and protection for the same purpose. The tattoo of the dancing girl is thought to signify the materialization of the spirit of man. The tattooed figure on his forehead is thought to act as a guardian "angel" when the tribesman is awake and in good health. It enlightens the intellect and aids him to be successful in his endeavors. [61]

Katu religious rites are cyclic (attached to the agricultural year) and crisis created. Normally the cyclic ones occur when bamboo sprouts begin to appear, when fields are to be cleared, and when rice is to be planted or harvested. Crisis rituals may be for the building of a house, weddings, sickness, death, omens and signs indicating

imminent danger, or when a taboo has been violated. All the ceremonies seem to involve invocations, sacrifices, heavy drinking of
fermented rice alcohol, dancing and singing. [62]

The Katu have resident priestesses or sorceresses. These
individuals have the power and ability to communicate directly with
the spirits. The Katu believe that sickness is spirit caused rather
than by dirt, filth or germs. The ill need the priestess to determine which spirit is offended and to ascertain the required sacrifice
for restoration of health. Sickness is caused by the evil spirit
taking one's soul or spirit from the head and hiding it in the jungle.
Until that soul is returned, the stricken individual cannot recover.
To achieve recovery of health, the sorceresses is sought as the
means to the troublesome spirit.

When her simple medications are not effective, a sacrifice is
required. If the sacrifice is a buffalo, it will be tied to the sacrificial pole. There the men will dance about the sacrifice pole and the
buffalo while playing their gongs and beating their drums. The
women dance with their arms held high in the air while the priestess
dances about with a bowl of rice on top of her head. When the buffalo
has finally died of its many and repeated spear wounds, the priestess
will take some of its blood and rub it on the sacrificial pole and on
the sick person. She chants to the spirits and performs incantations
all the time she is engaged in her priestly function. [63]

Little study has yet been devoted to the male sorcerers who
are found among the Katu. These may be either Katu tribesmen
who are thought to have much ae , charismatic and magical power,
or the wandering Laotian tribesmen who perform similar services
as does the priestess. In addition, these read the claws of a
rooster to determine the feasibility of a wedding, the necessity of
a blood hunt or the approval of the spirits for a proposed field.
These sorcerers may also sell the Katu tribespeople lustral
water as being efficacious for their various ills. Lustral water
is water thought to be endowed with the qualitites of the Buddha.
This lustral water is widely used by those who are Buddhist
oriented in house warmings, weddings, funerals, etc. Although
the Katu are not Buddhists and have been little exposed to Buddhism,
their animistic beliefs of the supernatural allow them to purchase
and use such items. [64]

The priestess and sorcerer act to prevent disasters for the individual or the village. They do this by being able to "read" the signs, communicate with the supernatural world and by serving as intermediaries. This is an accepted community service of value. This may include the interpretating of omens or signs, the reading of a rooster's right foot, the reading of the entrails of a sacrificial animal or the recitation of "magical words" over them so that they may have greater curative power.

Buffalo Sacrifice: The priestess, sorcerer or "witch-doctor" is requested to perform the essential service of determining what must be done for the patient when serious illness is present. If the patient continues to be ill, it may be decided that a blood sacrifice will remedy the ailment. The sacrificial blood may be of a chicken, pig, goat, buffalo or in extreme cases, that of a human being. The buffalo sacrifice follows a fairly standard pattern.

A large post or pole, perhaps eight to ten inches in diameter is planted in the large opening of the village. Various decorations may be tied directly to the post or to long frayed bamboo poles which have been tied and as are like wings to the post. The sacrificial buffalo is fastened to the post by means of a rattan line about the neck or by a nose ring. This rite is accompanied by the drinking of rice wine, singing, dancing and playing of tribal musical instruments so that all spirits may be alerted as to what is happening for them. During this tumult, the teasing and tormenting of the buffalo continues. When this has reached a certain level, one of the young men will use his sharp knife to slash the back and front leg tendons. Buffaloes being unable to bellow can only bleat, but these "cries" are thought to be pleasing to the spirits. When this has continued a sufficient time, one of the tormentors thrusts his long spear into the buffalo aimed at its heart. As soon as the buffalo falls, the participants rush to it with long reed-like tubes or slender bamboo tubes and attempt to draw blood from the vicinity of the heart as this blood is believed to be most effective. The blood is then placed on the sacrifical post, on the sick person, on or over the doorway, etc. as a means of gaining favor of the troubling spirit with a consquent release from sickness or whatever condition has caused the sacrifice.

The buffalo is thought to be a sacred animal as it belongs to the spirits rather than to any living individual who are merely stewards. The Katu, as a whole, formerly had taboos against selling buffalos to other than their own people. Nowdays they can sell and trade buffalo as they like with out fear. Likewise, they are not supposed to ever eat the buffalo as food unless it has been offered in sacrifice. Neither do they use it as a work animal. Once the buffalo has been sacrificed, its skull is kept in the communal house. It is believed that the spirit of this mighty skull will promote the productivity of the land and the prosperity of the village. The buffalo represents man in the collective sense, so the presence of this spirit can provide many blessings for the whole community. [65]

Blood Hunt: As a "rite du passage" into manhood and for the appeasing of angry spirits who will accept nothing less, the Katu men engage in the sacrifice of human blood in the rite known as a Blood Hunt. Blood Hunts are engaged in upon the approval of the village council under the mandate of the spirit world determined by a sorcerer or the oldest male in the village.

When other means of placating the spirits seem to have no effect, the right foot of a rooster is severed and careful attention is given to observe the curling of the toes or claws. If the toes curl and touch in a certain manner, it is indicative that the spirits approve and desire the blood hunt. When a hunt is supernaturally approved, the village begins the ritual with the beating of drums, pounding of gongs, the singing and shouting of the adults. The smaller children add to the din by pounding on pots and pans so that the spirits will be sure to know what is about to take place in their honor.

The Katu village spends the night in drinking rice wine, singing dancing, etc. As dawn comes stealing through the dark dense jungles of the highland, the Katu warriors take their crossbow, arrows, spears and other equipment and depart to find their sacrificial victim. Once located, he is quickly brought down. In order to meet the tribal requirement, each warrior must repeatedly jab the victim with his spear until the whole blade is covered. Then the warriors place their hands in the blood and smear it on their foreheads, cheeks and chin. The blood must be allowed to dry there.

162

Leaving their dead victim in the jungle (unrobbed as that would spoil its sacrificial value) the warriors return to their village communal house for a ritualistic animal sacrifice. Then, again with wine, song, dance and instruments several nights are spent. This is to be sure that all ancestral spirits, and any other who may be involved, may know what has happened for their benefit.

The high Katu prefer foreign blood as their sacrificial offering but rate the ethnic Vietnamese second choice, the lowland dwelling Katu as third, while the high Katu of other villages are fourth. [66] When other high Katu villages are involved as victims of a blood hunt, the Katu warriors attempt to steal small children of two years old or less. These will be carried back to their village in a back-basket which has a closed lid to prevent the child's spirit from escaping until it is sacrificed. Sometimes the Katu will waylay people passing through Katu areas, take their blood home on spears and rub some of it on the village sacrifice post. They may take the scalp of such a person and carry it back to the communal house. When they go forth on a kidnapping foray to kill another adult or kidnap a child, the scalp or skull may be taken with them. They do this as it is believed the spirit of the person is still sitting on top of the scalp or skull. It is thought that this spirit will be able to persuade the new victim for a sacrifice to come with them. [67]

The rhythmic beat of the drums and the haunting throb of brass gongs pulsating through the wet dark jungles create a sound that produces an unforgetable sensation to all who hear and understand this Katuic practice. While human sacrifice is forbidden by Vietnamese law, the South Vietnamese government has not been able to fully suppress this ancient tribal ritual of appeasement to spirits who are thought to have a thirst for human blood. Nearly all Southeast Asian tribal peoples believe that shed-blood is an essential element in appeasing the spirit world.

After holding important sacrifices, a Katu village becomes taboo, "dien", for three days so that no one is supposed to leave or enter the village. Katu signs of dien are placed in the roads or paths leading to the village. These signs may be a tree lying across the road or path, the notching of trees close to the pathway, or even hanging a leafy branch on a stake in the pathway.[68] A dien on the village always requires the sacrifice of a rooster, pig or buffalo to meet the desires of the ancestors. Anyone who violates a village dien is expected to pay a fine. Failure to comply with this expectation creates resentment, increased fear of angry spirits and results in greater hostility toward those who cause this uneasiness.

Other taboo or dien occasions include a three day dien for the house in which a baby is born; a one day dien for the village before it engages in selling its harvest or any other equally serious matter; a one day dien of the village before the start of a blood hunt; a dien of one or two days for the planting of the rice crop and also the harvesting of it at the end of the season. Evil deaths can cause a Katu village dien which may last anytime between one and six months.[69]

GUIDELINES FOR UNDERSTANDING

Never pacified by the French or the Vietnamese, the Katu have long felt themselves to be despised by all who are not of their ethnic group.[70] This has led them to exercise their hostility on other peoples so that the Katu are feared by other groups and by ethnic Vietnamese who live close to the Katu area.

In their isolated jungles, the Katu have learned the secrets of the jungle and use them in offensive and defensive ways against their fellow tribesmen, ethnic Vietnamese, and toward foreigners as opportunities permit. Combined with skill and cunning in a hostile environment strongly influenced or controlled by supernatural spirits, the Katu use punji stakes, traps, poison arrows, booby trap of jungle products and the fine art of jungle concealment. The poison most frequently used by the Katu is that made of a curare-like substance. Curare is produced by plants of the genus stychons, and is a black resinous substance derived from the bark of these plants. It causes motor paralysis when introduced into the blood stream. Incidentally, the same extract used for killing either animal or man, is used to reduce spasms and muscular rigidity in tetanus and spastic paralysis under scientific medication.

Taboos are protective methods to avoid stirring up the wrath of the spirits. The Katu, in his concern for the spirits, zealously guards against infractions either by himself or by others who may be in his area. Never deliberately do anything which will generate additional fears of the tribespeople as this will only retard acceptance of any proposals which may be made to them.

Music is a basic element of the Katuic way of life. From childhood to death, it forms part of their daily life. Lulled to sleep as a baby by songs; taught tribal traditions by melody and chant; they sing as they roam the forests or watch the buffaloes; as they court their girls during engagements which may extend for a period of two years; as they work in their padi-fields; as they mourn for their dead; in the rituals of their sacrifice; in the building of courage for approaching war parties; or in the setting forth of a blood hunt. When the animistic Katu becomes a Christian, he still sings, but with a harmony and hope incongruous with his former fears.

Typical Katu culture promotes the practice of two meals a day with the one being shortly before bed time and the other one being quite early of a morning. The wines of the Katu are made of different bases which include rice, palm juices, corn and manioc. Because wine constitutes so much of the Katu religious rites and of their social drinking, they may use up to half of their rice harvest for this purpose.

Blood Hunts among the Katu are events of importance because of their religious significance and social prestige. The Katu man who has led a blood hunt is considered an attractive "catch" as a husband. Katu girls tend to "chase" such a young male adult.

Because buffaloes are considered to be the property of the spirits, many are not normally used as work animals in any form so that it is best to leave them strictly alone. If on occasion, an enraged buffalo must be killed to protect human life, a quick satisfactory settlement with the Katu chief, the elders and the "owner" of the buffalo is urgent. Speedy arrangements are essential because of the Katuic fear of the spirits, and to avoid depriving the Katu of a very valuable status symbol and economic loss. Care to avoid increased hostility can prevent hostile propraganda that may prolong the war.

To the Katu, stealing is the worst crime of which man is capable. Rated to be more heinous than killing, repeated thievery can cause the death penalty. Among the Katu methods of execution is that of burying people alive. To do this, the person is placed in a small hole with enough air to last about two days so that death is both painful and slow. [71] Incidently, the Katu also bury alive any Katu with serious mental problems so that these deranged persons will not be able to destroy the village by fire or anger the spirits.

It is imperative that all military personnel pay the agreed price for any item or souvenir which they secure. Violations of this Katu standard by any American is a very serious matter and should promptly be handled by the proper authorities. Restitution must be combined with the information that the violator will be punished being relayed to the offended party. Of course, a wise procedure to avoid possible unpleasantries is to establish controlled "trading-centers" with fixed prices that have been agreed upon by the chief or village council and competent military authority. This combined with a requirement that all exchange of items between Americans and tribal peoples be through this media, including the laundering activities for personnel, could avoid some of the difficulties experienced elsewhere. This or similar procedures would avoid charges and counter charges of "robbery", "dishonesty", "double prices", etc., while promoting acceptable marketable items and services.

The loss of a simple crossbow or a basket may seem insignificant to Americans, but to the Katu, it may mean the loss of his livelihood. Moreover, the tribesman has so few possessions that each one has a value that may be little appreciated by those of the Western "civilized" cultures.

Americans must be extremely careful about actual or implied promises made to tribespeople. To promise safety to a village and then have the military unit move away after a few months leaves the tribespeople fully exposed to communist retaliation. The fear that this may happen again as it has happened before is a factor that may cause the tribesman to be very slow in showing friendship or cooperation with the Americans. To renege on promises to the Katu implies to the tribesman that the American cannot be trusted. One incident in which promises are not fully kept will require strenuous and extended efforts to repair relationships even when it does not result in the loss of life.

Truthfulness, honesty and sincerity are essential in American contacts with the Katu. The Katu have experienced the effects of incorrect or misleading statements in the past. They bitterly resent anyone attempting to take advantage of their primitive life. Likewise, the promise of a future fulfillment of aid, help, etc., carries little weight with the Katu due to unfortunate past experiences and their lack of a linear time concept.

Americans in the Katu tribal area ought to be informed of all taboo signs and markings so that they may be aware of and alert to them. If the American presence is not essential at the particular time of the taboo, it is wise to stay out of the field, village or house which may be involved. If military needs demand your immediate presence, be prepared to fulfill the amenties which can reduce Katu resentment, anger or fears.

Beware of involvements with women of the Katuic peoples. These create resentment throughout the community as tribal customs, family status and economic factors are involved. Moreover, a resentful Katu may decide to handle the matter through the use of a sharp spear when it is least expected. The Katu are human beings and are entitled to the same considerations which may be desired for our own relatives. Each American has moral obligations to himself, to fellow servicemen and to the peoples where military duty requires his presence. Unwise actions in this or other areas of human interaction can be used by unfriendly agents to influence the tribal peoples. This can prolong the war with a consequent loss of additional lives.

Never enter a Katu home unless specifically invited to do so and are accompanied by someone of your own sex who dwells in that particular house. To violate this custom will expose those who live in the house to harmful gossip. It will make you chargeable as a thief for any item later discovered to be missing from the house which was visited.

The Katu extended family system often requires time for decisions to be reached. Many courses of proposed action may require sacrifices and divinations beside extended periods of palaver by the tribespeople. Americans must allow for these factors, or be prepared for failure when cooperation is essential. Like most Montagnards peoples, the Katu do not "buy" ready-made solutions to problems or preconceived plans of operations in which they have had no valid part. Effective cooperation requires consultation and discussion with the appropriate tribal personalities and their assent to plans which involve action on their part. When this is done, the agreed plan can be executed with the assurance that when the critical moment of success or failure arrives, the American will not be alone.

Ideal leadership qualities in effective relations with the Katu include awareness of tribal life; preceptive intuitive understanding of Katu dynamics and temperament; patience; the ability to exercise forethought; and reasonableness of ideas with a willingness to modify plans as the need becomes evident. These qualities must be undergirded with a good natured willingness to "go-along" with practices which are not offensive to personal convictions or which are not detrimental to the assigned mission.

Before taking or showing pictures of the tribespeople, be sure of their attitude toward pictures of people. Many Katu believe that a picture is the result of the capture of the soul or spirit of the person whose picture is shown. Consequently, some fear to have their picture taken as they think that sickness or death through the loss of their spirit may be the result. Should a Katu become sick after his picture has been taken, the picture-taker may be accused of stealing his "soul" and be held responsible.

When offered food or drink by the Katu, accept it graciously. It may be unusual or different than that to which you are accustomed. Should it be unacceptable due to religious or other personal convictions, explain that the particular item is taboo or "dien" to you. The Katu will accept this, but then don't be seen using the same or similar items elsewhere. This is particularly true of their "home-made" rice wine, which is considered by the Katu to be special. If you are concerned about medical problems, be sure to keep your medication up to date. If there is the possibility of being poisoned, wait for your host to eat or drink and then eat or drink from the same item which he does. Normally the hot cooked foods will be safe as few dangerous germs survive the heat essential to have cooked foods. After all, the gesture of offering food to a foreigner is not lightly undertaken as food is too scarce. Therefore, be appreciative, gracious and thankful that you have been accepted by the tribesman as one worthy to share food with him.

Because the Katu are village oriented, it is well to have proposed "civic action" projects which directly benefit the village and its inhabitants. Never feel that the only success to be achieved among the rather primitive tribespeople must be done according to the "American plan". Try to ensure that cooperative projects provide tangible measurable results without long waiting periods. The Katu time concept does not include long range objectives, but require some fairly immediate benefits which can be seen.

The Katu demonstrate abilities to learn rapidly the mechanical crafts in which they can observe, participate and utilize. Because of the limited educational opportunities as they do not have any formal school system, the Katu do not readily grasp theory. Therefore the procedure by which demonstration and application is the teaching method seems to promise the quickest success. By moving from the known toward the unexplored unknown, it is much easier for the Katu to grasp the principles and procedures necessary for the mechanical age into which they are being ushered.

The village chief, the elders and their chosen counselors are the authority figures in the Katu community. For programs to succeed, the open approval or at least their tacit consent is essential. Thus it is wise to clear ideas with them privately before launching plans that seem to be revoluntionary to the tribespeople. Then be free to give praise and credit to the community leaders. The Katu knows little of what occurs beyond his immediate world. For that matter he does not much care either. It is essential that programs be of immediate community orientation, insofar as the Katu are concerned.

Most of the Katu area is presently under the influence and partial control of the Viet Cong. This is due to the inability of the Katu to successfully resist their encroachment, and in some cases, the tribespeople may be unaware of the implications of what is actually occuring all about them. Even so, it means that every American serving in the Katu area must realize the responsibility thrust on him by his assignment. He is a living witness of a different way of life with value systems totally unknown to the primitive peoples. Each American becomes the living embodiment of the concepts, dreams and practices for the tribesman who has yet to fully come out of an ancient past in spite of the jet, radar, and the wonders of the electronic age which now invades his world. Even while engaged in the dangers of war, each American by understanding the people; by appreciation of what they have done with

the little which they possess; by awareness of how one's own belief
determine value systems and behavior patterns; can aid in the long
march to a better tomorrow for the tribesman and for you the
American.

FOOTNOTES

1. Summer Institute of Linguistics, Saigon, Vietnam, "Vietnam Minority Languages" July 1966 List, "Katu"; Frank M. Lebar, Gerald C. Hickey, John K. Musgrave, Ethnic Groups of Mainland Southeast Asia, New Haven, Conn. Human Relations Area Files Press, 1964, p. 141.

2. LeBar et al, Ethnic Groups of Mainland Southeast Asia, p. 141; J. Le Pichon, "Les Chasseurs de sang" Bulletin des Amis du Vieux XXV (1938) pp. 359-61

3. LeBar et al, op. cit. pp. 94, 141

4. George Coedes, "Ethnography of Indochina" (JPRS/CSO: 6757-D.C. Lectures, 1950) Washington, D. C. Joint Publications Research Service, 1950, pp. 1-16.

5. Summer Institute of Linguistics "Vietnam Minority List of July 1966, "Katu".

6. Nancy Costello, 9 January 1966 Tape on the Katu for the Personal Response Project.

7. U.S. Army Special Warfare School, Montagnard Tribal Groups of the Republic of Vietnam, Fort Bragg, N.C. Second Edition 1965, p. 133, 138.

8. Costello Katu Tape; H. L. Josephsen (Christian Missionary Alliance) Katu Tape of 29 April 1966 for the Personal Response Project; LeBar et al, op. cit. p. 141; USA Sp. Warfare School, op. cit. p. 133; Summer Institute of Linguistics, Saigon, "Vietnam Minority Languages" List of July 1966 "Katu".

9. Costello, Katu Tape; Lebar et al, op. cit. p. 141; USA Special Warfare School, Montagnard Tribal Groups pp. 133;

10. Josephsen Katu Tape; Costello Katu Tape; Lebar et al, p. 141; US Army, Montagnard Tribal Groups, p. 133; Mole, 1965-6 Field-notes.

11. Josephsen Katu Tape.

12. Costello, _Katu Tape_ (9 January 1966); J. Le Pichon, "Les Chasseurs de sang", _Bulletin des Amis du Vieux Hue,_ XXV (1938) p. 363; Mole, _1965-6 Field-notes._

13. Le Pichon, _op. cit._ p. 363; Mole, _1965-6 Field-notes._

14. Le Pichon, pp. 364-6; Costello Katu Tape; Mole, _1965-6 Field-notes_

15. Josephsen, _Katu Tape_; Mole, _1965-6 Field-notes._

16. Costello Tape.

17. Mole, _1965-6 Field-notes_; Le Pichon, pp. 364-6.

18. Laura Irene Smith, _Victory In Vietnam,_ Grand Rapids, Michigan, Zondervan Publishing House, 1965, p. 97; Nancy Costello letter to author about Katu.

19. Le Pichon, pp. 364-6.

20. Costello, _Katu Tribal Tape;_ Josephsen, _Katu Tape_; Mole, _1965-6 Field-notes_; Le Pichon, _op. cit._ p. 366.

21. Le Pichon, pp. 391-393.

22. Le Pichon, pp. 365-73; LeBar et al, _op. cit._ p. 141; Josephsen, _Katu Tape,_ Mole, _1965-6 Field-notes._

23. Le Pichon, p. 370; LeBar, p. 141; L. I. Smith, _op. cit,_ p. 23; Josephsen _Katu Tape,_ Mole, _1965-6 Field-notes._

24. _Webster's Third International Dictionary,_ "Toucan" p. 2415.

25. Le Pichon, p. 397; LeBar et al, p. 141.

26. See "Blood Hunt" in section on religion for details of this still current practice.

27. Le Pichon, p. 386

28. Le Pichon, p. 378.

29. Le Pichon, pp. 376-9; Josephsen Katu Tape; Mole 1965-6 Field-notes .

30. Le Pichon, p. 377.

31. Gerald C. Hickey, "Comments on Recent GVN Legislation Concerning Montagnard Common Law Courts In the Central Vietnamese Highlands". Santa Monica, The Rand Corporation Memorandum June 8, 1965, pp. 1-4.

32. Le Pichon, pp. 357-8

33. Hickey, "Comments on Recent GVN Legislation" p. 1.

34. Hickey, P. 2.

35. Le Pichon, pp. 378-9.

36. Le Pichon, p. 378.

37. Costello, Katu Tape; Le Pichon, pp. 375-7

38. Costello Katu Tape.

39 through 71 are based upon Mole 1965-6/1967-8 Field-notes.

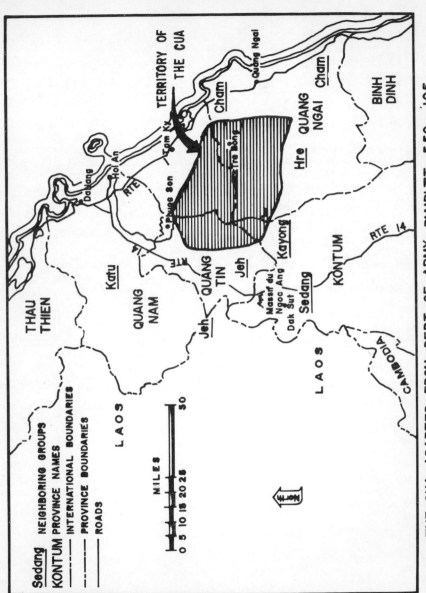

THE CUA ADAPTED FROM DEPT OF ARMY PAMPLET 550 – 105

CHAPTER VI

THE CUA

Names: The Montagnard ethnic group known as Cua has several other names also. The ethnic Vietnamese spell the name of this tribe as Khua while some of the other names are Kol, Kor, Traw, Bong Mieu.[1] The Cua who live in the higher mountains may also be known as Kor, Dot, or Yot, while the foothill groups may use the names Kol, Traw and Dong.[2] Similar to other tribal groups, the names may be explained by the close village identification which the Cua has with his place of residence. In other instances, the varying names are based upon changes and differences of dialect. An example of this is evident when it is noted that the final consonants "l" and "r" may fluctuate or interchange as the Cua near Tra Bong call themselves Kol while in the higher mountain area the Cua give Kor as their name.[3]

Language: The speech of the Cua has been classified as that of the Bahnaric subgroup of the Mon-Khmer. The Cua language is thereby related to the Bahnar, Sedang, Jeh and Hre. However, the Cua language is more closely related to that of the Hre than to any others in it subgroup.[4] Until recently, the Cua language had no written form and was used only in oral communcation. Current efforts, with Vietnamese government approval and or support, especially the Summer Institute of Linguistics, Saigon, to create a written alphabet and grammar are in progress. As progress is made in this effort, it will be combined with experimental attempts to teach reading and writing to the Cua in their own language.

Cua speech is primarily monsyllabic as are the other Mon-Khmer languages, although a number of polysyllabic terms have been borrowed from other peoples. Although the Cua speech has a wide range of tone sounds, it is not tonal in the sense that tone affects either meaning or grammer. The majority of the Cua know only their own language, although a few who deal with the Vietnamese have a speaking knowledge of the Vietnamese.[5] Some of the Cua young men who speak Vietnamese are believed to have been trained in Hanoi inasmuch as the Viet Cong have operated rather freely in most of the Cua tribal area for a number of years.[6]

Population Estimates and History: The estimated number of Cua tribespeople is anywhere between ten and twenty thousand persons.[7]

The unsettled conditions and their geographic isolation make an accurate census impossible. Only when peace is restored to Vietnam and a systematic survey is undertaken for all Vietnam will it be possible to determine exact figures.

The Cua as members of the Mon-Khmer family may have originated in the upper Mekong valleys in what is now South China. Due to the Southward push of the peoples within China, the tribes-people migrated down to their present location.[8] Little factual information pertaining to the early history of the Cua has been accumulated to date. But by the 11th century A.D., they had come under the domination of the Champa Kingdom, and were thereby involved in the almost continuous wars between Cambodia, Annam and Champa. In 1471, the Annamese ruler, Le Thanh Ton of the Tran dynasty, defeated Champa so decisively that Champa domination over the Cua was permanently removed. The Vietnamese undertook no strenuous effort to rule the Cua and left the tribespeople alone except for a few military colonies, a small number of guard posts and limited trade. The items which the Vietnamese desired from the Cua included elephants, medicines, herbs and aphrodisiac items for which they bartered metal pots, brass gongs, jars, buffalo, iron and salt.[9]

The royal Annamese Court also imposed a yearly tax or tribute on the Cua. This tribute was gathered by assigning cac-lai, "special traders", to serve as tribute-collectors in definite tribal areas. Even when punitive expeditions were dispatched to control and subdue tribal uprisings and revolts, only limited success marked such efforts. However, when Gia Long became the Vietnamese ruler in the early 19th century, he determined to rule and control the area. Therefore a definite pacification effort by military force was under-taken. The strife that resulted devastated the lowland tribal area and it was placed under direct Vietnamese administration. Never-theless, the higher areas of the Cua habitat were never successfully conquered or assimilated; even the French gained only a limited direct control over the area and its people.

Location: The Cua are located in the mountain terrain of Quang Ngai Province and the south-central portion of Quang Tin Province. The majority of the Cua seem to live in Quang Ngai province with about 3,000 living in the district and town of Tra Bong.

Others live in Tra Dong, Bong Mieu or farther west in the mountains. The Cua tribe is largely divided into three areas: those who live on the river road; those on the mountain road and those along the Son Ha road. Almost all Cua villages can be easily located and identified in relation to these three main travel routes.[10]

The Cua area is west of the city of Quang Ngai and the "Chu Lai" area. Chu Lai is the name given to the United States Marine Corps base which in 1965 was established in the southern section of I Corps, South Vietnam a short distance north of Quang Ngai City on the South China Sea. Chu Lai is the Chinese expression for "Little Man" which was the nickname which the Chinese bestowed on Lieutenant General Victor Krulak while he was serving in China. This name was given to the site of this large military base when it was discovered that the available maps listed no Vietnamese name for this particular area.

The tribal area starts about ten miles inland from the South China Sea and extends westward some twenty-five miles until it meets the Jeh tribal area. The northeast point of the Cua area is some six miles southeast of Tam Ky and the northern border gradually extends until it comes within a couple of miles of Phuoc Son as it goes west. Inasmuch as the north-south extremes of the Cua area are over twenty miles apart, the tribal habitat encompasses between 450 and 500 square miles.

Within this rectangular area is located the eastern portion of the Annam Cordillera known as the Massif du Ngoc Ang. The eastern part of this massif is composed of a series of eroded plateaus. The western part of this area contains a series of round hills composed of shale, slate and schist, with occasional isolated granite peaks that may reach a height of 8,000 feet. Schist is a metamorphic crystalline rock which has a closely foliated structure, and, while containing little if any feldspar, has a finer lamination than does gneiss. In the areas around Bong Mieu and Tra Bong, the rugged hills rise abruptly from the narrow coastal plains and are divided by narrow steep river valleys and short swift flowing streams.[11] These streams and rivers are not normally navigable because of the shallow water in dry seasons and the swift currents in times of high water while occasional typhoons add to the hazards of attempted water transportation.

The Cua area is affected by the Summer (May-October) and the

Winter (November - January) monsoons. The summer southwest prevailing warm moist winds often bring thunder showers and heavy local rain. The winter brings a northeasterly air flow which creates cloudy rainy weather as the moisture-ladden air rises up over the Annam Cordillera. The combination of these two seasons create an average rainfall of 150 inches on the higher slopes while 120 inches is the yearly average on the lower levels of the tribal area. While the full force of typhoons reach the Cua area only rarely, the winds and the heavy rainfall created by them do, and these cause serious flooding, uprooting of the forest and the loss of human life.[12]

Vegetation in the Cua area varies greatly. On the higher slopes of the Massif du Ngoc Ang, where some of the Cua live, only a tough grass about waist high is abundant. Below this area and yet in the almost inacessible regions of the steep mountains is a primary rain forest. Some of its trees may be a hundred thirty feet or more high. An almost continuous canopy of green is about all that is visible from either a low flying airplane or a hovering helicopter which attempts to stay above the range of small arms. Below this green canopy, however, is a middle layer of trees while even closer to the ground is a third level of saplings, etc. While little direct sunlight penetrates to the ground, lianas which are woody climbing plants, orchids and other epiphytes are common. Along the water courses where the sun does reach, rattan and bamboo are luxuriant. Although the rain forest is rugged, travel in it is not so impeded by thick ground cover as it is on the lower slopes of the Cua area where the primary forest has been cut in order to raise crops.

In those areas where the Cua have removed the primary rain forest in order to plant the various crops, a secondary rain forest quickly claims the abandoned fields. These have only a few isolated fallen trees, but do possess an abundance of small trees, heavy ground growth and many climbing vines or plants. Travel, except in the well-worn and often used paths, requires the constant use of the machete. Such an environment encourages the use of ambushes inasmuch as the noise of clearing new paths would quickly reveal the presence and exact location of any patrol.

Few, if any, of the Cua trails can be seen from the air. The secondary roads which once existed in the area are now largely unusable as they are full of potholes in the dry season and serve as beds for torrents of water in periods of heavy rain. Formerly, a secondary road left National Highway #1 just north of Quang Ngai city and went into the Cua area before becoming just another track. Another and formerly more important road started from National Highway #1 at Tam Ky and went through the Bong Mieu region to Tra My and then as a track continued to Kontum.[13] Because the Cua area provides infiltration routes which stretch almost to the South China Sea and overlooks the rich rice fields of the coastal plains and river valleys, it and its inhabitants are of strategic importance to any successful pacification effort.

Neighbors: The Hre tribe shares the southern Cua border for perhaps thirty-five miles. The Kayong tribal group are their neighbors on the lower western Cua tribal area while the Jeh occupies the balance of the western and northwest borders. The Takua or Duane are the northern tribal neighbors as are also the ethnic Vietnamese to the northeast and the east.

INDIVIDUAL AND TRIBAL CHARACTERISTICS

Like most Montagnards, the Cua are more similar in body build and color to the Philippine and Indonesian peoples than they are to the ethnic Vietnamese. The men are normally well-proportioned, stocky and muscular while ranging in height from five feet to five feet six inches.[14] The women are slightly smaller, and, when young, quite graceful with this trait particularly obvious in their dances which form a part of the Cua animal sacrificial rites.[15] Obesity never seems to be a problem for either sex of the Cua.

With deep set black eyes and dark skin, the Cua have heavy black hair. While a few of them have curly hair, most have bangs cut across the forehead and long straight hair which may be worn down the back or tied up into a bun. The Cua men often tie a cloth around their bun or wear a large tribal made silver comb in it. Because of the long hair worn by both sexes, some people may mistake young boys for girls.[16]

Occasionally a young Cua may have reddish-brown hair. This is believed to be due to a shortage of Vitamin A. Inasmuch as some Cua believe that the spirits may be angered if the hair is washed, and this anger result in death, opportunities for diseases of the scalp are prevalent.[17] The Cua in the Tra Bong area do wash their hair and bathe,

179

even if those in the most remote mountains may not. The latter simply have not been educated in such matters; and most likely do not think it is important one way or the other, so why bother? Sometimes the Cua women may wear a cotton headband or may have a number of beads about their hair. Blue is a predominate color for the Cua beads.

Clothing of the Cua may be that of the traditional dress; may be copied from the ethnic Vietnamese, or may be adapted western pants and shirt. The male may wear a plain or colorful loin cloth and nothing else; he may wear a loin cloth with an upper garment much like a T-shirt; sometimes a loin cloth with a short jacket in cooler weather; or he may wear western clothing. If he wears western style trousers, the ends of the loin cloth will be deliberately left exposed as a mark or sign of his tribesmanship; or, some may wear one of the uniforms of the National government as they serve in the armed forces.[19]

The apparel of the Cua women often consists of a dark knee-length wrap-around skirt; or a fancier Cambodian-type sampot with a halterlike blouse from neck to waist with the arms and back exposed; or Vietnamese pajama-like black pants and blouse.[20] Sometimes in cooler weather a cloth cape may be worn about the shoulders. Both men and women, due to a life-time of bare-feet, have such hard calluses on their feet that even the leeches cannot draw blood through them.

In addition to clothing, the Cua add to their appearance by the use of various jewelries. Men wear beads about their necks; sometimes have collars of turned or polished metal, while some wear long pointed pewter earrings or others made of fine black wire. They may also wear both bracelets and anklets.[21] The women may wear a bead belt about the waist or hips along with earrings, bracelets, anklets, necklaces and hair ornaments to the fullest extent that their financial status will permit. The beads may vary in color although blue is predominant. Other earrings and bracelets may be made of silver or other metals. While Cua women often wear a brass or metal ring about their necks, their waist-bands are hand-strung hip beads of many colors. The Montagnard women in Tra My who wear brass coils about their hips are not Cua women.[22]

The chewing of betel results in the dark discoloration of the Cua teeth, while some diseases result in the loss of teeth or of the teeth becoming unfunctional through looseness, etc. The Cua are excellent workers with both persistence and endurance in spite of nutritional diseases. Their ability to cover mountain terrain swiftly is well-known to military personnel stationed in the area. The tribesmen can carry packs of forty-five pounds or so as far as twenty-five to thirty miles a day even in their rugged tribal area. From childhood, many have carried huge bundles of cinnamon bark or green tea to the various towns which have markets for these items.[23]

The first ten years of life is most precarious for the Cua. Once these have been mastered, life expectancy has a span of forty to fifty years. Unlike some of the tribes, the Cua do not seem so attached to their villages and will travel great distances without showing "home-sickness". But for that matter, the Cua do not normally demonstrate strong emotions freely, even though some of their flamboyance may be demonstrated in personal choices of jewelry. [24]

Generally, the Cua are quite hospitable people and are not known to be warlike.[25] The Cua have the ability to quickly learn the rudiments necessary to cooperate with foreigners in their area. While there is distrust for the ethnic Vietnamese, this seems to be based on the feeling by the Cua that the ethnic Vietnamese consider them as "wild-men"; as "savages"; and as objects of scorn. This hostility has been engendered by the various commercial transactions with lowlands merchants and by the unwise behavior of military personnel on duty in the tribal area.

The Cua demonstrate the ability to maintain military gear with pride. This seems to be a factor that prevents the Cua deserting in time of stress and extreme danger. Moreover, the Cua have a remarkable ability to maintain a correct sense of direction and to know all of their tribal area. The ability of the Cua to track is almost unbelievable as they can determine the number of people on a trail, how heavily loaded they may be, how fast or slowly they are traveling, and the possibilities of successful interception. The willingness of the Cua to stick to a difficult task without constant supervision makes the tribesman a favorite to Americans who have served in "Cua country". [26]

181

THE VILLAGE AND ITS BUILDINGS

The normal site for a Cua village is on the side of hill or mountain near a stream or similar source of water. This location seems to be chosen as a method of better protection against enemies, high waters and to escape the valley floors.[27] If the village practices wet rice farming, it will be located at the foot of the slope that overlooks the wet rice fields.

The Cua village may consist of several simply constructed bamboo and wood long houses built on stilts. The long house may be seventy or more feet in length, be of heavy beam construction and have heavy bamboo thatched roofs tied into place with rattan, bamboo floors and plaited bamboo walls. Entrance into Cua long houses is gained by a notched log which serves as a ladder at the front end of the house for the floor may be three to six feet off the ground.

Cua villages may be arranged in a systematic pattern or be constructed in what seems to be a haphazard manner. The individual long house, called a palov, forms the dwelling for a patrilineally-linked extended family. The front part of the long house has a long large room that is the width of the house and is known as gol.[29] This room serves as the place where guests are entertained and as the sleeping space for the men and boys of the house.

Extending through the center of the house from this large room is a central hallway or corridor with rooms on both sides that have doorways into the passageway and window spaces on the exterior walls. The individual compartments are family "apartments" or "kitchens" as each holds an open mud firebox or hearth for cooking, smoking meat and provides heat for a nuclear family. The individual rooms also serve as "bedrooms" for the women, girls and small children.[30] In the areas where terrorists operate most freely, the houses are decrepit looking and badly constructed so that they will not be inevitably burned down.

Household possessions are few and may be kept in the large common room or in the individual family units. These items includes wine jars against the walls, crossbows and spears attached to the walls or roof, basket, hammocks, brass gongs, trays for sifting rice, cooking utensils and perhaps smoke dried meat, blackened almost beyond recognition, hanging from the ceiling.[32]

The area underneath Cua houses may be used as storage areas, as livestock pens and shady places to lounge when it is hot and sticky at midday.

The Cua often construct little thatch-houses on high posts outside of their long houses. These small buildings may be a yard or more in length and width. These serve as rice-store houses and reveal the Cua wisdom of not keeping their surplus grain in the long houses where accidental fires could easily destroy their food.

While some Cua villages have permanent sacrificial poles, others do not. When these post are present, they may be decorated with stripped bamboo, and may be painted with ornate designs thought to be pleasing to the spirits. On occasion of sacrifices, these posts may also be embellished with white cotton trimmed rope pennants.[33]

Due to factors that include beliefs about epidemics, deaths, and argicultural practices, the Cua change their village locations from time to time. However, these village moves are normally within a limited area as the tribesmen may return to reforested fields every few years. Such village relocations may be every two or three years when agriculture is the cause or at anytime when "unnatural" events seem to make a move desirable.

SOCIAL STRUCTURE

The Cua have a patrilineal kinship system so that ancestry is traced through the father. Thus, the man is head of the household, disciplines the children and has the only hammock. Upon his death, his elder son if old enough, or if not, a brother will assume the role of head of the family. Women show their secondary role by walking behind the men even if they do work in the fields, and must return home to fulfill their domestic chores. Subordinance is also evident when foreign vistors come to a Cua village. Men, boys and small children will come forth to "inspect" and visit, but the women and girls discreetly observe from semi-seclusion. Thus, like the ethnic Vietnamese, women seem to be relegated to lower status than that given to men.

Each long house is governed by a leader called jalang with this an inherited position through the eldest or youngest son. When a young boy inherits this responsibility, he is guided by his uncles until he can assume full responsibility. Inasmuch as a Cua long house may house up to a hundred families in some instances, a jalang has much the same function as a village chief would have in other tribes.[34]

The jalang is considered the owner of all family property and is responsible for keeping law and order in his long house. But in addition to the jalang, each long house has its own representative for the government who is a lien gia. Moreover, each small group of long houses is called a xa and these have a government representative known as dia dien. The next higher official, the khu truong, who oversees several xas or villages, is responsible to the District Chief with Tra Bong District having two Cua khu truongs.[35]

Thus, a comparison of Cua governmental structure to that of the Vietnamese would be the long house is like a hamlet, the long house community (xa) like a village, with several villages under the khu thuong being a sub-district. And as in all societies, crime and punishment is part of Cua life.

Justice: Crimes may be punished by banishment from the long house or village, repayment of value and a sacrifice with enough food for the entire long house. If repeated crimes are committed by an individual, he may receive capital punishment by being speared to death. To the Cua, stealing is one of the most serious crimes.[36]

Authority to administer punishment depends upon the offense. If the effect of wrong doing does not extend beyond the immediate family, the father administers discipline. If the whole long house is affected, the jalang and long house elders determine the punishment. When an offence extends beyond the long house, the jalangs and xa leader, dai dien, determine the appropriate action, and in more serious cases, the offender's entire family may be held responsible for the culprit's action.

Besides the foregoing, the Vietnamese Government in March 1965 decreed a system of tribal laws and courts. This law establishes courts at the village, district, province and national levels

for civil and criminal matters when all involved parties are Montagnards.[37]
The village courts composed of the village chief and two Montagnard
assistants who judge matters brought before it and render a decision.
If the involved parties accept the decision, they sign the judgement
which eliminates the right of appeal. But when this is not done, the
matter can be appealed to the district court. This court is composed
of the district chief and two Montagnard assistants and may hear appeal
cases or matters too serious to have originated in village courts. The
highest Montagnard court is at the province level where a Montagnard
Affairs Section is a regular part of the National Court. With a Montagnard judge and two assistants, the court may hear appeal cases from
Montagnard matters which are beyond the jurisdiction of the lower
courts.[38]

Alliances: Another factor of the Cua social structure is that of
alliances. These may occur in three different types. The first of
these occurs when an orphan or poor young person wishes to become
part of a family which can better provide or care for him. The second
type of alliance is when two feuding families wish to become reconciled
to the degree that their children can marry, while the third form of
alliance occurs when the tribe wishes to form an alliance with another
tribe.

The ceremony of adoption is quite similar to the rites held after
the birth of a new baby. Each person of the household places a small
symbolic amount of water, sugar, rice and meat on top of the head of
the person being adopted. Since the head is considered to be the residence of the "spirit", "soul", or "life stuff", this symbolic feeding of
the adopted person's spirit indicates their willingness to accept all of
their responsibilities for this new family member.[39]

The other two forms of alliances are generally sealed by the rite
in which a drop or so of blood is taken from each leader or person involved. These small amounts of blood are mixed with rice wine and
then drank by everyone present. This ceremony makes the participants
"blood-relatives". The new relationship is then expressed by exchang-
ing gifts of both clothing and food.[40] While only a few Americans have
been so "adopted", subversive agents have used the Cua adoption alliance
to their good advantage. Since religious value systems and taboos in a
spirit-controlled environment are involved, Cua tribesmen feel it impossible to break their pledge and fight once these alliances have been

formed. The long-time alliances found in many Cua mountain villages, with intermarriages cementing the bonds cause many of the tribesmen to be unwilling to engage in hostile acts against alliance-partners. This has been effectively utilized by communist agents for a number of years.

Marriage: Basically a monogamous society, the Cua have been influenced by contact with foreigners and ethnic Vietnamese, so that both marital unfaithfulness, promiscuity and polygamy appear to be increasing. The former stern tribal mores are slowly eroding by virtue of such non-tribal influences.

Cua marriages are arranged by the parents of both the boy and girl through an intermediary. This arrangement avoids embarrass- and "loss of face" in the event of difficulties during courtship. Because a dowry price is not involved involved in agreements of marriage, arrangements of marriages are times of sharing, good-will and happiness. Even though there is no formal bride price, the prospective groom, with a small group of friends, will go to the bride's parents to ask if they have need of anything. If they are "rich", they will say no. But, if they are "poor", the prospective groom will attempt to give them whatever they need in way of food clothing and money for the wedding feast. Cua marriage restrictions are quite strict and require that they be at least seven generations removed before relatives can marry.[41]

The wedding feast is a two-day affair with one day's feast at the groom's house and one day at the bride's home. Because the families are so deeply involved in weddings, the groom's family has the final authority in choosing the wedding date while the bride's family determines the number of wedding guests. These decisions are important inasmuch as the wedding is normally scheduled to include the sacrifice of a buffalo which precedes the wedding feast by one day. Like American weddings, the groom and bride have attendants. These may vary but must always be an even number.[42]

In instances of polygamy, the first wife has seniority and primary influence. Plural wives may or may not occupy the same "kitchen" or living space as this would depend upon their attitude toward each other.[43] In most instances man's plural wives would have their individual kitchens for themselves and their children with the husband and father taking turns in eating with his separate families. Second and subsequent wives have positions which are quite similar to the concubines or hand-maidens of Old Testament times.

Divorce: Should a man desire to divorce his wife because of her unfaithfulness or continual laziness, he must make his arrangements through the intermediary who arranged his marriage. The father retains custody of the children inasmuch as the Cua are patrilineal. If a wife wishes to divorce her husband, she must return to him whatever help he provided to her parents at the time of their wedding.[44] The women's inability to meet such economic requirements in her primitive society combined with the man's "right" to acquire additional wives helps to account for a low divorce rate. The struggle for physical survival where knowledge is limited and medical help remote is sufficiently severe that the breakup of a family only makes existence more difficult.

Birth and Childhood: As in other preliterate cultures, birth is met with, what appears to foreigners, simplicity and naturalness. The expectant mother continues her normal work until the time of her delivery. While a midwife may assist in the birth of a women's first child, many Cua women handle subsequent births by themselves. The new mother returns to the fields to continue her tasks about ten days after delivery. Like other Montagnards, the Cua family may be able to raise two or three children of every ten births.

As head of the family, the father is responsible for providing food and for teaching the children the ways of the tribe. Children begin contributing to the family work load at a very early age.

Since loud talking and rowdy behavior are thought to be inexcusable by the Cua, Cua children seldom quarrel with each other. Parents rarely raise their voices in discipline, so the effect on their children is instantaneous when this is done.[45] Cua parents resort to corporal punishment for their youth only on infrequent occasions as the tribal temperment does not make such actions necessary.

Funerals: When death occurs, the Cua sacrifice a buffalo so that the spirit which caused the death will not take the life of another person. Different than most Montagnard buffalo sacrifices, the Cua family providing the sacrifical buffalo at a funeral cannot eat the meat of the sacrifical animal.[46]

The Cua inter their dead in simple village cemeteries. Then after filling the grave, a small thatch or bamboo shelter or shade is erected over the grave about two to three feet above the ground. This shade is supported by frail stakes which along with the rest of the temporary shelter falls apart within two or three months. Under the shelter and on the grave may be found a small rice bowl, a open container for rice wine, etc. while simple cloth decorations may be tied to the shelter. The purpose of the shelter and the offerings under it include protecting the spirit of the deceased which may linger at the grave site for a little while; allowing the spirit to have shade from the sun as the graves are often in open areas; and to appease the "devil".[47]

ECONOMICS

Farming: The Cua, like other Montagnard groups, use the slash and burn or swidden form of agriculture except for a small amount of wet rice farming. Swidden farming is accomplished by cutting down the foliage in a given area, allowing it to dry, and then burning it just prior to the rains. The resulting potash acts as fertilizer for the various crops which are planted among the stumps and larger trees which are still standing. After two or three years, the field has lost its potency and must be abandoned. It is allowed to return to jungle, and a new area is prepared for farming.

New swidden sites are generally chosen by the village head man, the village elders and any sorcerers who may be present. The choice of the new sites is determined by examination of the natural vegetation combined with rites of divination so that a fertile field will provide good crops when "protected" by the relevant spirits. When the fields are to be planted, the men, holding dibble sticks in either hand, make holes for the seed. The women follow them dropping the proper amount of seed into the holes and covering the seed. Except for guarding the fields against wild animals and some weeding, the fields do not require much attention until harvest. The clearing, tending and harvesting of the fields are the responsibility of the individual family.

Besides the fields which may be some distance from the Cua village, the tribesmen also have gardens in which they may grow corn, cotton, tea, potatoes, bananas, betel nuts, fruits, leafy plants and vegetables.[48] Sugar cane is a rare delicacy as is salt which normally is gained by trade with other peoples.

Gathering: From the forests and jungle the Cua women collect herbs, edible roots, leaves, bamboo shoots and wild jungle fruits. The major commercial Cua input into the Vietnamese national economy is cinnamon bark. This is gathered and transported by the Cua into market areas such as Tra Bong.

Hunting and Fishing: While the Cua raise such domestic stock as chickens, pigs and buffalo, these are consumed as food only after they are sacrificed in rituals to appease and placate the spirits. However, the Cua are skillful hunters with their crossbows and traps and they hunt game and fish from the jungles all bout them. These may be cooked and immediately consumed, or else smoke cured for future need.

Crafts Trade: Cua women make mats, baskets, and in the more remote areas weave a coarse colorful cotton cloth on light looms. The cotton fiber may be either locally grown or secured in barter with Vietnamese merchants. The Cua women near the trading centers generally secure their clothing materials in the market place. The Cua use bamboo, rattan, palm leaves and wood in making their various containers, house walls, weapons, traps, mats and pipes. Besides being bead makers, the Cua also secure tin from Laos which is used in making their pewter items.[50] Most of the Cua manufactured items are for domestic use. Since the tribespeople are not too hard pressed for essential food or shelter, they are reluctant to dispose of long-time family possessions or heirlooms.

The chief item of Cua bartering is cinnamon bark which is traded in the various Vietnamese markets. An excellent cordial, carminative astringent aromatic oil or spice is derived from this Cua traded bark. Cinnamon is producted from several of the trees of the cinnamomum genus with the Cua source being that of the Saigon cinnamomum loureirii which has a more agreeable fragrance and flavor than the cassia bark exported by the Chinese.

Besides revenue earned through trade and limited commerce, some Cua earn funds through employment as wage earners. This opportunity is limited, however, as only a few foreign employers are in the Cua area.

DEFENSE

Due to the Vietnamese war, Cua defense is no longer a tribal community function. If the Cua live near a government or American Special Forces Camps, they look to these for protection. Since much of the Cua area is dominated by the communist forces, these have assumed responsibilities for this function. When the hostilities cease, it can be assumed that the Cua will tend to revert to tradition-al tribal defenses until better procedures offer the tribes people greater security.

RELIGION

As animists, the Cua live in continual fear of spirits. Much of their day to day living, therefore, involves elaborate ceremonies, sacrifices, taboos, attention to omens and recourse to magic, as means of placating and appeasing spirits believed to be angry or hostile. Animism provides the Cua with an explanation of the universe while also establishing methods by which the tribesman can live in peace with or control his universe. To the Cua, every significant event of life has some "spirit association". Therefore rituals and sacrifice are integral parts of birth, marriage, death, serious illnesses, and cyclic events as field choices, clearing of fields, planting and harvesting of crops. Should misfortune result due to unappeased spirits, it may be necessary to move the commu-nity to a new location. It is much easier to rebuild the village in a new locality than to continue facing the anger of unappeased spirits.

In addition to "crisis" situations, the Cua have three major cyclic family sacrifices a year conducted according to the lunar calendar. A chicken sacrifice is held in the fifth lunar month (August), a pig is sacrificed in the seventh (October); and the buffalo sacrifice takes place in the eleventh month (February).[51] The buffalo sacrifice is the most important and the ceremonies extend over a eight day period. The actual sacrifice of the buffalo takes place on the second day. The jalang (household head) strikes the first symbolic blow with the household long knife after which the buffalo is quickly killed by the thrust of a spear. The Cua, unlike some highland ethnic groups, do not torture the animal as a means of pleasing the spirits. After the animal has fallen from its death thrust, a bamboo tube is inserted to reach the area of the heart. This blood is believed to be the most powerful, so it is caught in a container and then painted on the door posts and lintels as a means of preventing evil spirits entering the home.[52]

The sacrificial animal is then consumed along with other foods and rice-wines accompanied by invocations, dancing and the playing of musical instruments. Because the Cua normally consider loud boisterous conduct improper, it is worthwhile to note this does not apply to the times at which sacrifices are made. At these times, they drink alcohol often to stages of intoxication. Then they claim they don't know what they are doing. They claim that their spirit leaves them to return "to the sky" where it cannot see their misbehavior. When the feast is over, the Cua have a ceremony by which they call their spirits back to them.[53]

In spite of a seemingly simplicity of life, Cua existence is complicated by their concepts of existence. The presence of both good and evil spirits who dwell in objects of the physical world, in people and even survive death requires appeasement. Since the tribesman is fearful of all spirits, he prefers to use an intermediary when possible. Those tribesmen with greater amounts of ae often act as sorcerers, as reciters of prescribed formula, as communicators with the supernatural world, and may preside in ceremonies, festivals and sacrifices. Sometimes he can heal the sick or cause a curse to fell an enemy; some can foretell death or other future significant events.

Taboos: These are protective rules for preventing offense to the spirits. Cua daily life is permeated with them. When a taboo is violated, the "cure" is the proper sacrifice. In all cases the remedy of a violation is determined by the seriousness of the particular offense.

Omens: These are portents of the future dreams or mysterious signs which notify the observer that he is about to suffer misfortune or enjoy good luck. Some omens are self-evident to the observer, but in most instances, a "reading" by a sorcerer is considered desirable. Omens are considered to be warnings from good or friendly spirits.

Cao Dai Beliefs: These have been superimposed upon some of the Cua basic beliefs in some of the lower land areas. With the exception of the foregoing and one world wide Evangelization Crusade Church at Tra Bong pastored by a Cua pastor, the Cua are animists.

GUIDELINES FOR UNDERSTANDING

Religious, cultural and social traditions formulate and determine Cua attitudes and actions. Generally, behavior is governed by the unwritten tribal law in the form of tribal and community sanctions or taboos. Failure to comply with the expected code, by either the Cua or an outsider always results in uneasiness or hostility. Normally, safety is secured by the execution of punitive justice.

Sacrifices or divination may be required by the Cua even in instances which appear minor to Americans. Even simple decisions may require consultation with the long house chief, the village leaders and or the sorcerer. A basic requirement for Americans is patience. Extended palaver may be necessary for the tribesman to reach binding decisions on proposed courses of action. But once these have been reached without external pressure or coercion, the Cua will strive diligently to follow through with the appropriate action. Under external pressures, actions agreed upon will receive only the feeblest of attempts.

Rice wine is freely used as a major hospitality drink by the Cua and is used in their festivals , reunions, social events and sacrifices. Strong coffee, made by hot water dripping over freshly ground coffee beans may be occasionally served also. The latter is sure to be rather free of serious germs and seems strong enough to tan elephant hides!

Never enter a Cua "Kitchen" without an invitation and even then only when accompanied by the man of the house.

Never touch or handle any article or item of Cua worship. These are normally kept on a shelf in Cua house.

Among the Cua it is good manners to leave a little beverage in the bottom of your hospitality drink to indicate that they have been able to satisfy you with what you received from your host. When refusing to eat or drink, it is very courteous to take a very little and leave the rest. This may be one, two or three kernals of rice, or by dipping the tip of your finger into the beverage and then touching your mouth with the dampened finger. Since all meats and drinks are first offered by the Cua to the various spirits, some Americans may not feel free to partake of Cua refreshments.

A small barrier of stakes outside of a house indicates a sacrifice is being conducted and visitors are not welcome.

When a village is taboo - forbidden to all non-inhabitants - signs indicating this will be placed on or near the paths leading into the village. Be it a bamboo stake suspended near the path, or any other item which seems "out of place" the meaning is the same: "STAY OUT"! Entry into a taboo village is permitted only by the direct invitation of the village leaders.

Cua tribespeople shake hands by holding your hands with both of theirs. If you do likewise, you are more readily accepted as this involves one's total personality according to Cua customs. So try to have both hands free when anticipating shaking hands.

Once the sacred or special objects have been identified, leave them alone. Should these be molested, the Cua believe that the spirits may be angered and cause harm to the whole village unless a sacrifice is made, and sometimes this fear may cause the village to be relocated.

The Cua appreciate the quiet soft spoken, semi-passive, polite individual and reject loud, boisterous, haughty or overbearing behavior patterns. Impatience by Americans will delay effective action more than extended tribal palaver! In fact, the Cua seem to have admiration and respect for people who can command and give orders with quiet authority. While they may take impoliteness and rudeness without outward signs of rebellion, the time of crisis will allow them to "gain" revenge as the tribesmen have "long" memories.[54]

Allow the Cua to return favors. Return gifts may be as small as a single banana, but it allows self-respect. To force items on the Cua, even for their own good, without their opportunity to give anything in return is detrimental to the Cua sense of well-being. Recognize this and provide opportunities for the tribesmen to demonstrate their acceptance of you. A genuine partnership can be achieved, if the American permits it.

Never promise to the Cua what you cannot positively deliver. Never lie to them or your usefulness among them is finished. Always remember that Cua culture may not have the same value or traditions as that of American. You will be judged according to Cua standards.

Never mock, ridicule or slight Cua beliefs. Such will not only tamper with Cua emotional well-being, but also threatens his very existence and may create unbearable tensions within him. Animism and animistic beliefs form the cornerstone of Cua life and establish the value-behavior systems of this culture. Sustained empathetic relationships with Americans can reveal to the tribesman a world which he does not know exists.

The Cua are sharp, quick and intelligent. Don't try to exploit them! Do not allow anyone to cheat them! Instead, communicate and reason with them! Learn a few Cua expressions. In so doing, you can better illustrate your desire to help achieve their individual destiny. As the Cua recognize a sincere desire and interest on your part, they will reach in the same responsive way that appreciative Americans would.

In one sense you, the American, are fortunate to have the privilege of duty among the Cua. Since you are not of the Cua spirit-controlled world, the burden of compassionate understanding essential for true rapport and acceptance is yours. Measure up to the opportunity and you will stand tall in the society of men who would build a better world.

FOOTNOTES

1. Summer Institute of Linguistics, Saigon, "Vietnam Minority Languages, July 1966, "Cua"; Richard L. Phillips, "Here Are the Tribes", Jungle Frontiers XVI (Winter 1962) p. 13; Laura Irene Smith, Victory In Vietnam, Grand Rapids, Mich. Zondervan Publishing House, 1965, p. 41; E.H. Adkins, A Study of Montagnard Names In Vietnam, East Lansing, Mich, Vietnam Advisory Group; Michigan State University, February 1962, p. 6; Jackie Maier, Member, Summer Institute of Linguistics, Saigon CUA TAPE TRANSCRIPTION of March 1966. p. 1 (Hereafter refered to as Maier Cua Tape).

2   "Vietnam Minority Languages", "cua".

3. Maier Cua Tape, p. 1.

4. David Thomas, "Mon-Khmer Subgroupings In Vietnam", University of North Dakota: Summer Institute of Linguistics, 1962, pp. 1-4.

5. Irene Smith, op. cit. p. 43

6. U.S. Army Special Warfare School, Montagnard Tribal Groups of the Republic of Vietnam, (2nd Edition, 1965) Fort Bragg, N.C., p. 59.

7. Smith, op. cit. p. 41; Adkins, op. cit. p. 6; U.S. Army's Montagnard Tribal Groups, p. 59; "Vietnam Minority Languages" July 1966, "Cua"; Maier Cua Tape, p. 1.

8. George Coedes, Ethnography of Indochina (JPRS/CSO: 6757-D.C. Lectures, 1950) Washington D.C., Joint Publications Research Service, 1950, pp. 1-16.

9. Georges Condominas, "Aspects of A Minority Problem in Indo-China", Pacific Affairs XXIV (March 1951) p. 79

10. Maier Cua Tape, p. 1; Mole, 1965-6 Fieldnotes made as a part of the on site research of the Navy Personal Response sponsored by the Commanding General, Fleet Marine Force, Pacific, The U.S. Navy Chief of Chaplains, and the Commander, Service Force, Pacific.

11. Mole, 1965-6 Field-notes.

12. Mole, 1965-6 Field-notes.

13. Mole, 1965-6 Field-notes. These observations are based on personal observation by air and on ground, and by extended interviews with both the indigenous and foreigners of the Cua area.

14. L.I. Smith, op. cit., pp. 38-44; Maier Cua Tape p. 1; Mole 1965-6 Field-notes.

15. Maier Cua Tape, p. 1.

16. Maier Cua Tape, p. 2.

17. L.I. Smith, op. cit. p. 42; Maier better to author of 17 May, 1966.

18. Maier Cua Tape, p. 2; Mole, 1965-6 Field-notes.

19. Mole, 1965-6 Field-notes; Smith, op. cit. p. 42

20. Maier Cua Tape, p. 2; Mole, 1965-6 Field-notes.

21. Maier Cua Tape, p. 2; Smith, op. cit. p. 42; Mole, 1965-6 Field-notes.

22. Letter by Miss Jackie Maier to author dated 17 May 1966, p. 1.

23. Smith, op. cit. pp. 41-43; Mole 1965-6 Field-notes.

24. Smith, op. cit. p. 46.

25. Smith, op. cit. p. 43.

26. Montagnard Tribal Groups, p. 64; Mole 1965-6 Field-notes.

27. Mole, 1965-66 Field-notes; Smith, op. cit. p. 43.

28. Maier Cua Tape, p. 2.

29. Ibid.

30. Ibid.

31. Smith op. cit pp. 44-45.

32. Mole, Field-notes 1965-6.

33. Smith, op. cit. p. 51

34. Cua Tape, p. 3.

35. Ibid.

36. Maier Cua Tape, p. 3

37. Confer Gerald C. Hickey, "Comments On Recent GVN Legislation
Concerning Montagnard Common Law Courts in the Central
Vietnamese Highlands" (Santa Monica: The Rand Corporation
Memorandum, June 8, 1965) p. 1.

38. Ibid.

39. Maier Cua Tape, pp. 243.

40. Ibid.

41. Maier Cua Tape,

42. Ibid.

43. Maier letter to author, May 17, 1966; Mole, 1965-6 Field-notes.

44. Maier Cua Tape, p. 4

45. Maier Cua Tape, p. 2; Mole 1965-6 Field-notes.

46. U.S. Army, Montagnard Tribal Groups of the Republic of Vietnam.

47. Maier Letter to author; also Mole 1965-66, Field-notes.

48. Maier Cua Tape, p. 6; Mole 1965-6, Field-notes, Smith, op. cit, p. 43.

49. Maier Cua Tape. p. 6; Smith, op. cit, p. 42.

50. Smith, op. cit, p. 42.

51. Maier Cua Tape, p. 5

52. Ibid.

53. Ibid, p. 2.

54. Maier Cua Tape, p. 6; Mole, 1965-6 Field- notes.

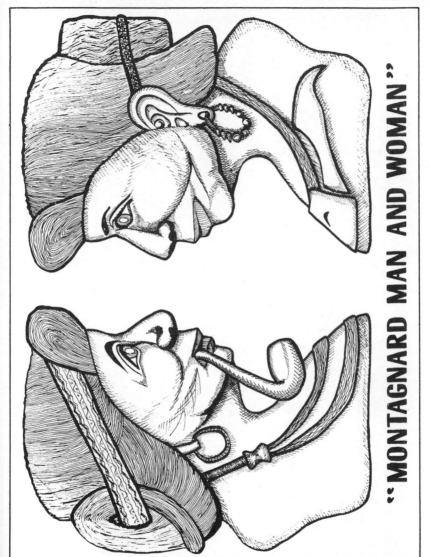

"MONTAGNARD MAN AND WOMAN"

199

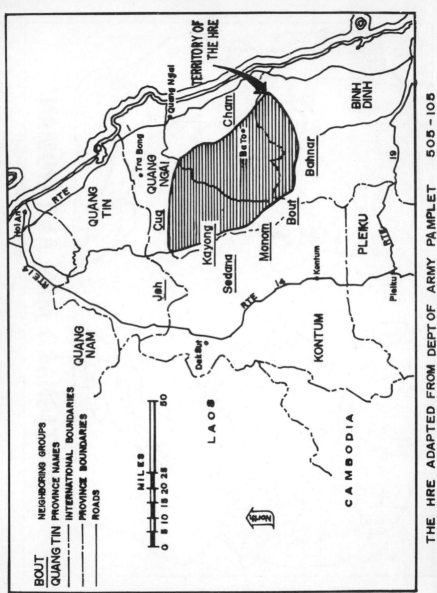

THE HRE ADAPTED FROM DEPT OF ARMY PAMPLET 505-105

CHAPTER VII

THE HRE

Most of the Montagnard peoples who occupy almost fifty per cent of Vietnam's geographic area come from two large ethnic groups: the Malayo-Polynesian and the Mon-Khmer. The Hre, by physical appearance, customs and language, are part of the Mon-Khmer group of peoples.

Names: Like other Vietnam tribal groups, the Hre have many names. These include Hre, Kre, Hrey, Bo-Vach, Tava, Kare, Kha-Re, Moi Cham, Moi Dong, Davak, and Rabab.[1] The Hre use the name "Hre" only for the tribal members who live along the Song (River) Re and the Song Hre. The other names are sub-tribal groups who live near other rivers in the tribal area. The major division, however, is that of the highland Hre and the lowland Hre.

Language: All the Hre groups speak the same basic language with variations of dialect and accent from village to village. The language is closely related to the Bahnar, the trade language of the area, and is therefore of Mon-Khmer origin,[2] although the Hre of the Song Lien and Song To areas are believed to speak Cham.[3]

The Hre basic language is largely monosyllabic with the Hre "r" being even more stressed than the French use of the same letter.[4] The Hre speech also contains many words derived from the Cham, the Vietnamese and Chinese languages. The Chinese terms are quite similiar to those spoken in Southwest China and by the Burmese Lisu tribes of the Upper Salween and Mekong valleys.[5] The few foreigners who know and speak the Hre language consider it very expressive with its four word combinations and the duplication of words which give emphasis and added meaning to the orginal terms used.

The Hre language is non-tonal, i. e. , the tone does not change the meaning of the words as does the Vietnamese. This quality is believed to make it "easy" to learn. Until very recently, however, the language was transmitted orally only as no written form of language or grammar existed. Now, through the cooperation of the Summer

Insitute of Linguistics, the Vietnamese government, missionaries
and some support from other Americans, the Hre language is being
transformed into writing also. By the streneous efforts of the
Summer Institute of Linguistics team, a thesaurus, a glossary of
terms and materials constituting an introductory course in basic
Hre has been translated into both English and Vietnamese. Some
of the lowland Hre speak Vietnamese, Bahnar and Cham. Some of
the Hre also serve as translators for U.S. personnel stationed in
the Hre area.[6]

Population Estimates: Estimates of Hre peoples vary greatly
as the numbers range from 27,000 to 210,000.[7] The more probable
population number would be between 90,000 and 120,000.[8] Regardless of the exact Hre census, the tribe consitutes one of the largest
Montagnard groups.

Geographic Location: The Hre are the tribal group which
inhabit the river valleys and mountainous area to the west of the
coastal city of Quang Ngai. The majority of the Hre are found on
the eastern portion of the Annam Cordillera in Quang Ngai and
northern Binh Dinh Provinces. The Hre tribal area, which starts
in the foothills west of the city of Quang Ngai, extends west to
Choung Nghai and Son Ha, south to An Lo in Binh Dinh provinces
and north to Minh Long.[9] The three principal divisions of the Hre
are the "highlanders" who live along both banks of the Hre Song,
a "middle group" that dwell along the Song To, and the "lowlanders"
residing along the Song Lien.

This is a mountainous area which has the Vo, Ba To, Kra No
and Hre rivers dissecting it as these drain the tribal area waters
into the coastal plain and South China Sea. The major Hre settlements are along the river valleys, and are thereby subject to rainy
season floods which occasionally create heavy damage. The heavier
floods may cover river crossings, wash out bridges and silt the
rice paddies while leaving huge boulders washed onto the paddy fields
so that the Hre food-raising opportunities are left in havoc.

Since paved roads are almost unknown in the tribal area, the
highland villages can only be reached by jeep in good weather. The

lowland villages are more accessible, although practically all foreigners must travel by small aircraft or helicopter due to the current war. The major means of travel for the tribespeople is that of walking, while pack animals, bicycles and horses, may serve as a means of transportation for goods too heavy to be carried on one's back. There is a "main road" from National Highway #1 at Mo Duc via Ba To and Gia Vuc to Kontum. It is both narrow, tortuous and dangerous as with rare exception the communists keep it interdicted. There are jeep trails from Quang Ngai to Ba To and to Gia Vuc along the Song Tra Khuc but few there be who ride these trails and live to tell of their deeds. However, most trails are practically invisible from the air.

The eastern edge of the Hre area overlooks the coastal plains and its ethnic Vietnamese dwellers. In the higher mountains of the tribal western regions, the Hre live in rather sparse settlements with these extending west almost to the Massif du Ngoc Ang and the Plateau of Kontum.

The Hre tribal area has two almost distinct belts of vegetation. The higher elevation primary rain forests form an almost continuous canopy of green about seventy-five to ninty feet in height. From the air, this gives the appearance of an uneven lawn with occasional green clumps of turf sticking up to break the otherwise sustained green blanket. Below this top canopy will be a second layer of trees with tops varying between forty-five and sixty feet. Closer to the ground will be an abundance of saplings and seedlings. Adding to this three layer growth will be a profuse supply of lianas (woody climbing plants) epiphytes, orchids and other herbaceous plants. Since little sunlight reaches through these dense layers there is little ground growth. This condition permits penetration by foot during the dry season with comparative ease.

After the primary forest has been removed to make room for ricefields the fields are allowed to return to their natural growth after two or three years. This permits secondary rain forest to develop. In this, the trees are dense with an abundance of herbaceous climbers, lianas and grasses. In such growth, one does not make much penetration without the almost constant use of a sharp machete. The noise of the machete will quickly reveal one's location. Yet, following animal-made trails, paths and tribally prepared trails can lead the unwary to booby traps or ambush sites.

Moreover, the secondary rain forest in this area is noted for the presence of malaria. It seems to be fear of malaria which has thus far kept most of the ethnic Vietnamese, excepting military posts, out of these regions rather than the presence of warlike tribes. Combined with this statement would be awareness that unimproved mountain areas offer much less opportunity for wet-rice farming than lowland plains and deltas. Wet-rice farming has been a farming trait of the Vietnamese for over 2,000 years so that it is most familiar to the ethnic Vietnamese.

The Hre area is a series of eroded plateaus with occasional high peaks that may be up to 5,000 or more feet in height. Rising sharply from the narrow coastal plain, the hills are composed of schist, slate, shale and similiar rocks. Schist is a metamorphic crystalline rock which has a closely foliated structure with more lamination than gneisses, but contains little feldspar. The tribal valleys may be meandering and comparatively broad even though most of its rivers are swift, short and dangerous as they vary in depth, currents and impeding rocks.

Basic to the Hre area geographic structure and way of life are monsoons and occasional typhoons. These bring winds and rain so that the higher areas average more than 160 inches of rainfall while the lower area receives more than half this amount. The summer monsoon (May - October) affects the western Hre region, while the winter monsoon (November - January) brings the rainy season to the Hre eastern tribal area. This climatic fact combined with the terrain of the area offer the potential of dams for irrigation and electric power for various light industries. In general, the weather of the Hre area is warm and humid with temperature averages of 60 - 65 degrees in January and 80 - 85 degrees in July. The high humidity makes the temperature more uncomfortable than the thermometer would indicate.

Neighbors: The neighbors of the Hre are the Cua to the north; the Sedang and minor tribes in the west; to the south and south-west are various Bahnaric groups, while the ethnic Vietnamese are on the east. The Hre tribal neighbors generally have customs, languages and economic conditions quite different than the lowland Hre.

History: The Hre have a creation story explaining the origin of their highland and lowland tribesmen. According to this legendary history, following the birth of both animals and people, a great fire destroyed most of the earth. This fire was either concurrent with, or followed, by a flood which engulfed all the earth except for two mountains. These two mountains were the Goong Din (East Mountain) and Goong Dom (West Mountain). On Goong Din were one hundred Vietnamese who formed the remants of a former boat-dwelling people. On Goong Dom lived a woman and a dog who eventually mated and produced a son. This boy through sexual relations with his mother was the father of the Hre people. As his descendants multiplied, they divided with one group living in the mountains and the others dwelling in the lower field areas. The tribes people tell this story to explain the Vietnamese numerically greater numbers as well as to explain their present geographic location.[10]

This primitive tribal tale indicates the Vietnamese were foresighted by living on boats and were surrounded by frogs, a delicacy much enjoyed by the Hre and the Vietnamese. While such were the Vietnamese fortunes, the Hre indicate the hard life of their forebearers who survived by living on roots gleaned from the jungles.

On the other hand, Hre traditions also relate that their early peoples lived in Laos and migrated to Vietnam many centuries ago where they created paddy fields like the old ones of their home land. Inasmuch as the Hre language has a number of Chinese terms which are not found in the Vietnamese, it may be that the legend of origin in the Upper Salween and Mekong Valleys has truth in it. As previously noted, the Hre have some words which are quite similiar to those of the Burma Lisu vocabulary.[11]

In spite of misty legends of the Hre, it is known from other sources that by the 11th century A. D. they came under the domination of the Champa Kingdom and were thereby involved in the almost constant warfare of Annam, Cambodia and Champa. The defeat of the Cham by Le Thanh Ton of the Tran Dynasty (1471) freed the Hre of Champa rule.

The internal problems of the Vietnamese dynasties precluded sustained conquest and rule of the Hre regions until Gia Long began to reign.[12] Then the Vietnamese military in 1819 began the erection of the Son Phong defensive wall from Tra Bong through Song Ha and Binh

Long and east of Ba To up to Nuoc Giap. Moreover, Hre youth were conscripted for the Vietnamese army while repeated rebellions by the Hre brought devastating retaliation on the Hre people. The Annamite Court continued to tighten its rule until the French pressures forced the Court at Hue to change its tactics toward the Hre in 1904.

Prior to this, the French had built military strongholds at An Lao (1900), Ba Ta (1901), and Tra My (1902). While the Hre had opposed these French efforts, their primitive weapons were harrassments rather than serious impediments. In 1940 the Japanese came into Vietnam. They eventually disarmed and imprisoned the French. Then the Viet Minh seized the larger towns of Quang Ngai Province. Through propaganda and force, the Hre were neutralized and the Viet Minh were able to establish Ba Ta as an administrative center.

From this base, the Viet Minh suppressed resistance, established de facto control, and drafted Hre youth as warriors or as labor conscripts. This procedure allowed a number of ethnic Vietnamese to settle in Hre lands and take physical possession. By 1949, the Hre reached the point of rebellion. By preplanning, they revolted and massacred all the 5,000 or so Vietnamese settlers in the area by killing them, throwing them into the rivers, or burning their victims as offerings to the spirits of the sky and earth. [13]

Following this, the Hre warriors requested French aid, and allied themselves with the French. However, the Viet Minh extracted terrible revenge by reoccupying the area, massacring, looting and burning everything. The Hre responded with guerrilla warfare, and by joining the French sponsored Doc Lap Hre (Hre Independent Movement). Nevertheless, the Viet Minh definitely maintained its rule of the Hre area until the Geneva Agreement of 1954. Much of the tribal area is still dominated by the communists as the central Vietnamese government and its allies have not yet effectively broken the domination of the Viet Cong forces for the whole area.

INDIVIDUAL AND GROUP CHARACTERISTICS

Like all the tribespeople of South Vietnam, the Hre more closely resemble the people of Indonesia and the Philippines in skin coloring, bone structure and physical build than they do the ethnic Vietnamese. Some Hre tend to have lighter colored skin than the peoples of other tribes, even though normally they have dark eyes and long straight black hair.[14] While taller than the Rhade or Jarai, the Hre are muscular, and seem to have short legs in relation to body length. Most seem to have strong well-formed backs, and since nearly everything is carried in baskets on their back by shoulder straps, their physical build seems appropriate.[15]

Some of the full-blooded Hre have chestnut brown streaks in their hair. However, this may reflect a vitamin deficiency more than a tribal physiological trait. Normally, the Hre of both sexes wear their hair long, even though it may be bound up with a cloth while they are engaged in heavy labor. Some contact with non-tribal peoples have created variations of hair style so that Hre women wear their hair in buns on back or side of the head occasionally. Either sex may wear graceful turbans, preferably yellow, while the older Hre people may dress their hair by tying it on top of their head.[16]

Filing or breaking the front teeth in puberty rites is an ancient Hre custom; and although the practice is dying out, a number of men and women still have this facial feature. Moreover, the majority of the Hre chew betel which discolors their teeth and mouth.

Wearing apparel among some of the Hre also comes under the influence of contacts with other tribes and the ethnic Vietnamese. Nevertheless, loincloths for the men and wrap-around skirts for the women are still common. The matron or married girls may be distinguished by the fact that the married woman does not have to wear a blouse or bodice in public as do the unmarried girls.[17] Generally, when non-villagers are present, a blouse or bodice is worn if such women are in public areas.

The dress of the younger Hre women is as colorful as possible. Their bodice may be white although the usual color is either blue or black.[18] Their jackets are usually embroidered on both sides of the front-buttons in red and white designs. Their skirts, also of blue and black, normally have two tiers with five to seven rows of white and red embroidery about 3/4 of an inch wide on each layer. The outer tier often extends to the middle of the calf while the inner one may reach the ankles.

The Hre younger women demonstrate a definite preference for rather ornate jewelry to match their bright colors in clothing. Poor women may wear a string or two of colored wooden beads, a small strand of metal beads or perhaps a necklace composed of yellow and red copper. The richer women may wear heavy collars, pendant silver coin necklaces, silver or gold earrings and necklaces of wood, amber or silver beads. Some of the Hre women complete their apparel by adding copper or silver bracelets on their wrists and ankles.[19] Hre men do not show a strong preference for bright colors or ornate jewelry. Thus, the male necklace is composed of heavy dark beads as amber is reserved as the correct beads for the Hre sorcerers.[20]

Hre men still wear the loincloth and a short jacket. Many tribesmen, affected by the nearness of the Cham and the ethnic Vietnamese, wear a short jacket, a pair of trousers or short pants. Some of the more wealthy even wear a shirt under their jacket. In most instances where Hre men wear western style clothing, the ends of the loincloth are left exposed as a sign that the wearer is a tribesman. Upon occasion the Hre tribesman may wear a woven blanket as a shield against climatic conditions as the night can be quite chilly in Hre "country".[21]

The Hre seem to have an excellent physical endurance. Moreover, they demonstrate abilities to lift heavier weights than men of other tribes and can move over mountainous terrain rather swiftly.[22] Because village sanitation and knowledge of personal hygiene practices are rudimentary, a very high infant mortality rate is common and all Hre adults have been exposed to numerous endemic diseases. Thus, only the most healthy can survive to adulthood. With the following diseases - malignant and benign tertian malaria, typhus carried by rats, fleas, mites, and lice; cholera, dysentery, typhoid, tuberculosis, leprosy, yaws and other parasitic sickness so prevelant, one is amazed to find that so many do survive and have some degree of good health. In addition to the things already mentioned, there are widespread nutritional deficiencies which compound the Hre difficulties of survival. The Hre do keep their water sources much cleaner of impurities than is customary among other Vietnamese tribal groups. Moreover, the Hre love to bathe in running streams of fresh water which helps to reduce incidents of skin disease.[23]

The Hre have long memories which do not seem to even desire to forget any injustice. They may wait a long time for the right moment of revenge as they feel that only the foolish and angry will fight against overwhelming odds. Should the wronged individual die before he is avenged his children and grandchildren may continue the feud. While the Hre seems to bear physical pain with much stoicism, his tribal pride rebells against offences against himself, his family and community so that he seeks revenge.

The Hre are not a warlike people that demonstrate aggressive traits against other Hre communities or non-tribesmen. Yet upon occasion they can be "blood thirsty" as the Viet Minh and other ethnic Vietnamese have discovered.[24] Normally, the Hre are both generous and hospitable, and have enduring close friendships.[25] As the occasion occurs, most Hre seem to wholeheartedly participate in community dancing, singing and drinking of rice wines. The use of rice and wine extends to the rather small children also.

Inasmuch as most Hre are pre-literate, they share the concepts of time prevalent among such primitive peoples. That is, they seem concerned only with the present, "the here and now", except when feuds are concerned. Consquently, the concept of thrift and saving for a distant "tomorrow" is not widely held or practiced. Instead, their value system is based upon terms of present use and status rather than what a future requirement might be. This is a dominant feature and seems to be a rather universal trait of most pre-literate peoples.

HRE VILLAGES

The lowland Hre rarely move their villages inasmuch as their valley paddy fields are generally fairly fertile and productive. Although serious epidemics may force the temporary abandonment of a village, it is usually reoccupied when the danger is believed to have passed.[26] The highland Hre, who practice "ray", "swidden", (slash-and-burn) agriculture, are migratory to the extent that their farming requires. That is they must prepare new fields as the soil wears out, but even then the village remains in the same place.

In either case, the Hre prefer to build their villages near streams or rivers as water sources. Sometimes the location of a spring provides a settlement site, while the absence of all three may require the digging of wells to provide water. When location near flowing water is possible, the Hre often construct aqueducts of bamboo or areca tree-trunks to gravity-flow water into the settlements "water point". Here a large stone basin may be prepared for the water which is used for drinking, cooking, bathing, laundering, etc. As noted earlier, the Hre prefer to keep this basin free of all debris.[27] Located on hillsides, most Hre lowland villages have ten to twenty houses unless they are resettlement communities. Each house may have a family of five to fifteen members so that there may be two hundred or so Hre in the community. Normally, these lowland homes will be surrounded with gardens composed of beans, corn, manioc, oranges, breadfruit or jack fruit, grapefruit, known as pamplemousse, in French and as Qua Buoi in Vietnamese, and areca (betel nut) palms. Manoic is a tropical plant of the cassava family that has edible starchy roots which have a taste similar to sweet potatoes when roasted in hot ashes. The starch from manoic roots may be used to make either bread or tapioca.

Deeper in the mountains among the highland Hre, the houses are more scattered with only two or three houses forming the community. These isolated settlements are normally protected from wild animals and unfriendly men by double bamboo palisades with sturdy bamboo gates, punji stakes, concealed animal traps, etc. Most of these settlements do not have extensive gardens nor cultivated fruit trees due to geographic location and migratory requirements.

The highland Hre houses are built on sturdy pilings five to seven feet above ground. Occupied by the Hre extended family, a house may be eighteen feet wide and forty-five to fifty feet in length. There are rare houses which may be up to one hundred feet or more in length. The wealth or size of the family would be the factors that determine the length of a house.[28]

Hre resettlement villages are miniature caricatures of the prewar villages and family homes. The Hre follow no prescribed pattern of building houses except in the resettlement communities. Houses are constructed according to land contour rather than being controlled by religious forces as is the case in many other tribes. While a few Hre build houses on the ground, or with pilings so that one part of the house is at ground level, the majority of the homes are five to seven feet above the ground.

The normal Hre house is constructed with beams of bamboo or wood, floors of whole or split bamboo, the walls of plaited bamboo and the roofs composed of a thick thatch. Ceilings in Hre homes are utilized as storage areas for spears, fishing traps, cross-bows, food, etc. Windows are often cut in the plaited bamboo, with bamboo used to shut the window space when so desired. The roofs are tied to the house framework by rattan.

The Hre house normally has two open roofed or unroofed porches. Access to these is gained by notched logs or homemade ladders. Both verandas permit entrance into the Hre house by means of a doorway hung with thin bamboo or wood strips. A few of the more wealthy homes may have wooden doors, but these are quite rare.

The Hre front porch, "ben chin", is the reception area when guests are received and entertained. Normally, it is also the area where guests sleep except when there is serious danger. It is here that the family wine jar is located. This jar is firmly tied to a porch post to prevent accidental spilling. The Ca Ra subgroup of the Hre have a high post set in the middle of their veranda for this purpose.

The back veranda, "ben gioang" is the workspace for Hre servants and the "family recreation room". Both of these porches are about nine by twelve feet in size, although some Hre make the front veranda larger and keep it much neater.

Often the doorways of a Hre home are the sites of chicken feet, feathers, fishtails, etc. as means of preventing the entrance of evil

spirits.[29] The room nearest the ben chin is considered to be
sacred so that only the man and his first wife and their small children may sleep there. A second wife or subsequent wives, servants,
married children, etc. require their own room and hearth. This
sacred room contains the sacred mortar used in rice grinding .
The hearth in this room can be utilized only in the preparation of
sacrificial food by the man as he alone cooks this. No one else may
touch the hearth or the spirits will be angered. Both the fireplace
and the rice mortar are built in place.

A broken mortar means that the house has been abandoned
while two cords hanging over the sacred hearth is a sign that the
family is temporarily away from home.[30] The number of hearths
in a Hre house is an index of wealth inasmuch as the poor have one
or two, the middle class three or four while the wealthy have more.
Actually the hearths are just fireboxes of mud on four posts which
pierce the floor and are normally about two by two feet in size. [31]

A number of the Hre homes will have nearby "bombshelters"
built into the earth. Generally, one can slide off the porch into a
short tunnel which leads into a larger space covered with beams,
brush and dirt. This provides shelter against light weapons and
also prevents lifestock from falling into the protective pits. [32]

Sometimes the Hre make houses for their cattle that resemble
their own houses except that these are at ground level. The grain
storage practice of the Hre includes small grain houses. These
small houses, about the size of a refrigerator, are also on posts.
They are covered with wet clay which is allowed to dry and forms
a protective shield against fire should nearby houses be consumed
.by flames. Each time grain is required, the mud has to be broken
open and then replastered once the cereal has been removed. [33]

Hre Spirit Houses: The Hre construct small huts for the
spirits of the dead just outside the village enclosure or village area
if the village is not enclosed. These will often have small saucers
of food or drink in front of them. Normally, the nearby twigs will
have small streamers attached to them. A white piece of cloth
flying at the end of a thin bamboo pole is indicative of a recent
death.

Another feature of the Hre village is the secret hideouts for family treasures. These dugouts are completely concealed and generally known by only the father of the family. In these secret hiding places, the Hre put earthenware jars that contain their valuable Laotian urns which represents their "gold reserve". These Laotian urns may sell for several thousand dong (piasters) among the Hre tribe. Should the man of the house be killed suddenly by a tiger or in war, the family treasure may be lost completely. A few Hre, through foreign and ethnic Vietnamese contacts, keep their wealth in actual gold or in coins and currency.[34]

SOCIAL STRUCTURE

Hre social structure, like that of other Vietnamese tribespeople, centers about the family and village rather than the clan or tribe. Frequently the extended family forms the village core. Some larger villages may contain several extended families. In any case, the major identification is with the village rather than any external socio-political organization.

The Hre family structure is patriarchal in that the oldest male is accepted as the head of the extended family. Economic factors may radically alter the impact of this structure as when the youthful Hre groom lives with his wife's parents due to inability to satisfy the various requirements.

Political: Normally, the Hre have an allegiance to their family and to their own independent village.[35] The latter is often led by a chief, called "ca ra", and a council of elders. The council functions as an advisor to the chief, and with him acts as a tribunal for settling disputes and internal village problems. Because the chief and council are selected by the tribe on the basis of age, experience and apparent wisdom, they are held in high esteem and respect by their villagers. The chief is generally the wealthiest and most influential man in his community. As one who possesses much "ae", charismatic powers, the villagers believe the spirits give him skills in hunting, war, leadership and knowledge of tribal customs.

The sorcerer, "ba giau", is a prominent figure in nearly all Hre villages. Even when he is not the village chief, he is a powerful

213

figure inasfar as the villagers are concerned. Because of his accepted communication with the spirit-world, he is often reputed to be able to foretell future events, length of life, time of death, to cure sickness, etc. The animistic Hre, living in a world thought to be controlled by spirits, may allow feared sorcerers to acquire and exercise despotic power so that the sentence of death may be executed upon his pronouncement. [36]

Justice: To date, the Hre system of traditional justice has not been written. Rather, Hre oral traditions are interpreted by the ca ra and his council with judgements rendered in accord with their interpretations. The only recourse against an unfavorable decision is to leave the Hre village permanently. Since Hre traditional law is based upon the concept that man is free, he must answer for violations of tribal traditions and customs. If an offender runs away from "justice", his next of kin, wife, children or relative may be held responsible. In some instances, the sentence of punishment imposed upon an offender may be lifelong slavery to the party against whom the crime was committed. [37]

Since March 1965, the Vietnamese government, through its decree restoring the legal status of tribal laws and tribunals, has attempted to operate courts in the village, district and provincial levels for all tribespeople. These courts handle civil affairs, penal offences and other legal items when all parties are tribespeople. Village courts, consisting of the village administrator and two tribesmen as assistants, hear local cases and render decisions. If all involved parties then sign the decision, the right to appeal to a higher court is eliminated. If settlement cannot be reached, the matter is referred to a higher court. District courts, with the district chief and two tribesmen as assistants, hear appeal cases from the villages and those matters deemed to be serious according to tribal customs. The provincial court, which is a part of the Vietnamese National Court with a tribespeople section, composed of a Montagnard presiding judge and two assistants, hear all appeals from the district courts and other matters beyond their jurisdiction. [38] Until the Vietnamese government exercises effective control over all the Hre territory, the 1965 decree can not be applied in every instance. Moreover, it will require time, diligence and patience for the impersonal application of the law to have its full effect in the lives of this preliterate people.

Social Structures: While the Hre are patriarchal, many of their marriage customs seem almost matriarchal. Thus, among the Hre a married woman has significant authority in her family and is respected in the community. A widow, however, is rather badly treated in comparison.[39] Hre tradition and customs permit polygamy so that the well-to-do men may have several wives. Customarily, however, a second wife is not acquired by the ordinary man unless his first wife remains childless. If a wife is either pregnant or capable of pregnancy, she must give her consent before her husband can aquire additional wives.[40]

Birth: Among the Hre pregnancy is considered to be honorable while the barren woman is thought to be most unfortunate. Customs of delivery vary between the lowland and highland Hre women. In the highland areas, birth is thought to be a contamination so that it must take place in the forest outside the village. The baby is delivered with the mother in a squatting position with several old women acting as midwives and receiving the baby. The baby's umbilical cord is cut, tied and poulticed with herbs and the baby immediately washed with water. The mother is responsible to look after her own needs as well as the secret burial of the afterbirth. After the baby has been wrapped in cloth, the new mother and baby live for one month in special quarters for women with new-born babies. While the husband and father may visit during this period of purification, he does not live with his wife.[41] Incidentally, in a society where so little knowledge of cleanliness, sanitation, germs, etc. is understood, these primitive procedures may save more lives than they destroy.

Among the lowland Hre women delivery occurs at home assisted by a tribal midwife who cuts the umbilical cord with a sacred knife. Normally, no medication is known or used during delivery although after the baby is born the new mother drinks water containing salt and a solution made of forest plants.[42] For fifteen days after giving birth she must abstain from eating meat, even though three days after her delivery she bathes in clean water, and after five days returns to her normal tasks.[43] If the birth is a difficult one, the village sorcerer may be called upon for assistance which is rendered by the sacrifice of a pig or a chicken. This is believed to appease the spirit causing the trouble so that the spirit will then release the baby and allow its birth.

Childhood: Hre babies are breast fed as the use of animal milk for them seems to be unknown. If the new mother has no milk, or dies, a wetnurse is obtained. Should one not be available, the infant is given a rice-water solution until it can eat a powdered rice mixture. Then as it grows older, it can begin to use cooked rice as a basic food. [44]

When the new baby is a month or older, the father on a fixed day, will take the child and present it to the village. At this time the village sorcerer conducts rituals at a special altar containing wine, tobacco, rice, meat, vegetable, etc. These are offered so that any wandering spirits who are present may participate in the celebration, be satisfied, and refrain from harming the small child.

When a Hre child is born, it is given a false name in order to mislead the evil spirits. Many Hre seem to feel that if their child is not given the special rites just mentioned, the uninitiated child while asleep will reveal its given name to the spirits who may use this knowledge for harmful purposes. When a girl begins to show puberty or when a boy is about eight years old, the parents tell them their real names which have been kept secret in order to protect them from evil spirits. [45]

Children begin to work at an early age as is typical of almost all primitive societies. Some even marry at thirteen and fourteen. Sometimes, poor parents may offer a child or children as security for a debt or a loan. If the debt is not repaid, the child can remain in service, "slavery", the rest of his or her life.

The Hre have a custom of allowing a young bride and groom to live with the parents of either one of the in-law families. Since only the well-to-do can afford to accept a daughter-in-law, the new couple normally live with the bride-parents and thereby furnish extra help to them. Consequently, the Hre seem to think that a baby girl is a greater blessing to them than a son would be. This is in marked contrast to those societies where girl babies are not desired.

216

MARRIAGE: The Hre have several ways of determining marriage partners. Young people may use drinking parties, community sacrifices or festival events like those of New Years, as opportunities to establish bonds, reveal sentiments and make tentative marriage plans. If the young couple agree to marriage, they proceed to determine with which parents they wish to live. Then they seek their parents counsel and consent.

Should a young couple decide to marry without parental consent, they may simply go into the forest and live together for a time. When they return to the village it is imperative that they set up a new and separate household. In such cases, there is no formal wedding or party for the family or village.

Sometimes a young Hre male who is very poor or who comes from a "deserted village" will offer to provide several years of free labor to the family of a girl he wishes to marry. When the obligations have been met, the promised marriage takes place, and a new family becomes fact.

In contrast to free choices of mates, many Hre families make marriage alliances for their children. Sometimes these are made before the children are even born. These alliances can create quite a disparity of age between the groom and bride. However, these marriage alliances are not final and can be broken before the marriage or shortly thereafter. The one who desires to "break" the alliance is required to pay compensation. This may be one or two buffalo if the marriage has been consummated, and one or two pigs to the family of the "jilted", with wine for the whole village if it has not. [46]

The marriage ceremony among the Hre is quite simple. This includes joint-family wine drinking; an exchange of gifts between the families of the espoused, and wine for the whole village.

After the wedding the couple move in with the parents where they have agreed to live. They may stay in the family home until several children have been born. However, if too many children die at birth or shortly thereafter, the couple may move to the home of the other parents or into their own houses in an attempt to get away from the evil spirits which are causing these misfortunes.

When an individual, who is widowed, plans to remarry, Hre customs demand that payment be made to the family of the deceased before the marriage takes place. This payment may be as much as one water buffalo and 3/10 of an acre of land in the village. This is necessary in order to liquidate all claims by the former spouse's family.[47]

When a husband dies, his widow loses her social status and must wait at least one year before remarrying. Because men, who are financially well-fixed, prefer to marry young girls, a widow can seldom marry anyone except a poorer member of the tribe who has no qualms about acquiring a "ready-made" family.[48] Sometimes, these are desired by men who are acquiring additional wives as it provides a shorter waiting period before extra hands are able to contribute to the family welfare. It is hardly necessary to stress that plural wives may prevent the one-to-one relationship in marriage considered to be most ideal in the Judeo-Christian concepts.

Adultery and Incest: The Hre are a family people and their customs tend to protect the family. While Hre young people seem to be quite free and easy in their sex relations, the tribesmen do not approve or condone unmarried girls being friendly with non-tribal men. Thus, unmarried girls should be spoken to only in the presence of their families or other women. Any clandestine meeting with foreigners will be sure to bring swift retribution.

Adultery: When adultery is detected, the village intervenes in order to punish the guilty. This village action is believed to be essential inasmuch as adultery is a serious infraction of tribal taboos. Penalties for adultery may be as much as one buffalo and five copper pots, or may be as low as three copper pots to be paid to the village or offended party by the guilty party. If one of the guilty pair is still unmarried, the punishment may be reduced to a fine of one pig.[48]

If a Hre male has an affair with another man's wife, which is detected, it may start a feud which can last for generations. Should he "repent" in time to save his life, he can demonstrate his "change of heart" by a public apology to the village, a wine-feast for all the village and payment of three to five buffalo to the wronged husband. When all this has been done and accepted by the village and the lawful husband, hostility and danger are over and peace is restored. The offender may now keep the offended husband's wife for himself.[49]

Incest: The Hre have strict taboos regarding the family and sexual relations among relatives, due to family bonds, village structure and fear of the spirits. Misconduct which involves incest is thought to bring misfortune on the guilty party and disaster to the village. To avoid the anger of the spirits, the Hre have taboos which prohibit marriage between members of the same ancestral family. Other taboos prevent a daughter-in-law eating from the same common dish as her father-in-law, and prohibits a young man sharing the common platter with his mother-in-law. Numerous other taboos exist to prevent incestous affairs.

When, in spite of these taboos, incest does occur, drastic penalties are imposed on the offenders. The spirit of the ancestors must first be asked forgiveness through a sacrificial ceremony in which a chicken, goat, etc. are offered by the village sorcerer on the bank of a nearby stream. The male offender is required to also stab the sacrifice with a sharpened stick and sprinkle some of the blood in the water and along the stream's bank. The village elders do likewise as they plead for the various spirits and their ancestors to forgive this terrible wrong and implore their protection and blessing instead of wrath. After being forced publicly to eat from a pig trough, the offending couple are banished forever from the village. Then, the village seizes all the property of the parents of the guilty couple and divides it among the remaining relatives. In earlier times, detected incest resulted in a tribal death sentence.[50]

Sickness: The Hre. like most Vietnamese highland dwellers, know little of scientific causes of sickness, disease or germs. In their animistic culture, these agonies of body and mind are thought to be caused by displeased or evil spirits. These supernatural forces are believed to be easy to offend and quick to take revenge, but are manageable through the use of the proper magic formula and the correct sacrifices. Therefore, the sorcerer is often the practitioner of "medical arts" among the Hre. The following rites for healing the sick are typical when "foreign" medical skills and medicine are not known or readily available.

An altar is placed in a specially erected bamboo shelter, and "flowerlet s" prepared from beaten and frayed bamboo are dyed red with the blood of a chicken, dog, goat or pig and hung at the same level as the altar. When all is in readiness, the sorcerer stands before the altar while the village sick in their best garments stand, sit or lie behind him. Calling upon the demons in rapid succession, the sorcerer gives particular emphasis to those who may have caused the illness. He then throws handfuls of rice over the altar, and studies his hand to determine if the spirit of the sick person has returned to him or not. If the sickness is thought to be more serious or threaten the patient's life, it may be necessary to sacrifice a buffalo to the spirits. This sacrifice is accompanied with wine drinking and feasting. Local or itinerant sorcerers are the only persons who may offer sacrifices for various illnesses. The spirits are thought to give permission to sorcerers to prepare and administer medication prepared from certain leaves and roots gathered from the jungles.

Death and Burial: When death visits the Hre, its arrival is announced by the beating of brass gongs so that friends, relatives and even strangers may offer condolences, weep, feast, and drink wine. Funeral customs vary according to geographic location and wealth. Poor families keep the body one day and then bury it while the more wealthy may keep the deceased three or four days before burial. The poor may be able to sacrifice only a pig while the rich may offer six or seven buffalo for sacrifice. [51]

Poor families normally inter their dead, while the richer Hre may utilize above the ground tombs for their deceased. In both instances, the preferred coffin is a hollowed out loang lang tree trunk due to its resistance to decay. Personal effects of the dead are placed over the body and then the top half of the coffin is sealed in place with beeswax and resin. The body is not placed in the coffin until the time of burial. Normally, the burial site will then have a miniature thatched house erected over it, but this falls apart within a few months as it is left unattended. [52]

The Hre, like other Vietnamese peoples, believe the dead continue to exist, but in another form. Thus, the Hre consider the deceased to still own a share of family goods so that approximately one square meter of riceland is allotted to the deceased among lowland Hre. This "spirit-land" must not be entered or cultivated under any circumstances. This having been done, and the property of the deceased distributed among his family with all feasting completed, the grave site is abandoned permanently.

If several members of a highland family die in a short time, the Hre interpret this as an omen that the spirits desire the family to move. If five or more deaths occur in the village during a lunar month, the whole village will be abandoned by the highlanders. The lowland Hre do not abandon their villages, but offer pigs and buffalo sacrifices to appease the spirits.

ECONOMICS

Farming: The Hre economic base is agriculture with rice being their primary crop and basic food. The Hre cannot recall, even by legend, a time when they did not have paddy-fields. The Hre do not have written title deeds for their lands and fields, although tribal tradition of ownership is fully recognized among them. When ownership changes are necessary through death, etc. the matter is settled by the local Hre village council. Generally, the various Hre families cooperate in their irrigation requirements so that the lowland Hre do well in their paddy-fields.

Due to contrasting features of terrain, the lowland Hre irrigate the lowland valleys while the highland Hre still practice swidden or ray, i.e., slash-and-burn, dry-rice cultivation. This procedure involves the selection of a field-site, cutting down all vegetation in the area and after it dries, burning it to clear the land and having the ashes serve as a natural fertilizer for three or four years. When the soil no longer produces well, the field is allowed to return to jungle with other sites being cleared for farming.

The lowland Hre cultivate wet rice by the aid of primitive irrigation. With a keen appreciation of rice qualities, the Hre seek seed suitable for climatic conditions, water supply and the particular soil so that seldom do they have a complete crop failure. Moreover, many plant two rice crops annually. Mua, the important seasonal crop, is planted in August and September. Mua rice is exclusively used to make rice wine, rice cakes and in sacrificial rites. Moreover, it may not be cooked or eaten after its harvest until all the members of the family are present. Chiem rice is the second crop and is planted in March and April since typhoons in October and November require that crops be harvested by late summer. Chiem may be eaten immediately after harvest but must never be stored, mixed with or cooked with Mua rice.[54]

With farming techiques adopted from the Cham, the Hre use oxen and buffalo to plow and harrow their fields, with buffalo dung as natural fertilizer. When the rice seedlings are one to two months old, they are transplanted from the seed beds to the prepared paddy-fields. Three to six months later the rice is harvested by hand-sickle. After being carried home, it may be threshed by buffaloes treading it or by simply storing it until the grains loosen and fall from the stems. If the latter occurs, the rice may be black by the time it is cooked after being husked by a heavy wooden pestle in a tree trunk mortar.

Highland Hre grow dry-rice with one crop per year and harvest it much as do their lowland kinsmen. In addition to rice, both groups of Hre grow cotton, beans, corn, red peppers, cabbage, pumpkins, cucumbers, tomatoes, gourds and manioc. Manoic, also known as cassava, is a tropical plant which grows either wild or cultivated, and has edible starchy roots which may be used as bread or for the making of tapioca, or baked like a potatoe.

The Hre often sell green cocoanuts inasmuch as they have not adopted the Vietnamese procedures for handling the dried fruit. They also grow, gather and sell tea to the Vietnamese, along with such cash crops as broomstraw, hemp, cinnamon, tobacco and ramie. Ramie is an asiatic plant with heart-shaped flowers having many rod-like fibers which can be used for making a fine cloth.

Forest Products: The ever present jungles with their various tropical fruit trees, provide the Hre with additional forest products for food, trade or sale. Cinnamon trees near Tra Bong have commercial value as does the clear white honey of the Ba To area which is prized for its unadulterated unprocessed natural sweetness.[55]

Scented leaves, bamboo shoots, bulbs, wild vegetables and mushrooms are products of the forest also. Wild game provides food and items of trade as the Vietnamese prize, as aphrodisiacs, both tiger bones and deer antlers. Fish, crabs, snails, etc., all contribute to the Hre larder to the extent that war conditions permit the exploitation of the forests and jungles.

Domestic Animals: The Hre raise water buffaloes for plowing and for sacrifices. Some goats, oxen and pigs are raised. Normally, animals are utilized as food only after being sacrificed to the spirits. Chickens are a natural part of almost every Hre village.

Arts and Crafts: The Hre use bamboo, rattan, palm leaves and wood to make recepticals, traps, walls, matting, weapons, pipes, tobacco, salt and water containers. Almost every Hre village does some basket weaving in spite of the belief that the Hre are not skilled in craft work. Moreover, Hre women, using looms, weave coarse cloth of ramie, cotton or with fiber from outside the tribal area.

Commerce and Trade: The Hre use the barter system as their primary method of commercial transaction except when dealing with the Cham. Gems, silver and gold to the Hre are for ornaments and not for currency. Often Hre prices are fixed in terms of gongs, jars, copper pots, buffaloes or other common items.[56]

In spite of often receiving a lower price the Hre seem to trust the Cham and prefer trading with them. In their long time bartering with the Cham, the Hre have acquired copper pots which have become family heirlooms. These along with precious jars and gongs passed from parent to child inasmuch as only the direst circumstances will force a Hre to dispose of their family heirlooms. Particularly is this true since antique jars may cost as much as would twenty water buffaloes. These treasures are usually hidden outside of the home, and often are carefully and secretly buried in order to protect them from breakage, fire or theft.

The Hre dispose of beeswax, honey, ivory, cinnamon, bark, deer, antlers, cocoanuts, rattan, tobacco, betel, tea, paddy, hemp, broomstraw, and other forest products in trade. In exchange they acquire salt, pigs, dogs, dried fish, copper pots and jars, agricultural tools, iron for weapons, cotton and silk cloth, etc. Normally, barter arrangements are completed upon the advice of the ca ra who is the richest and most influential man of the village. Often, bargaining agreements are sealed by the invitation to the elders to drink wine. Written papers are not necessary to make a binding arrangement. [57]

DEFENSE

The crossbow is the favorite weapon of those Hre who do not have firearms. Their favorite version is one which has a stock shaped much like the handgrip of a pistol. This may be cocked by standing on one foot while using the knee of the free leg to strain the bow in order to place the string behind the trigger. This crossbow is in contrast to the rifle stockbutt which some tribes, including the Lisu near the Chinese border, use. The latter crossbow, like the straight stick bow, may be cocked by placing the butt against the stomach and pulling the string back to the trigger. To "fire" any of the bows, aim is taken along the cross of the bow.

Like other tribes within Vietnam, the Hre use spears also. Their version is five or six feet in length rather than the longer seven to eight foot spears preferred by some of the highland dwelling peoples. Moreover, the Hre spear point may be shaped more like a bayonet blade than the two edged sharp pointed tip spear of most tribes. The spear is shaped and sharpened so that the tribesman can thrust it completely through the body of the sacrificial buffalo in one swift motion after the buffalo has first received a knife cut with the sacred knife which is used only for such rituals.

In order to increase the effectiveness of their traditional weapons, arrows, spears, punji stakes, etc. the Hre have a variety of poisons which may be used against man or beast. These poisons may be secured from other tribes such as the Bahnar of Kontum or produced within the Hre tribal area. Within the Hre area, the Ba To region is known for the preparation and use of poisons. These poisons may be used on the various instruments to enhance their effectiveness, or may be placed in food and water. Friendly Hre relate that sometimes an individual may poison his enemy's well, or that one village may destroy another through secretly poisoning their water source provided that it is not a stream or other body of flowing water.

Some of the animistic Hre believe that evil spirits live in poisons so that the tribesmen must perform certain rites of placation. This includes the offering of the blood of a white rooster on a moonlit night at least once a year. The Hre believe that if this ritual is not performed, the evil spirits will turn on members of any household possessing poison. Some also believe that the greater the number of deaths by poison, the more content the evil spirits become. Moreover, the tribesmen believe that if poison is stored within a household the children will be weaker than normal, stunted, bloated or be jaundiced.[58]

Perhaps the most deadly Hre poison is the yellowish grey powdered do, which has such a nauseating odor that it must be stored in tightly sealed containers. This particular poison is obtained from the Bahnar and is sufficiently potent that a few grains sprinkled in food or drink will kill a man when he eats or drinks it. Depending upon the amount of do used, death may take a few hours or a week. In the longer period, the victim suffers with severe stomach cramps, vomiting, foaming at the mouth, passing blood, and prior to death develops a bluish color. When used in a liquid form, do causes very similar symptoms while the victim may live ten days or longer. At the present time, there is no known antidote for either form of do.

A second poison frequently used by the Hre is fatal if it touches an open sore or wound. There is no known antidote for this poison which is always fatal, yet the flesh of animals killed by its use is safe for human consumption.[59] This particular poison is prepared by mixing and cooking resin from the cam tree (which resembles the wild persimmon tree) with red pepper, serpent teeth (rang ran) and centipede teeth (rang ret) over a hot flame. Cooking continues until the concoction has a shiny black thick ointmentlike quality. It is tested by placing a small drop about one inch away from a fresh cut on the tribesman's arm or hand. If the flow of blood stops, the poison is strong enough to kill elephants, tigers or man. Arrow points, spears and punji stakes or sticks are dipped into the mixture and then allowed to dry. Apparently this poison has curarelike substances in it since it causes a very rapid respiratory paralysis. The tribesmen declare that the poison will kill a man within a few steps, a tiger within a few meters while an elephant may live to move a kilometer. [60] This poison may also be used in still water to kill fish which may then be used as food. Incidently, the use of natural jungle poisions to gather fish is a common practice in may jungle areas of the world.

The Hre also utilize a third poison. This poison is called rin. Normally, it is secretly grown and resembles ginger or saffron. Its leaves are picked, dried and finally crumpled. When the tribesman is to be away for sometime, he may take the finely crushed material and sprinkles it on whatever he wishes to protect during his absence. This may be his garden, fruit trees or his household items. Should anyone come in contact with this fine powder, by touch or in handling the items, the symptoms are loss of appetite, severe pains, yellow skin, swollen legs and arms, eyes swollen shut with a red enflamed face. Internal symptoms include the urine becoming a definite brownish color, the passing of blood and if the skin is scratched, the lymph is yellow and foul in odor.

This poison, rin, has an antidote. The application of a special leaf from the jungle on the affected areas aids a gradual cure to take place. [61] Since the Hre believe that ivory chopsticks placed in poisoned food will cause it to start boiling, the offer of ivory chopsticks to a guest is a sign of sincerity. [62] If the foreigner eats only what his host eats, there is little danger of being deliberately poisoned through food or drink. Moreover, the tribespeople do not normally desire to feed a foreigner to kill him so that there needs to be little anxiety as to this being a source of danger. Instead, the tribesman's offer to share his food may be accepted as a clear indication that he has accepted you for otherwise this privilege is not extended lightly.

RELIGION

The Hre have a complex religious/spiritual life filled with deities, spirits, taboos and rituals even though they lack a "theology" as understood in the West. The supernatural good or evil spirits dwell in objects of the physical world, in animals and in man, be they living or dead. These supernatural forces are everpresent, creating constant threats so that rites of placation, appeasment and supplication are believed to be essential. Only by performing

226

these rituals does the Hre feel that he can meet and overcome the problems of daily life. His beliefs of the supernatural are expressed in formal rituals and in daily life routine.

The religious beliefs of the animistic Hre form an attempt to meaningfully relate to the world about them. This essential requirement is often sought through religio-magical behavior which may allow the tribesman to "control" his world. These beliefs and practices help the Hre to meet those critical life events such as the danger of tigers, deadly snakes, etc. without a disintegration of personality in a hostile environment where other aids are unknown or beyond one's reach. While animistic beliefs and practices are non-ethical and non-moral, they are binding upon those who know no better way of life.

The Hre have several types of spirits. These include the spirits of ancestors, "bien", earth spirits, "trau" and heavenly spirits, "vya". Additionally, the hearth spirits, "vay vna", fire spirits, "vya un", mountain spirits, "vya vang", water spirits, "vya diak"; and evil spirits or demons, "kiet choc", are ever present. [63] Evil or displeased spirits are believed to be responsible for sickness, death, droughts and other complications of life,

Although the Hre believe in the presence of both good and evil spirits, only the ba giau, sorcerer, can act as the intemediary between man and the spirits as the latter are dangerous. Only the sorcerer can determine the spirits that may be involved in a particular situation. The ba giau knows the times of sacrificial days, festivals and appropriate rituals believed to be necessary. He therefore, is the central figure as he presides over and generally conducts all ceremonies related to the spirit world.

The ba giau is believed to have many essential faculties vital for every day life among the Hre. He can read and interpret evil omens, "bo rinh", which require sacrifices. These omens may include occurrences such as someone bumping into a tribesman carrying charred firewood, lightning striking a house or some other obstacle within the yard, a rat gnawing on cloth, birds flying into and within a house, or any other event which may seem strange to the tribesman. [64] The ba giau can also foretell sickness, life, death and other future events so that he is a very important personality to most Hre. Nevertheless, the respect which the tribesmen render the sorcerer is dependent upon his successes in healing and prediction.

In order to determine which spirit is causing a particular illness, the Hre may cut off the feet of a chicken and place them in boiling water. Then the ba giau "reads" them in order to know just "who" is causing the sickness. This also helps to determine the appropriate sacrifice. [65]

The buffalo sacrifice, "ta reo po", is the principal community sacrifice among the Hre as the buffalo may represent any spirit. [66] Its importance is shown by the ba giau choosing the exact location for the sacrificial post. When he has done this, each of the community elders take turns removing one spadeful of dirt after which the young men of the village complete the task. The digging of the hole for the sacrifice posts and placing the post requires an odd number of men assist the ba giau. When the sacrifice is for a petition, "ta reo po", or for general thanksgiving, "cham gieng", a tall center post bracketed by two smaller ones is used. When the rituals are for expressing gratitude for the recovery of health or for a blood pledge of friendship, the central post is bracketed by four smaller posts. The posts are often beautifully carved for the Hre by Vietnamese artists while the wood cross arms of red and black Hre designs is of Hre workmanship. [67]

Prior to actually slaying the buffalo, one or more pigs are killed as a part of the rite. If there is an insufficient number of pigs available, chickens and geese may be added. Any uneaten portions of the sacrifices are carefully left at the site so that hungry demons will not follow the participants to their homes. The blood of the sacrifices is dubbed on the sacrificial posts, perhaps on the sick, other appropriate places, and on bamboo chop sticks as a symbolic invitation to the spirits to join in the feast in their honor. Blood may also be mixed with rice wine and then poured over the sacred gongs.

Before planting a new crop and prior to harvesting it, blood sacrifices are offered in the rice field or paddy. The site of this ritual is at the place where water enters the paddy field or near the entrance of the dry-rice fields. In a very small plot of ground, a pig is sacrificed with some grain of the previous harvest of the sacred plot. When the sacred grain has sprouted in this plot, then the rest of the field or paddy is planted. At harvest time, another sacrifice is made in the same plot, and the grain of the sacred ground harvested. Then the balance of the grain is gathered in a regular harvest. After all the grain has been brought to the village a thanksgiving sacrifice may be made also.

Candles made of beeswax and betel, "ghinh gu", are essential items for Hre sacrifices. For a chicken sacrifice, one candle is used; two are used for a pig and seven to ten for the buffalo. These candles are normally placed on a small woven bamboo ceremonial table about one square foot in size. Also on the table is a small jar which symbolizes the wind which either helps or hurts the Hre in its seasonal movement. [68]

Other sacred items utilized for Hre rituals and ceremonies include the sacred hearth, "mnu uan t'teo", the sacred mortar and the sacred sack of salt. The sacred hearth is believed to be the dwelling place of the hearth or fire spirit or god. The sacred hearthstone, "mo pan renh", forms the front part of the hearth, and should it be touched by anyone except the man of the house, a pig sacrifice is urgently in order to placate the anger of the fire spirit and to prevent diseases or other tragedies from striking the family. Even the house owner may touch the sacred hearthstone for religious purposes only. This hearth can be used only for the preparation of ritual food even as only the man, his wife (and if he has more than one, only the first one) and their small children can sleep in this room. [69]

The sacred salt bag which may weigh anywhere from three to fifteen pounds hangs over the sacred hearth. Salt from this bag may be used only for ritual foods and under no circumstances can it be used for ordinary use.

The room with the sacred hearth contains the sacred mortar which is carved from a tree trunk. In the corner near the hearth may be found stored the pots and pans which can be used only for sacred foods. To use them for any other purpose would be a challenge too great for mortal Hre to risk.

In front of the hearth and to its right is found the, "de reng-kia", sacred sacrificial post. Attached to this post is a small bamboo tray which serves as the site where small family sacrifices are placed. Near this post is where the man and his wife store their personal property also. When either of them die, their personal property is buried with them or placed on their grave for use by their spirits. [70]

These graves are perhaps the most sacred place to the Hre. Yet because of the fear of offending the spirits, graves are generally taboo so that the Hre do not have much to do with a grave once the funeral has taken place. It is wise for Americans to avoid Hre grave sites when possible so that needless fear, anxiety and consequent resentment will not be created.

Most of the Hre are animists. However, some three thousand or more have been definitely influenced by the Christian teachings of the Worldwide Evangelism Crusade with Vietnam headquarters in Danang. The medical work of this Protestant organization has aided it to win acceptance among this tribal people to a remarkable degree. The Cao Dai have adherents among the Hre also, but to a lesser degree than do the Protestants.

GUIDELINES FOR UNDERSTANDING

The Hre celebrate the New Year with a festival that may last for several weeks. The Hre gather from far and wide to visit, eat, drink, sing and rejoice with one another. The various families of the community take turns in being hosts for relatives and friends. A special feature of this festival are the rice cakes. These rice cakes, wrapped in special leaves, are especially prepared to be eaten at this time by each Hre. Before eating their individual rice cakes, the leaves are removed to be later tied to the roof of the house above the main floor. Since each individual has his or her own place to tie the leaves, it is possible to know the times that each individual has celebrated the New Year by simply counting the leaves in a collection.

The Hre often sit about the evening fire and tell stories. Most of these stories are of the spirits and the reasons for some of the Hre taboos. Typical of their folklore is the story of the Cha

<u>Rap</u>. <u>Cha Rap</u> is an erect manlike spirit-animal who is covered with monkey-hair with feet that are turned with the toes to the rear. Eating only tender bamboo shoots and living in dense forests or on the highest mountains, the Chap Rap is rarely seen. The Hre think that meeting the Cha Rap will bring death as it tries to decapitate its victims with knifelike arms. Children are therefore cautioned to travel in groups as it seems that several voices shouting at the same time confuses the Cha Rap and allows victims to escape. While the Cha Rap cannot speak, it does understand human voices. Thus, if in meeting the Cha Rap, one quickly shouts "dam, dam, dam", (stab, stab, stab), the animal becomes confused and gives opportunity for one to escape. However, if one in excitement shouts "chem, chem", the spirit responds by immediately cutting off the victim's head. [71]

Another of the frightening tales of the Hre is that of the <u>diam dia</u> which is a spirit-animal resembling a tiger. When it sees a human being, it is said to sit down, remove skin from its chest and begin to eat it. If one sees this and remains quiet he is safe. However, if someone cries out, "Heavens. What a horrible sight!", the diam dia jumps on its victim and kills him. [72] A third story helps to explain Hre prohibitions against certain taboo foods. In this instance, in olden times, a Hre caught an eel which he ate. Soon thereafter disaster struck his village so that it completely disappeared. Because the Hre still fear a similar fate if they eat eels, the eel is taboo. [73]

In contrast to some tribal groups where toddlers seem to start smoking while still nursing, the Hre appear to prefer betel chewing to the use of tobacco. Moreover, the Hre give betel chewing a functional value in that distance may be measured in the number of betel chews required to cover a fixed distance - at the normal rate of "one chew" per half hour.

Generally, the Hre rise early, work their fields until noon, take a siesta, then work until dusk and go to bed soon after darkness comes. Normally, their two meals a day does not include an early breakfast. Hre food is often served in baskets, containers or large leaves placed on the floor. The hands are normally the instruments used to eat with since knives, forks, etc. are not yet common. However, some of the richer Hre may use bowls, copper trays and chopsticks.

The basic Hre food is rice. This is supplemented with manioc, yams, vegtables, corn, bulbs of the forest, etc. Green foods may be gourds, pumpkins, or herbs of the forest. But the Hre seldom use leafy greens, wild mustard, bindweed known as "ren", or wild lettuce. Hre bindweed is a member of the Morning Glory family, which, when properly prepared, can be a tasty dish.

Although chicken and pork are normally only for New Years and feast days, fish and other meats are used when available. Frogs, crayfish, snails and crabs may be prepared by roasting, boiling, salting, drying or cooking with bamboo shoots. Sometimes these items are placed in a container and allowed to decay into a gummy mixture and then served as food. Only those Americans with strong will power and "cast-iron" stomachs can face such a Hre dish without flinching.

These Hre foods may be consumed with either water or rice wine as drink. Tea is rather expensive in the Hre area so that only the wealthy Hre can use it from time to time. Ca ro, rice wine, is important to the Hre as almost all Hre men and women drink it. Normally, the rice of the first harvest is used for making wine, but if this crop is poor or fails, substitutes are used. These may be the roots of the forest, green beans, manoic or corn. The alcoholic content of Hre wine is low since fermentation lasts only four or five days and there is no distillation. The fermentating process is speeded up by the use of a special root of the forest of the thao genus of the ground vine that is called ko xi blo. Because the preparation of fermentation cakes is believed to be degrading, only the poorest Hre make the cakes for sale. The cake is prepared by scraping, then drying and grounding the outer bark of the ko xi blo root, mixing this powder with ginger and ground rice powder to form an egg-sized cake. To start the fermentation process, one fourth bushel of rice, one-half of a fermentation cake are put in a large earthen-ware jug with enough water to well cover the rice. Then on top of this, banana leaves are placed to keep out the dirt and protect the wine.

Hre wine drinking is quite an elaborate custom. Four to five feet straws or bamboo tubes are normally utilized after these have been prepared by having the pith removed and several additional holes cut in the lower end. Drinking starts after the host symbol-ically offers wine to the spirits by dipping a straw of his house-roof into the wine. The drinking tube must always be extended to the guest with the right hand after the host is sure the end of the tube is in the wine as offering the wrong end of the tube to a guest would be a very discourteous act.

When all have been given drinking straws, the host and his wife place their index finger on the jar and say together, "May this wine give you good health.". Then they sip from their straws and those of their guests and spit the liquid on the floor to show that the tube is unobstructed and that the wine is not poisoned. The guests are expected to spit their first sip on the floor of the porch also. Often the heathen Hre, in good faith, like to see how much wine their honored guests can drink before reaching the absolute limit. This may even include inviting the guest to start drinking, and then the host begins to carefully pour water into the jar to keep it full. Unless the guest keeps drinking rapidly, the jar will overflow. However, for those who do not drink, it is sufficient to say that it is taboo for you, and no pressure will be exerted to force you to violate a taboo. [74]

Because the Hre accept the American's word at face value, never attempt to deceive him. Never make promises which you cannot keep. Practice caution in all commitments as these bind you and your successors in the eyes of the Hre. Be prepared to bargain long and hard for the cost of labor, services or products, but having reached an agreement, live up to it and do your best to see that others do likewise.

The Hre prefer to be buried in the area of their home village if possible. If deceased Hre cannot be returned to such places due to the unsettled conditions, burial next to another Hre village is a satisfactory substitute. The Hre are practical people and practical considerations are valid for them. Seldom will the foreigner find a Hre making impossible requests of him.

It is well to remember that Hre villagers are aware of the emotional and political status of their fellow villagers. However, the absence of a common language with the foreigner often precludes sharing one's knowledge since the tribesmen often distrust the ability and motives of translators who are not of their own people. This is a common trait of all peoples who have suffered from time to time because of such media.

The Hre seem to feel inferior to the Vietnamese. Thus, they
appear to resent any tribesman who seeks to emulate or copy
Vietnamese clothing, customs or speech. Often such tribesmen
are objects of ridicule, scorn and distain. Moreover, the history
of past unpleasantries between the Hre and ethnic Vietnamese often
creates barriers hindering effective utilization of Hre abilities in
the current conflict. Consequently, some Hre are reluctant to
fully confide valuable information or emotions when non-tribesmen
serve as translators.

The Hre, like most primitive people, are basically honest.
They appear to be highly affronted by either dishonesty or thievery.
If the American gives his word, it is anticipated that he will live
up to his statement or promise. Therefore, never make promises
which cannot be fulfilled regardless of difficulties. For once you
fail in your word, the tribesman will not readily trust you again.
Likewise, make sure that all Hre souvenirs are either freely offered
gifts or are purchased through mutually agreed prices or barter.
Numerous difficulties can be avoided through the establishment of
trading centers with fixed prices which have been agreed upon by
the Hre village chief and the military commander.

This ethnic group has the ability to maintain their grudges
for long periods of time. Circumstances may force the Hre to bide
their time for revenge, but redress of grievances and wrongs will
undoubtedly be attempted through direct or indirect means. Only
thus do many feel that they can maintain their honor.

Americans who serve among the Hre consider them to be
good workers. They seem to work steadily and cheerfully at their
assigned tasks and do not require constant attention or supervision.
Their life, similar to other subsistence societies, is simple,
slow-moving and almost casually deliberate. Their feasts and
ceremonies are the bright events of an otherwise almost monoto-
nous existence.

It is wise to always strive to win the friendship and cooperation of the village chief. Through private conversation, persuasion

and planning conferences, teamwork can be achieved that will permit public praise to him and his people.

After all, the basic goal of our attempts to help these folk is to make our presence no longer a requirement. Therefore, remember that the opportunities for success in even the most limited of projects are most abundant when the "felt" needs of the people are considered and utilized. Effective changes in tribal existence must be predicated upon such short range goals that the people can recognize and gain tangible benefits within longer time concepts and goals.

Among the Hre, it is a mark of respect to refer to an older tribesman as dooc, (old). Likewise, when leaving a Hre, one does not just walk away. Instead, it is good Hre manners to say "Khae le a-lem", "Goodbye, I am going".

The Hre have a certain stone which they collect from the forest that they believe will cause bleeding wounds to heal. To achieve this, the stone is dipped in water and rubbed over the wound.[75] It is appropriate to note that the Hre seem to have considerable stoicism when it comes to bearing pain. However, they will attempt to avoid any action or activities which may offend the spirits who cause pain, injuries and death.

Among the Hre customs which foreigners can note with benefit are: (1) side doors in Hre houses are for members of the family only; (2) never enter a Hre home without being accompanied by a member of the family as this is both good taste and wisdom to avoid misunderstandings about women or property; (3) guests usually remove their shoes and leave them near the entrance-way, before seating themselves on mats; (4) guests are usually received and entertained on the Hre front porch; (5) when the house is taboo for some reason, green branches will be on or over the door and even the family must use the side door rather than the front one; (6) when presenting anything to a Hre with one hand, use the right one as it is more honorable than the left as anything offered with the left hand may be considered an insult or rude; (7) obtain permission if you desire to attend Hre ceremonies and religious rites; (8) act with discretion, common sense, appreciation of cultural differences and a value of people even though quite different from yourself, and you can be accepted with grace and friendliness.

Courtesy requires that nothing ever be used or taken from the Hre community without permission. Damage to fields, houses or people should be settled as rapidly and directly as humanly possible to reduce anxiety, fear, resentment or hostility and financial loss. Pause long enough in dealing with the Hre to realize that this primitive society is being thrust into the twentieth century so rapidly that it is undergoing a bewildering transition. The many things that we Americans take for granted are to the Hre as mysterious miracles.

The Hre are just as human as are the Americans. Their basic needs are the same as all other human beings. However, a different belief system has created cultural patterns that create behavior systems radically different to those which most Americans take for granted. But in spite of graphic differences, awareness, understanding and appreciation of the Hre as human beings can create a valid basis for positive action. Such can aid the Hre to also have hope in a better tomorrow, and for him this would not take much.

FOOTNOTES

1. Summer Institute of Linguistics, Vietnam Minority Languages List, July 1966, "Hre"; U.S. Army Special Warfare School, Montagnard Tribal Groups of the Republic of Vietnam, Fort Bragg, N.C., (Second Edition, March 1965), p. 67.

2. David Thomas, "Mon-khmer Subgroupings in Vietnam", (University of North Dakota: Summer Institute of Linguistics, 1962, p. 4; Summer Institute of Linguistics, "Vietnam Minority Languages", "Hre".)

3. Bui Dinh, "Customs and Habits of the Hre Tribes", (JPRS: R-2341-D, translated from the Vietnamese, Phong-tuc-Tap-quan Nguoi Hre: Ba-to-quang-ngai, by the Joint Publication Research Service, 1956), p. 3.

4. Stuart Harverson, "The Hre Tribe", Navy Personal Response Tape, #31, p. 2; C. Trinquet, "Essai de vocabulaire francasise", Revue Indo-chinoise, (July-December, 1912), p. 309.

5. Harverson, op. cit.

6. Mole, 1965-66 Fieldnotes of research for the Navy Personal Response; also Bui Dinh, op. cit., p. 3

7. Bui Dinh, op. cit., p. 3; Frank LeBar, et al, Ethnic Groups of Mainland Southeast Asia, New Haven, Human Relations Area Files Press, 1964, p. 140.

8. Stuart Harverson, Hre Tape of February 1966 for R.L. MOLE, research for Navy Personal Response, p. 1; Laura Smith, Victory in Vietnam, Grand Rapids, Michigan, Zondervan Publishing House, 1965, p. 47; U.S. Information Service, Montagnards of the South Vietnam Highlands, Saigon, USIS, July, 1962, p. 18.

9. Mole, 1965-66 Fieldnotes; U.S. Army, "Montagnard Groups" p. 67.

10. H.I. Philips, "Creation Story", (Unpublished research paper, pp. 1-3.), cited by U.S. Army, Pamphlet No. 550-105, Ethnographic Study Series, Minority Groups in the Republic of Vietnam, 1966, p. 165.

11. Harverson, "The Hre Tribe", p. 2, of Navy Personal Response Tape, #31.

12. Bui Dinh, op. cit., p. 35

13. Rene Riesen, Jungle Missions, translated by James Oliver, New York; Thomas Y. Crowell Co., 1957, pp. 22-23.

14. U.S Army, Montagnard Groups of South Vietnam, p. 72.

15. Harverson, Hre Tribe Tape, #31, 14 March 1965, p. 1.

16. Ibid.

17. U.S. Army, Montagnard Groups; Mole, 1965-66 Fieldnotes.

18. Bui Dinh, op. cit., p. 27.

19. Riesen, op. cit., pp. 154-163; Mole, 1965-66 Fieldnotes.

20. Riesen, op. cit., pp. 154-163.

21. Mole, 1965-66 Fieldnotes.

22. Bui Dinh, op. cit., p. 3; Harverson, Hre Tape, #31, p. 1.

23. Harverson, Hre Tape of February 1966.

24. Confer section on "Hre History" of this chapter

25. Bui Dinh, op. cit., p. 5; also Harverson, "Hre Tapes"; Mole, 1965-66 Fieldnotes.

26. Bui Dinh, op. cit., p. 3.

27. Bui Dinh, op. cit., p.19; Harverson, "Hre Tape of February 1966".

28. Laura I. Smith, Victory in Vietnam, p.53; Bui Dinh, op. cit.,
    pp.8-15; Harverson, "Hre Tape, #31 of March 1965."

29. Smith, op. cit., p.53.

30. Bui Dinh, op. cit., p.16.

31. Mole, Fieldnotes.

32. Harverson Hre Tape, #31.

33. Mole, 1965-66 Fieldnotes; also Harverson, Hre Tape, #31.

34. Harverson, Hre Tape, #31.

35. H. Haquet, "Notice ethnique sur les moi de la region de Quong
    Ngai", Revue Indochinoise, (July-December), p.1419; Rene
    Riesen, Jungle Missions, translated by James Oliver, (New York;
    Thomas Y. Crowell Co., 1957), pp.158-163.

36. Riesen, op. cit., p.154-163.

37. Bui Dinh, "Customs and Habits of the Hre Tribes", (JPRS-R
    2341-D, A translation of a Vietnamese language publication,
    Phong-tuc-tap-quon, Nguoi Hre: Ba-to quang-nqai), (Washington
    D.C. Joint Publication Research Service, 1956), p.23.

38. Gerald C. Hickey, "Comments or Recent GVN Legislation
    Concerning Montagnard Common Law Courts in the Central
    Vietnamese Highlands", (Santa Monica: The Rand Corporation
    Memorandum, June 8, 1965), pp.1-2.

39. Bui Dinh, op. cit., p.22.

40. Riesen, op. cit., p.52.

41. Riesen, op. cit., pp.64-65; Mole, 1965-66 Fieldnotes.

42. Haquet, op. cit., pp. 14-24.

43. Bui Dinh, op. cit., p. 27.

44. Mole, 1965-66 Fieldnotes.

45. Riesen, op. cit., p. 87; Mole, 1965-66 Fieldnotes.

46. Bui Dinh, op. cit., p. 26; Montagnard Tribal Groups, pp. 69-70; Mole, 1965-66 Fieldnotes.

47. Bui Dinh, op. cit., p. 26.

48. Bui Dinh, op. cit., pp. 22-23.

49. Bui Dinh, op. cit., pp. 26-27.

50. Mole, 1965-66 Fieldnotes.

51. Bui Dinh, op. cit., pp. 26-27; Mole, 1965-66 Fieldnotes.

52. Bui Dinh, op. cit., p. 28.

53. Ibid; Mole, 1965-66 Fieldnotes.

54. Bui Dinh, op. cit., p. 31; Mole, 1965-66 Fieldnotes.

55. Mole, 1965-66 Fieldnotes, Bui Dinh, op. cit., pp. 4-10.

56. Bui Dinh, op. cit., p. 15.

57. Bui Dinh, op. cit., p. 121; Mole, 1965-66 Fieldnotes.

58. Bui Dinh, op. cit., pp. 20-21; Mole, 1965-66 Fieldnotes; Harverson, "Hre Tape, #31, p. 5."

59. Bui Dinh, op. cit., pp. 19-22; Mole, 1965-66 Fieldnotes; Harverson, "Hre Tape, #31. p. 5."

60. Mole, <u>1965-66 Fieldnotes</u>; Harverson, "Hre Tape, #31, p.5."

61. Mole, <u>1965-66 Fieldnotes;</u> Bu Dinh, <u>op. cit.</u>, pp.19-22.

62. Bui Dinh, <u>op. cit.</u>, p.19.

63. Bui Dinh, <u>op. cit.</u>, p.30.

64. Bui Dinh, p.29; Mole, <u>1965-66 Fieldnotes</u>.

65. Bui Dinh, <u>op. cit.</u>, p.29.

66. Harverson, "Hre Tape, #31" of the Navy Personal Response files.

67. , Bui Dinh, <u>op. cit.</u>, p.8.

68. <u>Ibid</u>, pp.26-27.

69. <u>Ibid</u>, pp.16-17; Mole, <u>1965-66 Fieldnotes</u>.

70. Bui Dinh, <u>op. cit.</u>, p.16.

71. <u>Ibid</u>, p.33.

72. <u>Ibid</u>, p.34.

73. <u>Ibid</u>, p.33.

74. Mole, <u>1965-66 and 1967-68 Fieldnotes</u>; confer also U.S. Army Special Forces, <u>Montagnard Tribal Groups in Vietnam</u>, Fort Bragg, North Carolina, (Second Edition), pp.77-79.

75. Bui Dinh, <u>op. cit.</u>, p.33.

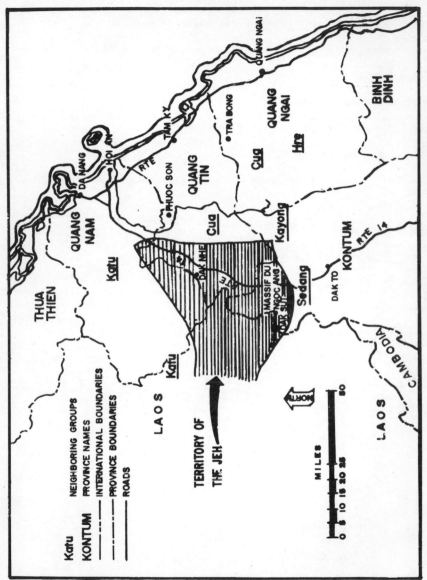

THE JEH MAP FROM/CRESS/CINFAC R-0426.

CHAPTER VIII

THE JEH

Several names have been given to this ethnic group: Die, Yeh, Dram, Langya, Brilar and Jeh Derale are names which are sometimes used to identify the Jeh tribe or particular portions of it. Being one of the more isolated and primitive tribal groups, an understanding of the Jeh is essential for those who serve in their territory or have either military or civilian activities among them. Also, pertinent information about the Jeh may have significant value to various religious and philanthropic organizations in their desires to assist this ethnic group to best adjust to the twentieth century.

Language: The Jeh are considered to be a part of the Bahnaric subgroup of the Mon-Khmer.[1] Incidentally, language is the major means used to classify the highland ethnic groups. While the various Jeh groups seem to have three or four different dialects, all are sufficiently related to be understood by their fellow tribesmen and by a few of the Vietnamese who dwell among them. A few Jeh men speak Vietnamese. Those who cross the Laotian border frequently also speak some Laotian. Because of the proximity of the Sedang, the size of this larger tribe and the fact that Sedang territory must be crossed by the Jeh to reach the city of Kontum, Sedang is a prestige language for the Jeh.[2] A few Jeh understand some French as they may have attended French mission schools, served in French led military units, or worked with the French a sufficient period of time to communicate with them.

The spoken language of the Jeh is currently in the process of being developed into a written one. This very difficult task is under the direction of the Summer Institute of Linguistics, Saigon. The Vietnamese Ministry of Education is also interested in this project and provides encouragement and support from time to time. However, it must be remembered that it requires time, effort and persistence for a language that is merely spoken to be accurately developed into written form. It also requires time and facilities so that sufficient study can permit those who speak Jeh to read and write it also. The difficult conditions under which this gigantic task must be accomplished is merely another condition which must be met and mastered if the Jeh are to ever take their rightful place in the society of all Vietnamese citizens.

Population Estimates: The estimate of the number of Jeh, as for all the Montagnards, is merely an educated guess. Guesses by various authorities vary from six to eighteen thousand people. [4] When peace again becomes a fact in Vietnam, a census will be feasible. Until then, the conflict combined with geography and psychological fears of the Jeh will effectively prevent an accurate count.

Location: The Jeh tribal area is located in both I and II Corps of South Vietnam besides crossing the Vietnamese-Laotian borders into Laos. In South Vietnam, the Jeh are located in the three provinces of southern Quang Nam, western Quang Tin and northwest Kontum. An imaginary line drawn from the city of Quang Ngai on the South China Sea almost due west through the town of Dak Sut and across the border of Laos would mark the approximate southern border of the Jeh. This means the Jeh tribal area starts about sixty miles north of the city of Kontum. The Jeh's northern border reaches to the Katu southern border. The northern-most point of the Jeh is perhaps some twenty miles north of Dak Nhe, but the greater portion of the tribal area would be within the southern border line and one drawn almost due west from Tam Ky. The eastern limits of the Jeh seems to be the Dak Polo River which is just east of National Highway #14. The Jeh area extends into Laos to the eastern edge of the Bolovens Plateau. Thus, the basins of the Poko, Se Kamane and the Dak Main in the narrow long strip within Vietnam and Southern Laos form the home of the Jeh. [5]

Neighbors: The Jeh have various Laotian tribespeople around their tribal area in Laos. Within South Vietnam the Srieng are to the northwest, the Katu on the north, the Cua and the Duan in the east and the Sedang on their southern tribal border. The Duan have not been fully classified or closely studied so that they are still a mystery inasfar as detailed knowledge about them is simply not yet known.

The Jeh have trade relations with some of the Laotian peoples;

little, if any, with the Katu, and only infrequently with the Cua. By geographical location creating the necessity of crossing Sedang territory frequently, Jeh relations with the Sedang are good. This relationship is best symbolized by the prestige granted by the Jeh to one of their tribesman who speaks Sedang fluently. [7]

History: The Jeh have legends of their tribal origin, about spirits, and their tribal heroes. They also have proverbs, tribal laws and anecdotes. The Jeh use verse as the best means of transmission for these are all related by memory. Recitations may be parts of religious ceremonies as invocations or when gathered about the family hearth as entertainment and for instructional purposes.

Little is known of the actual history of the Jeh. What little is known is indicative of a weak people being forced deeper and deeper into the remote hinterlands by stronger tribes and other ethnic groups. At one time oppression by the Sedang was so severe, that the Jeh almost became extinct people. Their way of life disintegrated to the extent that longhouses were discarded about 1850, and they moved even deeper into the inhospitable mountains they now call home.

When French administrators finally reached the Jeh area about 1927, the Jeh fearing them to be allies of the Sedang, fought them for almost ten years. But as the French pacified the area, the Jeh began to recover as a people; to rebuild their long houses, to plant fields, produce articles for trade, etc. Some of the Jeh helped to build National Highway #14 through the tribal area. They would accept only salt or blankets as payment at first; but by 1940, they had become the first Montagnards to use paper money. [8]

The Jeh live in some of South Vietnam's most difficult terrain. It is characterized by narrow valleys with razor-back ridge lines and steep slopes. The tribal altitude varies from 2,000 to 6,000 feet with some hillsides so steep that footholds are required in order to ascend or descend them.

Vegetation is thick and varied while the rivers are generally swift, narrow and dangerous. Bamboo thickets and tall tough grass predominate along the rivers. The slopes may have forests of hardwood or pine trees with dense undergrowths of fern, etc. The rain forests, in some areas, have an abundance of moss and other plant parasites. In many instances, the growth is so heavy that visibility is severely limited. In some parts of the tribal area, the jungle is so thick that little light penetrates, and vision may be limited to ten or thirty feet at most. However, from the higher ridges, one may be able to see five to ten kilometers. Nevertheless, except in the areas where the jungle growth has been removed for farming, it is almost impossible to see any ground movements from the air, or to accurately sight air-borne craft from the ground.

Due to the on-going strife and difficult geographical factors, road construction seems impractical. The area has no east-west roads and only one acceptable north-south one. This is National Highway #14 which runs through Kontum, Dak To, Dak Sut, Dak Gle and turns east at Thuong Duc to reach the coast at Hoi An. The Jeh in their north to south travel use foot paths along the river banks with perhaps ninety per cent of all movement being by foot. Other Jeh trails seem to be the shortest distance between two points regardless of the obstacles. The Jeh seem to prefer to climb straight up and down a two thousand foot mound covered with trees, rocks, dense grass and vines than to follow a more circuitous route that might take the same time with much less effort.

While the Jeh have shallow draft canoe-like rafts, these seem to be mostly used in setting fish-traps than for transportation along the rivers. When all factors are considered - including the rocks, flow of currents and consequent difficulties of going upstream - the primitive tribesman may be wise in his choice of walking. Although this is the "Air Age" in Vietnam due to the continuing armed conflict as of 1968, the terrain is too rugged to permit the practical construction of large airfields at the present time. However, there are some small airfields near some of the larger settlements along Highway #14.

The annual rainfall in the Jeh area is about 150 inches. The winds of both monsoon seasons affect the Jeh, but it is the summer monsoon (Mid-April to September) season that brings most of the area's water. The major affect of the two monsoon winds is that when combined with altitude, the Jeh area is usually about fifteen degrees cooler than the lowland coastal plains and Mekong Delta.

CHARACTERISTICS

The Jeh are typical Mon-Khmer in build and coloring. Most have light-brown skin, black hair with vitamin deficiency occasionally causing reddish tints, and brown-eyes that seem perpetually "bloodshot". Most of this tribe seems to have smooth skin with high cheekbones and broad noses.[10] Muscular and stocky-built, the Jeh range from about five feet four inches to five feet ten inches in height.

The loincloth is the male Jeh's normal apparel, while the women wear the blue cotton tribal skirt. This skirt extends from the waist to below the knees. Frequently, the women wrap their legs with white cloth bands from the knees to the ankles. A major additional item of clothing for both men and women is an all-purpose blanket worn as an upper garment.

Some of the Jeh, who have been more exposed to Western influences, may wear foreign clothing from time to time. Many seem to suffer a clothing shortage as the Jeh do not weave their own cloth. What they do have is gained through barter and purchase from other ethnic groups or the Vietnamese.

Although men may wear an occasional multicolored head net about their hair knot, they are not particularly jewelry conscious. The women, however, do wear earrings, bracelets, necklaces, etc.[11]

The Jeh seem to be exceptional when carrying heavy loads in the mountains. They seem to have very strong legs and backs even if their arms seem to tire rapidly. However, their diet is too poor to give them endurance for steady operations that continue for several weeks. Excessive prolonged activities seem to make them prone to infections and sickness.

The Jeh have been described as being discreet, upright, dignified, responsive to kindness, capable of deep devotion, and rather fatalistic.[12] They are also intelligient, naturally curious, and capable of excellent imitations, industrious, basically honest and sincere in spite of living in what they believe to be a hostile spirit controlled world.[13]

Comparatively aggressive in nature, the Jeh play some rather rough games with bamboo swords and goatskin shields. The goal of the game is to disable your opponent by striking his ankles while protecting your own. However, they have little concepts of time, distance, cause of sickness, or even of conception and child birth.

THE VILLAGE AND ITS STRUCTURES

Jeh villages may consist of one to ten long houses which may vary from 150 to 600 feet or more. Built with one side on the ground, the other on pilings, the houses are oriented by the contour of the slopes. Normally, the villages are built close to permanent sources of water and may have bamboo tubing for bringing the water into the village itself.

Generally the long houses have a central corridor with family rooms on either side. Sometimes the roofs are so constructed that they may be lifted a little in order to give light or allow smoke from the family fire to escape. Besides an entrance way from the central passage, each family room has a doorway on it outside wall also. The long house may have a communal room or the village may be large enough to have a communal house.[14] Generally, such a communal house will have the skulls and tails of sacrificed buffalo and other items pertaining to the spirits on its interior walls.

While the Jeh are notable for their lack of sanitation and personal hygiene, they do take pains with the village water source. This area is kept clean of all trash. Even their animals must be watered elsewhere.

SOCIAL STRUCTURE

The Jeh appear to have a bilateral system of living patterns even though the patrilocal system seems to predominate. This may be illustrated by observing that the newly married couple usually go to the husband's family home first. Here they may remain for two or three years before going to the home of the bride's parents for about the same length of time. If they are staying with the groom's parents and one of their children dies at birth or during infancy, the couple may move to the house of the other parents. When one set of parents die they often live with the other parents and when these die then set up their own home.

The Jeh consider that all beds within a long house are related. "Beds", in Jeh terminology, are one husband, wife and children. Normally, the dwelling will contain grandparents, married couples and their children. [16]

The Jeh do not seem particularly conscious of any clan structure as loyalty seems restricted to the family and village. Incidentally, the Jeh do not accept any authority above the village level, in law, religion or power, except as imposed by the Vietnamese government in tribal areas where it has de facto rule. Within the tribe, stratification of social structure is created by degrees of wealth, measured in rice-land holdings, water buffalo, jars and gongs. Wealth seems to be possessed by the whole family, rather than a single individual. Thus, death reshapes the family and village, but does not cause a major re-adjustment of property. An additional reason for this custom is the sense of equality which seems to exist between men and women within the family.

Being patriarchal in social patterns, the Jeh are often exogamous in marriage. That is, their wives are from other villages generally. A major reason for this is that most Jeh villages are composed of one or more extended families with sexual relations in the extended family considered as incest up to the fifteenth cousin. The eldest man of the extended family is its leader. If there are several extended families in a village, their leaders serve as village elders. In such villages marriage partners may be of the same community.

Generally, the Jeh do not have a village chief as a formally elected position. When villages have several extended families, the head of each one must be consulted for any matter that affects the village. The Jeh judge the validity of an elder's opinion by his wealth, etc. Normally, such elders are respected by the village as a whole. Their prestige is enhanced by their role as interpreters of traditional customs. These ruling figures normally interpret tribal law infractions and determine penalties based upon "what is good for the family or village". Economic sanctions seem to be the major procedure utilized against an offender and his family. When fined for violations, the offender and his family must contribute livestock and food to be consumed by all other villagers except themselves.

Marriage: There seems to be a difference of opinion about Jeh marriage practices, [17] but in general, marriage takes the following pattern. Some tribes build a communal room or house for the boys and unmarried men. Others build a second such place for girls. The Jeh permit both boys and girls to sleep in the same communal room or house on opposite sides of the building.

Normally, the Jeh girl makes the first obvious move by asking a boy to come and sleep beside her. If she is particularly bold, she may go over and take him by the hand and lead him to her sleeping place and invite him to sleep beside her. She may even get her friends to go and bring the boy to sleep beside her by force if necessary. Later the girl may sleep beside her chosen one on the male side of the room, but this is rarely done. Even though all the unmarried people in the communal house know of this "romance", they do not make it a matter of gossip, nor do they reveal it to the parents of the couple. Eventually, someone will go to the parents secretly as a go-between to ascertain if they will agree to an engagement. As the parents become aware of the interest of their son or daughter, they normally agree. When they do, the go-between will get the other young people together, capture the young couple and perform the Bla ceremony. This is but the first of a series of ceremonies in the process of marriage.

The Bla ceremony begins by all drinking from the same wine jar through long straws. The go-between with the boy and girl drink from their straws. Then the go-between taps the wine-jar mouth while reciting phrases of good luck, happy wishes, etc. Next, the three hold a live chicken between them while the go-between continues reciting good will phrases. During this part of the engagement ceremony, everyone at the party, which is usually the whole village, will attempt to touch either the chicken or someone who is touching the chicken. This permits them to then take part in eating this and other chickens killed at the same time. If they are not in physical contact with the chicken or its proxy; they cannot eat of the food prepared in this ceremony. Should a child fail to take part in this ceremony, the food is taboo to its parents even though they took part. However, the child touching the chicken or its proxy, even though the parents did not, allows the parents to eat of the food.

The chicken is then killed along with enough others so all present may eat. The go-between must kill the chicken and cook it with rice, etc., but as many call themselves go-betweens, they also help with the preparation of the food. When the food is cooked, the main go-between takes two fists-full of rice mixed with chicken liver and gives one to the boy and the other to the girl. The two exchange their portion, and then eat. When they have eaten their rice and chicken, the go-between gives them each a bowl of wine. They exchange their bowls with each other and drink the wine to complete the first ceremony of their engagement.

The second of the ceremonies is called <u>Taya</u>. Only the families, who are directly involved, and the go-between take part in it. Normally, this involves killing a pig with all concerned having their hand on the knife or on someone who does. The pig is butchered with half going to the boy's family and half to the girl's family. Each will take their portion home, cook it and trade it to the other family before cutting up their share and distributing it to the village. Taboos prevent anyone with small children eating any of the one pig which is sacrificed. This does not prevent them from accepting and eating other foods offered at the same time.

<u>Talu</u> is the third ceremony of the Jeh marriage customs. Again its major elements are wine and chicken, but without formal exchanges of any type. Normally, it consists of drinking wine and reciting phrases of good will while tapping the lip of the wine-jar, and then eating chicken.

The fourth step in the marriage customs is that of the log or wood ceremony. In this, the girl's family will bring wood on their backs, for two or three days and stack it in front of the house of the boy's family. When this will be a sufficient amount to satisfy the boy's family, they will have a feast of pig for the family of the girl. The feast is begun by having the original go-between sprinkle the wood with wine, tap the wine-jar mouth and recite phrases. Then the go-between eats and drinks a bit of wine. The go-between then goes to bring the girl's family to the site. When they have arrived, they tap the wine jug, recite various phrases and then eat of the prepared food. This is followed by an exchange of gifts between the two families. The family of the boy presents baskets and other woven items, while receiving shirts, blankets, loincloths or other cloth-made items. This seems normal as men are the primary basket weavers while girls are the ones who make cloth by weaving.

251

The fifth and last ceremony is the "home-going" or <u>Chooyong</u> ceremony. At this time the go-between will lead the bride to the groom's house. There at the house, the bride, groom and go-between will hold onto a chicken or a pig while reciting phrases. Then the animal or fowl is sacrificed with some of its blood being smeared on the bed of the couple. The go-between also takes wine and sprinkles this on their bed while continuing his recitation. Then all eat and drink. This completes the ceremonies for marriage. Henceforth, the boy and girl are recognized as husband and wife.

Marriage seems to have a basic economic motive. The man wants someone to grind his rice, cook his food and chop and carry firewood, besides working in the fields, etc. The girls desire a husband in order to build them a rice house to store grain when it is harvested, to build a temporary shed in the fields, to build them a house with the various household implements. They both seem to desire children who may take care of them in their old age, as there is no other social security system at present.

While the Jeh have divorce, it seems to be rather rare. Divorce may be because of incompatibility, but seldom happens to such an extent to necessiate divorce with all its problems. While polygamy is also permitted, it is also rare. The major reasons for its general nonpractice may vary, but economic considerations are always involved.

Marriage among the Jeh occurs when the girl is about sixteen to eighteen and the same for the boy. As long as their ages are approximately the same, no one seems to worry about the age factor, or as to who may be the oldest. This unconcern may be related to a rather haphazard concept of time also. Normally, when death occurs, the remaining mate is expected to wait at least a year before marrying again. If one does not wait, the Jeh believe the new partner will certainly soon die also.

<u>Children:</u> There are no sacrifices to the spirits after the wedding ceremony for some time. This is due to the belief that ancestral spirits are not too concerned with them until they have lived together about a year. Normally, sacrifices are not made to ancestral spirits until the first pregnancy is obvious. This is in spite of the Jeh's belief that ancestral spirits return home to haunt

252

the living and demand sacrifices of chickens, pigs, goats, etc. The young couple, who are expecting, begin to appease the Kanam, ancestral spirits, by offering fish tails. During the normal year, they may make appeasment sacrifices of fish tails between ten and thirty times. Additionally, every two to three years, their sacrifices for spirit appeasement will be with chickens, pigs or goats.

The Jeh believe if they offer sacrifices early and "get the jump" on the spirits, they will remain well and healthy. Should the couple be slow and the spirits get ahead, then sickness and other troubles will be constantly present. For the sickness of a child, sacrifices will be determined by the medicine man who consults the spirits. When a couple have no children or only one child, the Jeh believe that they will often be sick. To them, a sure remedy for preventing sickness is a number of children. Then the ancestral spirits doesn't seem to bother them too much, although the exact reasons are not too clear to the average Jeh.

Incidentally, it is taboo for the bride or groom when living in the in-law's house to either sit or lie down on the bed of the in-laws. Likewise, the parents must not sit on the bed of their newly-wed children. In the same manner, it is taboo for the parents of a new baby to enter their regular home for eight to ten days even as it is taboo to give birth within the house.

For delivery, the husband is supposed to build a little shelter near the house when the expectant mother is to deliver her young. There she will stay several days until permitted to re-enter the home. She must wait an additional ten day period before renewing her work with kitchen chores and food preparation. Due to another taboo, the new mother must not eat hot peppers or any type of fruit for a month after delivery.

About twenty to thirty days after birth, the baby normally has its ears pierced. For ten days following this event, it is taboo to give rice to any visitors. The ears are pierced so that earrings, etc. may fool lurking spirits, and they will not steal the child's spirit causing it to die.

Normally, the Jeh nurse their children until two or three unless a new edition precludes this. When about six months of age, the baby is carefully fed precooked and prechewed food. Often carried on the parent's back, the child soon reaches the stage of being able to run and play completely oblivious of its nakedness.

Soon, the carefree days are exchanged for the time of learning. Small tools, weapons, bows and arrows are used first just to annoy the domesticated animals. Then gradually they become effective for hunting, fishing and other livelihood crafts. Girls remain at home, tend the fires, help with household chores, cultivate garden plants and learn the duties which will be hers throughout life.

There is little, if any, formal education among the Jeh. Almost all are taught their basic skills by example and practice in the family group. Occasionally, some will participate in an apprenticeship-like training to learn special weaving or iron forging, etc. Nevertheless, the Jeh can quickly learn to perform various manual tasks as they are excellent mimics. At puberty, the youth move into the communal room or house where their education continues to develop as they learn of tribal lore and legends. But all to soon, the Jeh is faced with the realities of death.

Death: When a Jeh is seriously ill and death is anticipated, the villagers come into his house, watch over him while playing tribal guitars in mourning, and drink wine. The dying are not left alone. As he gasps his last breaths, each member of the family and others of the community will grasp his hands to express their pity and then depart. The act of grasping the hand of the dying is not to keep death away, but to bid the dying farewell.

Once death has occurred, salt is spread on the body of the corpse, in its mouth, etc. The body is dressed and left lying on its deathbed for a day or two while the whole community comes to pay their respect and to eat rice, meat and drink wine. For the "wake" they bring drums and gongs. Whereas a guitar is played before death, afterwards, only the drum and gongs are utilized.

For the actual funeral, several mats are placed in a hewn

log casket with the body placed face up and a blanket laid over the body. Then the lid is placed on the casket and sealed with resin or mud. Then four to six men, usually relatives, carry the coffin to the gravesite. There it is placed in a shallow grave with the casket lid still above ground. Over it, the Jeh erect a small shelter and a fence about it. Then about the grave are placed various material items such as wine jars, knives, ax handles, baskets, pots, etc. While in times past, these were useful items, the Jeh now normally place useless items on the grave to prevent thievery. When this has been done, a pine torch at the foot of the grave is lighted so that the dead person's feet may stay warm. After the funeral is completed, the mourners return home and carefully wash their clothing which they wore to the gravesite in order to wash away the spirits who may have followed them home.

Incidentally, the same coffin may be reused again. If someone of the same family dies after four or five months, their corpse may be placed in the same casket. A shorter time lapse than this will require another casket. When the casket is reused, the normal procedure is to leave it partially buried, but simply take off the lid. If a widow is to be buried, the bones of her husband are placed at her head in the casket; if a widower, the bones of his former wife are placed at his feet as it is taboo to reverse this custom. The casket can be repeatedly reused until no space remains.

Some ten days or so after the funeral, the mourners will kill a chicken and recite phrases to the deceased. Normally, they will plead that they have offered a chicken; and not to haunt the living; nor to return to the house, but just stay in the cemetery. Then, anytime between two months and a year, depending upon the acquirement of a pig, they will sacrifice the pig and again recite phrases. Two to three years later, they will do the same with a goat. The Jeh say the dead consider the goat as a buffalo and if it is a man, he will give his wife something to eat. Should they actually sacrifice a buffalo the deceased would think it a goat and eat it all by himself without giving any to his wife, for it is taboo for a woman to eat goat. After this, every several years, the family will have occasional sacrifices of goats or pigs. Sometimes when eating chicken, they offer the liver, or when it is fish, the tails are offered.

Within a few days of a burial, the Jeh also perform another ceremony. In this one, they weave a very small mat perhaps one square foot. On this, thorny leaves are positioned in a circle with the thorns sticking up. Then small bits of tobacco, liver and cotton are placed on the leaves. In the middle of the circle formed by the leaves, the Jeh place a small bamboo quiver in which wine and water are poured and then a long straw inserted. This prepared platter is then taken and placed in the jungle. The significance of this procedure includes the thought that when the dead person's spirit tries to gather the tobacco, liver, cotton, etc., he will be stuck by the thorns. This will cause the spirit to realize that his owner is dead and that the spirit ought stay in the cemetery. Until this occurs, the soul of the dead is thought to be still living in the house. Thereafter, it is thought to go and stay in the cemetery. [19]

According to the Jeh, the body dies first, and the soul remains by the fireplace until a chicken sacrifice is prepared for it. Then it will go to the cemetary, but return periodically to haunt and plague the household until it has received sufficient sacrifices. Eventually, the soul dies after an indefinite period of time. To the Jeh, death is thought to be a blessed state since the dead no longer have to work. To them, there is no expectation of any punishment or suffering after death. [20]

Another Jeh custom related to death is that of the preparation of one's own coffin. Some Jeh prefer to make their own coffins. These may hire other villagers to help them hew a log coffin, or may hire others to do the work for them. In any case, the coffin is prepared under the communal house or room where it is left until its owner dies.

The first day of work on a coffin must be accompanied by the recitation of good wish phrases for the coffin owner. It may take five or six days or longer to prepare the coffin. During this time the owner must provide rice and six or seven chickens each day as food for the coffin-builders. When the coffin is completed, its owner must give a feast with the major ingredients being wine and pig. On the feast day, the coffin owner will take a live chicken and go under the communal house by himself in order to scratch the chickens feet against the coffin. Then he bleeds the chicken and catches in a bowl the blood which is mixed with wine and sprinkled on the coffin. All the while, he is supposed to recite various phrases to himself. This ceremony is then repeated once a year until the coffin-owner dies and uses his product. [21]

Social Attitudes and Mores: Jeh moral standards appear to be strict even though one communal house or room serves for both boys and girls. Punishment for violations of sexual codes is rather severe. Should a girl become pregnant before marriage, she with her guilty partner must leave the village and dwell in the forest. They are unable to return to their village until their period of exile is over and the village invites them back. Should there be any illegitimate children, their parents are banished from the communtiy.

Formerly, they could be re-accepted into the community only after requesting permission and the village warriors had killed someone of another village or in Laos, and had returned with the severed finger as proof of their deed. Currently, this violence is symbolized by throwing a spear into the woods and then admitting the couple with their child.

When someone is detected as a thief, the major action is being forced to give compensation to the person from whom he stole. Usually, the result is returning that which he had stolen. Other offenses against the individual may require giving them gongs, wine jugs, pigs or a buffalo. There is little sense of offenses against a community that requires action by the collective society as practiced in Western society.

The Jeh consider it good to be brave, but not foolishly so. Their general attitude toward fear is to have one brave ear and one that is afraid as if to say "discretion is the better part of valor". This is also reflected in their feelings about war, feuds and violence in general. Thus, it is thought good to attack another village first and show them that you are brave. But there is sufficient violence due to the current war that few Jeh now voluntarily engage in strife for the joy of battle.

Generally, the Jeh look upon death with a submissive resignation. For the one already dead, it is thought good for him. But many are afraid of death in that they fear the ancestral spirits won't accept them. And the Jeh feel that to be prevented from joining the ancestral spirits would be a most unfortunate fate.

The Jeh don't seem to worry about "face" very much. Their lot in life has always been humble, so they are not overly concerned that others give them special considerations. They do want to be treated as people and not as worthless objects.

Most Jeh seem to believe that illness, sickness and disease are the work of the spirits. It may be either ancestral or inanimate spirits who haunt them, demanding appeasment by the sacrifice of a chicken, pig, goat, buffalo, etc. Some ill are thought to be caused by spells being cast by someone else. In some cases, the Jeh think that illness results by the magical implacement of a stick or bone in their bodies. To such, the use of modern medicines are merely more powerful spirit treatments.

When the central Vietnamese government is concerned, the Jeh have not really been active for or against it. They have passively accepted such things as tribal courts and government rule, but have been too isolated and too small to create a major force for the government or against it.

LIVELIHOOD

Typical of most preliterate peoples, the Jeh are slash-and-burn farmers. Mountain or dry-rice is their major crop. Slash-and-burn farming, also known as "swidden" or "ray", consists of choosing a forest or jungle site; cutting the growth and then burning the cuttings when it is sufficiently dry. In these small cleared sites, the various grains, fruits and vegetables are grown until the fertility of the soil is used. Then the fields are abandoned and other places cleared for farming.

The Jeh must consider the spirits when choosing field-sites. There are some areas, varying in size from a few square meters to large sites where it is taboo or "tultul" to prepare fields. Normally, this area will have a number of large trees thought to be spirit-inhabited so that anyone preparing a field there would die.

This tribal group has one practice accompaning the harvest of rice that is different than most other Montagnards. This ritual includes the collection of resin or pitch of the Gugul tree for use in the harvest. Gugul trees grow in the high mountains and reach three to four feet in diameter with leaves about the size of a man's hand. To obtain the black resin, the tree bark is slit and the pitch allowed to slowly ooze much like a pine tree does. Where a sufficient amount has been collected, it is placed in a small bamboo tube about the size of one's little finger. This is heated until it begins to liquid and begins to boil. It is then allowed to cool and harden. Sections of the hardened resin in the bamboo one half to three quarters of an inch in length may be bartered for a chicken so that it is rather expensive.

Just prior to going to the rice field to be harvested, the Jeh will take a bit of this pitch, about half the size of a grain of cooked rice, and light it. Smoking like incense, the pungent odor permeates the house. Other houses nearby all know that the rite is being performed. As the fragrant smoke ascends, the Jeh take all their harvesting implements, including their baskets, and hold them in it. Then they place their hands and feet into the smoke also.

This particular pitch is thought to possess magical powers to that passing their implements through its smoke prevents their crops being diminished. Otherwise, the Kra spirits will enter the rice field with the harvesters and deprive them of some of their rice. The Jeh think the smoke prevents their crops being diminished. Otherwise, the Kra spirits will enter the rice field with the harvesters and take some of their rice. The Jeh think the smoke of the resin is repulsive to the spirits so that the spirits will not cling to them or their harvest tools.[22]

The Jeh only burn this particular incense on two occasions beside that of the rice harvest. The first of these occasions is when someone is sick and the medicine man, "Magua", is unable to determine the cause. For this, a bit of resin is placed on the ground in the center of a crude circle drawn in the earth which has spokes radiating to the circle from the center. Around the circle at the spokes, there will be chickens, pigs, etc. The pitch will be lighted and the animal or fowl over which the smoke flows will be killed and eaten. This is done because the Jeh believe the spirits of animals can enter people and cause sickness. The cure for this affliction is to ascertain the offending animal; kill and eat it so that the ill may be restored to health.

The third time the pitch of the Gugul tree may be used is for trials. If one Jeh accuses another of some offense and the accused does not admit guilt, additional steps are required. The accuser and the accused will go to the bank of a stream with witnesses and spectators, and there incense will be burned.[23] This seems to be the equivalent of oaths in the American court system. Then the two principals go down into the water and submerge themselves with a pole placed across their necks. In theory the guilty will have to come up for air first. The fact that the magical incense had been burned will confirm guilt or false accusations in the minds of the Jeh observing this trial.

Additional foods grown by the Jeh include corn, pineapples, guavas, bananas, papayas and some vegetables such as sweet potatoes. These items may be planted near the dwellings or even in the fields so that the fruit may be gathered long after the field has been abandoned for growing rice.

The Jeh earn part of their living by hunting, fishing, trading and some crafts. While hunting may be conducted throughout the year, it is most intensive when the rice supply is low. This would be true in regard to fishing also. These Jeh arts have a number of taboos. For instance, it is taboo for anyone to carry a container of any type to a dam which has been made to catch fish. If this is violated, the Jeh believe no fish will be caught. It is also taboo to show anyone where you have set an animal trap, be it for a rat or tiger. To do so will make failure almost certain. However, to set a trap or build a dam near where someone else had already done so is believed to be the cause for neither party to have success in getting fish or animals. While most Jeh set their traps secretly, there are occasions when two people of kindred spirit may hunt, fish or trap as a team.

At one time the Jeh panned gold from their rivers. This would be taken into Laos and used to secure buffalo or other things which the Jeh desired. Cinnamon bark is gathered by the tribesman and carried to such trading centers as Tra My and Tra Bong. But seldom, if ever, have the Jeh been able to have a surplus of food, tools or items for trade.

There are only a few of the Jeh who are skilled in making metal tools such as hoes, axes, knives, etc. Most of their metal tools are made of truck springs or iron brought in from Laos. Such items are normally bartered for as rice, wine and meat from other tribesmen. Interestingly, the craftsmen divide their work into "large" and "small" items with the larger being made first. Large implements are axes, large knives, crossbows, big hoes, etc., while small things are harvest implements, little knives or garden hoes. The reason of this practice may be to conserve metal or because of tribal beliefs inasmuch as practically every phase of Jeh life is colored by them.

Jeh women weave clothing from their home-grown cotton while the men are known as basket makers. They also make umbrellas for themselves, and some make musical instruments used in their various rites or for social singing.

Defensively, the Jeh make spears and shields besides their crossbows. Poison may be used with any of these tools. Generally, however, the Jeh have poverty as a constant resident in their midst. Few could be considered economically above the subsistence level.

RELIGION

The Jeh are animistic for the most part. Some have accepted the beliefs and practices of Christianity, but the cultural patterns of most Jeh communities are predicated upon animism. Living in a world they do not understand and which often seems hostile, the Jeh venerate, appease or worship may spirits. Making no clear distinction between animate and inanimate or tangible and intangible, all natural forces are believed to possess spirits. These must be dealt with in daily life if the tribesman is to have any peace of mind and meaningfulness in life.

Many Jeh seem motivated by fear primarily. Some feel helpless and at the mercy of capricious spirits who create adversities. One deals with such forces by placating them and through skillful manipulations gains desired benefits.

The Jeh have a primitive ancestral spirit veneration, and use rites to keep them appeased. But other than in funeral rites, they do not

261

seem to give them too much attention. More concern is given to other spirits, who, thereby, seem more important. While beliefs seem to vary from settlement to settlement, beliefs are in two catagories of spirits outside of the animal world. These categories are the <u>Kanam</u> and the <u>Yang</u> or the earthly and the heavenly spirits. <u>Ra</u>, the Jeh heavenly spirit, is the paramount spirit over all nature. But he is too mysterious and remote to be understood even though the thunder is thought to be his voice.

The earth spirit is more intimately associated with daily life. He watches after the individual Jeh and often dwells in the hearth stone regardless of who may live in the house. Thus, the hearth stone is left undisturbed when the Jeh move lest the spirit be offended. While many Jeh beliefs are unknown, it is known to be taboo to call upon the spirit of the sky and the spirit of the earth in the same ceremony. Each demands a ritual for themselves.

As with other Montagnards, the principle animal used for ritual sacrifices is the buffalo. However, the Jeh standard of living makes this a genuine sacrifice perhaps equivalent to the loss of an uninsured expensive automobile to the average American. Because the Jeh believe the buffalo to have special significance that exceeds its economic value, the skull and tail are saved when sacrifices occur. These are often placed in the communal room or house. Their movement across water becomes taboo and death will afflict the village which tries to do so.

When the Jeh sight a taboo animal, such as a tiger or leopard, they refuse to use the trail until they have performed the essential rites. Some even carry a tiger tooth as a magic charm against personal harm. But when one considers their comparatively hopeless plight, perhaps their solution is the best one available to them.

GUIDELINES FOR RAPPORT

Foreigners and ethnic Vietnamese need to realize the Jeh have lived in their particular area for generations. Generally, their boundaries have been respected by other tribes and by neighboring villages in the tribal area. Their unwritten law makes practical sense to them, so wisdom dictates that others who come into the area ought to learn these factors and observe those not in conflict with duty or moral obligations.

While the Jeh may hold foreigners somewhat in awe, this does not imply an automatic acceptance of them or their ideas. Effective results necessitate that foreigners ascertain the real feelings of the Jeh as these are often hidden in various guises. While the Jeh may be illiterate, this is due to lack of opportunities rather than inability to learn. If the non-Jeh will have the patience to deal wisely with the tribesmen and really listen, he may learn many wise ideas from these children of the jungles.

The Jeh, like all human beings do not like to feel degraded. They resent any sense of inferiority reflected toward them by others. Sure, they may be little among the peoples of the world or even of Vietnam, but they are still people. All too often foreigners - or non-tribesmen - come into the area with plans, designs and methods for projects already determined. They are baffled and dismayed at the lack of interest by the tribesmen.

If such plans were discussed with community elders and other leaders and they were asked for suggestions about the problems, the results might be startling. Generally, it is wise to plant ideas in tribal minds and allow these to ferment a while. Sometimes the solutions may be the same as the foreigners, while at other times the tribal approach may be unique. In either case, careful handling of the matter can provide the whole-hearted cooperation so vital for permanent success. After all, the single greatest good that we can do for any people is to help them to help themselves.

Again, foreigners ought to utilize the knowledge and abilities of the tribal people, even as the wise use of these can help to build a strong nation in Vietnam.[24] Thus, the use of tribal translators who are well trained in English and Vietnamese would be an excellent step in the right direction. Perhaps only the time, interest and ability to learn the tribal language by all who deal with the Jeh would have a more significant value. By utilizing tribal talent, numerous doors into the modern era are being provided to these people which time seems to have passed by.

FOOTNOTES

1. Frank M. Lebar, Gerald C. Hickey, John K. Musgrave, Ethnic Groups of Mainland Southeast Asia, New Haven, Human Relations Area Files Press, 1964, p. 140; July 1966. "Ethnic Minorities of Vietnam". List by the Summer Institute of Linguistics, Saigon, Vietnam; Navy Personal Response Tape #35, by Dwight L. Gradin about the Jeh. (Mr. Gradin's transcribed tape will be here after referred to in this chapter as Gradin, op. cit., with page number. This tape was prepared on 30 October 1966.)

2. Gradin, op. cit., p. 2

3. Robert L. Mole, 1965-66, On-site Fieldnotes (Unpublished).

4. Gradin, op. cit p. 2; Lebar, et all, Ethnic Groups of Mainland Southeast Asia, p. 140.

5. Gradin, op. cit. p. 1; Lebar et al, op. cit, p. 140; J. Hoffet, "Les Mois de la Chaine Annamitique", Terra, Air, Mer: La, Geographie, LIX (1933) p. 21.

6. Gradin, op. cit. p. 2

7. Ibid p. 2

8. H. C. Darby (Editor) Indo-China Cambridge, England, Geographical Handbook Series, 1943, pp. 83-4

9. Gradin, op. cit, p. 2; Mole, 1965-6 Field notes,

10. Gradin, op. cit. p. 2; U.S. Army Special Forces, Montagnard Groups of South Vietnam, Fort Bragg, N.C. . 1966 Edition, p. 119; Mole, Field-notes.

11. Gradin, op. cit p. 2

12. Louis Coudominas, "Notes sur les Mois du haut Song, Trang", Bulletin de la Societé des Etudes Indochinoises XXVI (1951) p. 34.

13. Mole, _Field - notes_

14. Lebar et al, p.140; Howard Sochurek, "Viet Nam's Montagnards", _National Geographic_ April 1968, Vol 133, No. 4 - pp. 443 -487.

15. Gradin, _op. cit_ p. 6

16. Gradin, _Ibid_.

17. Gradin, _op. cit_ pp. 6-9; Condominas, _op. cit_ pp. 27-29

18. Gradin, _op. cit_ pp. 6-9

19. Gradin, p.15

20. _Ibid_

21. Gradin, p.16

22. _Ibid_, p. 5

23. _Ibid_, p. 5

24. Gradin, pp. 22-23

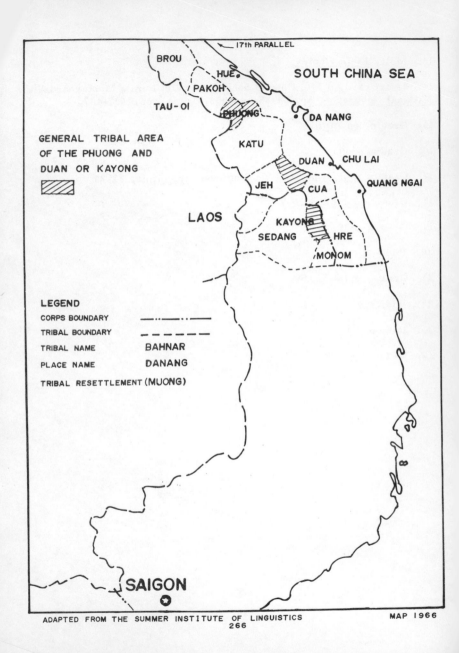

17th PARALLEL

BROU

HUE

SOUTH CHINA SEA

PAKOH

TAU-OI

PHUONG

DA NANG

GENERAL TRIBAL AREA
OF THE PHUONG AND
DUAN OR KAYONG

KATU

DUAN

CHU LAI

JEH

CUA

QUANG NGAI

LAOS

KAYONG

SEDANG

HRE

MONOM

LEGEND

CORPS BOUNDARY   ——·——·——

TRIBAL BOUNDARY   —— —— ——

TRIBAL NAME   BAHNAR

PLACE NAME   DANANG

TRIBAL RESETTLEMENT (MUONG)

SAIGON

ADAPTED FROM THE SUMMER INSTITUTE OF LINGUISTICS
266

MAP 1966

CHAPTER IX

THE PHUONG AND THE DUAN

Little is known of either the Phuong or the Duan. No foreigner observer seems to have lived among either ethnic group. The current military and political conditions prevent more than hasty visits into their tribal areas now. Moreover, the massive military support required for even brief visits distort observations beyond a useful purpose.

The Phuong are a fairly small group located in western Thua Thien province just east of A-Shau. They are located between the Pacoh and the Katu so that another name for them is Huu River Van Kieu. By language the Phuong are considered to be in a Katuan subgrouping of the Katuic subgroup of the Mon-Khmer language family.

The Duan are also know as Takua, Kayong and Halang Daksut. They are in northeastern Kontum Province and in I Corps. The exact identity of the Duan make the exact identification of their tribal borders impossible. Generally, they seem to have as their neighbors the Jeh, Katu, Cua, Hre, Sedang and the ethnic Vietnamese.

Until additional information is obtained, it would seem wise to treat these people in the same manner recommended for other Montagnards. The application of the Golden Rule or Golden Mean can never be harmful and may help these tribespeople to develop a hope in tomorrow in spite of todays problems.

If the American is to understand the Montagnard, and hope that the Montagnard will begin to understand him, he must become aware that they are moved by the same dynamic forces and needs that make Americans "tick". Human wants and human needs are quite similar the world over as all men search for the "right" answers. It is also essential to realize that while human needs and drives are universal, basic differences in belief-value systems provide differing solutions to the problems which confront all people.

One of the basic needs of all people is emotional security. This urgent need requires a sense of belonging or identification in a meaningful relationship with others. The absence of this reassuring communion with others is a by product of cultural shock that all sense to some degree as a part of the normal process of growth or when changes are made to cultures which have radically different logical and behavior systems. Often, the individual in a "strange" culture may seek security by "fading" into the environment, or by an almost compulsive whirl of activities. These activities are engaged in with little or no reflection for the immediate goal nor long range goals and with regard to the permanent effect of such activities.

REMEMBER:

Belief-value systems create difference of customs and behavior patterns.

Behavior patterns of different cultures may differ just as radically as do their languages.

While the various components of a culture are many, man's concept of himself and his place in this universe (world-view), united with geography, economics and history are basic to all human behavior patterns

Social conventions, superstitions, misconceptions and natural human conservatism tend to make the less developed culture extremely sensitive about the values of the traditional culture versus the new. This emotional reaction is normal to all people even if it does create restrictions on radical and rapid changes for a "better" society.

An initial inability to understand and appreciate new ideas, new objectives or new methodologies based upon that which was previously unknown, is not restricted to people of Southeast Asia as it seems universal.

Success depends more upon personal attitudes and interest than upon policies and written instructions. Patience, good humor,

268

freedom from false pride or superiority combined with a friendly inspirational outlook will enhance success more than many books, including this one.

Most tribespeople, like other Southeast Asians, are practical psychologists and will quickly spot and reject deception on the part of Americans just as they do a patronizing superiority complex. Wisdom and experience reveal that a simple, natural friendly attitude "opens" doors to the minds and hearts of the Montagnards that otherwise cannot even be pried open.

Before attempting to provide help for problems or conditions it is imperative that these be understood in the context of their culture. Effective success in aiding people is dependent upon the awareness and ability to help them satisfy their basic needs. This includes appreciation of the "interest of the people in their own development", their "felt" needs, their opinions, aspirations and expectations.

Community participation in both the planning and the execution of all projects having local interest or value is essential if these become of personal interest and concern to the people.

Alertness is essential for those religious beliefs and concepts held by the individual or the community which may promote or hinder all proposed developments of ideas or procedures. As perceptive insights are realized and utilized, community concepts may be changed or modified to harmonize with the acceptance of "New" ideas.

Knowledge of the relationship between local peoples increases dexterity in your relationships with all peoples. Be observant, discreet and perceptive in formulation of plans, recommendations, suggestions, observations or even in general comments.

Avoid the impression that "the Americans have landed and have the situation in hand". Rather, Americans have come to help the citizens of Vietnam to the extent they desire and as much as we are able to. When an opposing position is taken to a proposed "civic action", let the subject rest until you can analyze the matter. Then you can gracefully reintroduce the subject from different angles acceptable to needs and values. After all, for any development to be both permanent and sound, there must be an attitude of independence which permits rejection, acceptance and modification of ideas to meet local needs.

Never attempt to "force" projects, devices or ideas upon people before an interest is created inasmuch as a sense of need is essential for valid success.

Try to create an awareness that life can be changed, that conditions can be altered and improved if careful planning and persistence are combined. Successful inspiration requires perspiration. When humanly possible, seek the agreement, cooperation and support of local leaders in the community. When such is not practical, seek to neutralize efforts so that it will not be necessary to oppose the "program". One excellent way of doing this is to be willing to modify plans or projects to conform with their wishes to the greatest extent possible.

Never try to create projects beyond their skills and available resources as failure creates discouragement, disappointment and frustration. It is better to start small and develop to large things than it is to start as a big "BOOM" and finish as a mere fizzling "firecracker".

All really successful transcultural help must be based on the premise that the foreigner's presence will not always be required or desired. To the extent that we Americans become indispensable, we have failed. Especially is this true once projects are in operation and local talent has been properly indoctrinated with "on the job" experience. Be careful to give only assistance which is beyond the level of "your" people to help themslves. In this way, indigenous technical talents may be developed and utilized for a developing community without despair or frustration. Maximum utilization of local talents, skills and resources is a basic requirement for any successful cross-cultural program. Never allow your presence to be more oppressive then absolutely necessary and this can be best accomplished by using tact and dexterity with peoples of other cultures.

Never make fun or mock traditional ceremonies or rites and symbols no matter how strange they may seem to you. To those who use them, they are vital and are held in sincere esteem and value. When possible respect all customs that do not violate sovereign integrity or personal convictions of conscience. When refusal is necessary, this ought to be done with courtesy and consideration of those who hold different viewpoints.

Gifts and presents as "charity" may pervert and spoil the character of many simple hard working people. Normally the tribal-people react to gifts by giving you something in return. Therefore care must be exercised in this matter. Anything given with even a faint patronizing air is humiliating to the receiver and may give a sense of disgrace. Only to the extent that American help is viewed as a partner-ship interchange, can permanent benefits be realized

BIBLIOGRAPHY

BIBLIOGRAPHY

Adkins, E. H., A Study of Montagnard Names in Vietnam, East
    Lansing, Michigan, Vietnam Advisory Group, Michigan State
    University, 1962

Bernard, Nole, "Les Khas, peuple inculte du Laos français:
    Notes anthropométriques et ethnographiques", BULLETIN
    DE GÉOGRAPHIE HISTORIQUE ET DESCRIPTIVE, 1904

Bourotte, Bernard, "Essai d'histoire des populations montagnardes
    du Sud-Indochinois jusq'à 1945", BULLETIN DE LA SOCIÉTÉ
    DES ÉTUDES INDOCHINOISES, n. s. XXX, 1, (1955)

Burling, Robbin, Hill Farms and Padi Lands, Englewood Cliffs,
    New Jersey, Prentice-Hall, Inc., 1965

Bui Dinh, "Customs and Habits of the Hre Tribes", translated
    from the Vietnamese: Phong-tuc-Tap-quan Ngoi Hrey:Ba-to-
    quang-ngai, by the Joint Publication Research Service,
    (JPRS: R-2341-D), 1956

Bui Tan Loc, "Creation and Flood in Bru Legend", JUNGLE
    FRONTIERS, News Magazine of the Vietnam Mission of the
    Christian and Missionary Alliance, 260 West 44th Street,
    New York, Summer 1961

Cadiere, Leopold Michael, "Notes sur les Mois du Quang-tri",
    BULLETIN DE L'INSTITUTE INDOCHINE POUR L'ETUDE DE L'HOMME,
    Vol. III, 1940

Coedès, George, "Ethnography of Indochina", Washington, D.C.,
    Joint Publications Research Service, (JPRS/CSO:6757 - D.C.
    Lectures), 1950

Condominas, Georges, "Aspects of a Minority Problem in Indo-
    China", PACIFIC AFFAIRS, XXIV, 1951

Condominas, Louis, "Notes sur les Mois du haut Song, Trang",
    BULLETIN DE LA SOCIÉTÉ DES ÉTUDES INDOCHINOISES, XXVI,
    1951

CRESS, Minority Groups in the Republic of Vietnam, Ethnographic
    Study Series, Department of the Army Pamphlet No. 550-105,
    1966

274

Dam Bo (Jacques Dournes), " Les Populations montagnardes du Sud-Indochinois," FRANCE-ASIE, Special Number, Spring 1950

Darby, H.C., Indo-China, Cambridge, England, Geographical Handbook Series, 1943

Daupley, M., "Les Kha Tahoi", L'ETHNOGRAPHIE, n.s., 1914

Dowdy, Homer, E., The Bamboo Cross, New York, Harper and Row, 1964

Gerber, T., "Coutumier Stieng", BULLETIN DE L'ECOLE FRANÇAISE D'EXTREME ORIENT, 1951

Guilleminet, Paul P. "La Tribu bahnar du Kontum," BULLETIN DE L'ÉCOLE FRANÇAISE D'EXTREME-ORIENT, XLV, 1952

Haquet, H., "Notice ethnique sur les Mois de la région de Quang Ngai", REVUE INDOCHINOISE, July-December, 1905, 1419-26

Hickey, Gerald, C., "Comments on Recent GVN Legislation Concerning Montagnard Common Law Courts in the Central Vietnamese Highlands", Santa Monica, California, The Rand Coroporation Memorandum, 1965

Hickey, Gerald, C., "The Major Ethnic Groups of the South Vietnamese Highlands", Advanced Research Projects Agency Memorandum, 1965

Hoffet, J.H., "Les Mois de la Chaine Annamitique entre Touran et les Boloven", TERRE, AIR, MER: LA GEOGRAPHIE, Janvier, 1933

Kroeber, A.L., (Editor), Anthropology Today, Chicago, University of Chicago Press, 1953

LeBar, Frank M., Gerald C. Hickey, John K. Musgrave, Ethnic Groups of Mainland Southeast Asia, New Haven, Human Relations Area Files Press, 1964

Luzbetak, Louis, J., The Church and Cultures, Techny, Illinois, Divine Word Publications, 1963

Malinowski, Bronislaw, Magic, Science and Religion, Garden City, New York, Doubleday Anchor Books, 1948

Mangham, Evelyn, "Superstitions", JUNGLE FRONTIERS, 1960

Maspéro, George, M., Montagnard Tribes of South Vietnam, Washington, D.C., Joint Publications Research Serivce, 1962

Nguyen, Huyen Van, Introduction a l'etude de l'habitation sur pilotis dans l'Asie du Sud-East, Paris, Librairie Orientaliste/Paul Geuthner, 1964

Nida, Eugene, A., Customs and Cultures, New York, Harper and Row, 1954

Nida, Eugene, A., Introducing Animism, Friendship Press, 1959

Nuttle, David, A., The Montagnards of the High Plateau of South Vietnam, Saigon, USIA, 1962

Le Pichon, J. "Les Chasseurs de sang", BULLETIN DES AMIS DU VIEUX HUE, XXV (1938)

Riesen, René, Jungle Mission, Translated by James Oliver, New York, Thomas Y. Crowell Co., 1957

Robequain, Charles, L'Indochine Francaise, Paris, Librairie Armand Colin, 1935

Sabatier, L., Recueil des Coutumes Rhades du Darlac, Hanoi, Imprimerie d'Extreme Orient, 1940

Smith, Laura, I., Victory in Vietnam, Grand Rapids, Michigan, Zondervan Publishing House, 1965

Sochurek, Howard, "Viet Nam's Montagnards", NATIONAL GEOGRAPHIC, 1968

Special Operations Research Office, Ethnographic Studies Series: Selected Groups in the Republic of Vietnam: The Bru, Washington, D. C., SORO, 1966

Trinquet, C. "Essai de vocabulaire francais-moikare", REVUE INDOCHINOISE (July-December) 1912

U.S. Army Special Warfare School, Montagnard Tribal Groups of the Republic of Vietnam, Fort Bragg, N.C., 1965

U.S. Department of State, The Geographer, Office of Research in Economics and Science, Bureau of Intelligence and Research, International Boundary Study No. 35: Laos, Vietnam Boundary, Washington, D.C., U.S. Dept. of State, 1964

U.S. Information Service, Montagnards of the South Vietnam Highlands, Saigon, USIS, 1962

Webster's Third International Dictionary, Springfield, Mass., G & C Merriam Co., 1961

NAVY PERSONAL RESPONSE - TAPE FILE

Costello, Nancy, The Katu, 1966

Harverson, Stuart, The Hre, 1967

Haupers, Ralph, The Stieng

Johnson, Eugenia, The Bru, 1966

Josephsen, H.L., The Katu, 1966

Maier, Jackie, The Cua, 1966

Miller, John & Carolyn, The Bru, 1965 and 1968

Smith, Less, The Primitive Tribes of South Vietnam

Watson, Richard, The Pacoh, 1968